THE PALLADIUM
OF CONSCIENCE

A Da Capo Press Reprint Series

CIVIL LIBERTIES IN AMERICAN HISTORY

GENERAL EDITOR: LEONARD W. LEVY

Claremont Graduate School

THE PALLADIUM
OF CONSCIENCE

CONTAINING

Furneaux's Letters to Blackstone.
Priestley's Remarks on Blackstone.
Blackstone's Reply to Priestley.

DA CAPO PRESS • NEW YORK • 1974

Library of Congress Cataloging in Publication Data

Main entry under title:

The Palladium of conscience.

(Civil liberties in American history)
Each part has special t.p.
Also published under title: An interesting appendix
to Sir William Blackstone's Commentaries on the laws of
England.
Reprint of the 1773 ed. printed by R. Bell, Philadel-
phia.
1. Religious liberty—Great Britain. 2. Dissenters,
Religious—England. 3. Great Britain—Parliament—Elec-
tions. I. Furneaux, Philip, 1726-1783. II. Priestley,
Joseph, 1733-1804. III. Blackstone, Sir William,
1723-1780. IV. Blackstone, Sir William, 1723-1780.
Commentaries on the laws of England. V. Series.
BR758.P33   1974   323.44'2'0942   74-122161
ISBN 0-306-71972-X

This DaCapo Press edition of *The Palladium of Conscience* is an unabridged
republication of the first edition published in Philadelphia in
1773. It is reproduced from microfilm prepared by Harvard Law
Library from a copy in its collections.

Published by Da Capo Press, Inc.
A Subsidiary of Plenum Publishing Corporation
227 West 17th Street, New York, N.Y. 10011

THE

PALLADIUM of CONSCIENCE;

OR, THE

Foundation of RELIGIOUS LIBERTY DISPLAYED, ASSERTED, and ESTABLISHED, agreeable to its true and genuine principles, above the reach of all petty TYRANTS, who attempt to LORD it over the HUMAN MIND.

CONTAINING

FURNEAUX's Letters to BLACKSTONE.

PRIESTLEY's Remarks on BLACKSTONE.

BLACKSTONE's Reply to PRIESTLEY.

AND

BLACKSTONE's Case of the MIDDLESEX-ELECTION;

With some other curious TRACTS, *worthy of high Rank in every* Gentleman's Literary Repository,

Being a necessary Companion for every Lover of

RELIGIOUS LIBERTY.

AND

An INTERESTING APPENDIX

TO

BLACKSTONE's COMMENTARIES

ON THE

LAWS OF *ENGLAND*.

AMERICA:

PRINTED FOR THE SUBSCRIBERS,
By ROBERT BELL, at the late UNION LIBRARY, in *Third-street,*
PHILADELPHIA, MDCCLXXIII.

CONTENTS OF THIS VOLUME.

Particular Contents of each Letter.

LETTER I. Dr. Blackſtone's opinion concerning the Act of Toleration, that it only frees Diſſenters from the penalties, not from the crime of nonconformity, ſtated, page 1,—5. The reaſon aſſigned for this opinion conſidered, p. 5. The contrary opinion, That the crime of nonconformity is aboliſhed together with the penalties, with reſpect to thoſe who are qualified as the act directs, proved, (1) from the mode of expreſſion in that clauſe of the act, which repeals the penal ſtatutes with regard to ſuch perſons, p. 6,—8. (2) from thoſe clauſes which protect the diſſenting worſhip: the argument of a noble Lord in a high department of the law upon this head, p. 7—8. (3) from the unanimous judgment of the Commiſſioners Delegates, and of the Houſe of Lords, in the ſheriff's caſe: the grounds of their judgment ſtated, and ſhewn to be, that Diſſenters are freed from the crime as well as penalties of nonconformity, p. 10,—12. Further conſideration of the ſtate of Diſſenters, and of diſſenting worſhip, under the toleration: The opinion of a noble Lawyer, and of the late Speaker Onſlow, p. 12,—14. Concluſion, p. 14,—15.

LETTER II.

POSTSCRIPT

CONTENTS.

Letter VII.

REMARKS

ON

SOME PARAGRAPHS

In the FOURTH VOLUME of

Dr. BLACKSTONE'S Commentaries on the
LAWS OF ENGLAND.

RELATING TO

THE DISSENTERS.

By JOSEPH PRIESTLEY, LL. D. F. R. S.

——— *Quis tam ferreus, ut teneat fe,*
Caufidici nova cum veniat lectica Mathonis.

JUVENAL.

Who can behold religious liberty curtailed, and remain fo infenfible to the danger of being
bereaved of the ineftimable blefling as not to defend and enlarge it. ANON.

o

AMERICA:
PRINTED FOR THE SUBSCRIBERS;
By ROBERT BELL, at the late UNION LIBRARY, in *Third-ftreet;*
PHILADELPHIA. MDCCLXXIII.

REMARKS

ON

Some Paſſages in the Fourth Volume

OF

Dr. BLACKSTONE's Commentaries on the Laws of England, &c.

A T the time that I was engaged in writing on the ſubject of *church-authority*, in anſwer to Dr. Balguy, I
was informed that a paragraph or two in the laſt volume of Dr. Blackſtone's Commentaries, which was
juſt then publiſhed, deſerved the notice of Diſſenters. Accordingly I procured the book, and found the paſſages referred to,
contained the moſt injurious reflections on that part of the community to which I belong; but as they are altogether deſtitute
of candour, ſo they are unſupported by truth, or even a decent
appearance of argument, I own that I have been the more ready
to animadvert upon this writer, leſt, (as he is ſuppoſed to poſſeſs
the confidence of the preſent miniſtry) his ſentiments ſhould be
confidered

confidered as a notification to Diffenters, in what light they are regarded by thofe who are in power; and it fhould be imagined,
that fome defign is formed to eftablifh a fyftem of civil and ecclefiaftical tyranny ; but when my readers fee how groundlefs are all
his infinuations to our prejudice, and how exceeding futile are
the arguments he produces in favour of the obfolete ftatutes a-
gainft the Diffenters, I am perfuaded they will afk for no other
proof, of there being no intention, in any fet of men, who are in
their fenfes, to revive and enforce them.

T HE manner in which Dr. Blackftone has treated the Diffenters, is fuch as I fhould not have expected from a perfon of a
liberal education, who has gained a confiderable fhare of reputation as a writer, and who being fo perfectly fkilled in the *laws* of
his country, fhould have been better acquainted with the *inhabi-*
tants of it. Having done juftice to the former, in his truly admirable Commentaries, he fhould not have traduced the latter,
and have infulted his fellow citizens, who refpect his abilities,
and never gave him any provocation.

B ESIDES, this writer's good fenfe fhould have informed
him, that, in the prefent fituation of public affairs, it is peculiarly
unfeafonable to irritate and difunite the fubjects of this realm. It
is now particularly requifite, that every thing fhould be faid and
done, that may tend to make all the different claffes and denominations of people think well of one another; that, laying afide all
illiberal and party prejudices, we may unite together for the public good. But I am forry that I cannot help confidering Dr. Blackftone as a man, who, finding a houfe already in flames, either
wantonly or wickedly, throws another faggot into it.

Section. I.

IN vindication of the ftatutes of Edward VI. and Queen Eli-zabeth (ftatutes which nothing can even account for, but the groffeft ignorance of the nature and purpofes of the chriftian in-ftitution, of the natural rights of mankind, and of the proper objeƈt of civil fociety and government; together with the moft pitiable bigotry, and the moft violent party rage) ftatutes, which enaƈt, that *if any perfon whatfoever fhall fpeak any thing in derogati-on, depraving or defpifing of the book of common-prayer, he fhall forfeit, for the third offence, all his goods and chattles, and fuffer imprifonment for life*; he fays, p. 50. " Thefe penalties were framed in the
" infancy of our prefent eftablifhment, when the difciples of
" Rome and Geneva united in inveighing, with the utmoft bit-
" ternefs, againft the Englifh liturgy: and the terror of thefe
" laws proved a principal means, under providence, of preferv-
" ing the purity, as well as decency of our national worfhip.
" Nor can their continuance to this time be doomed too fevere
" and intolerant, when we confider, that they are levelled at an
" offence, to which men cannot, now be prompted, by any laud-
" able motive, not even by a miftaken zeal for reformation;
" fince from political reafons, fufficiently hinted at in a former
" volume (fee vol. 1. p. 98.) it would now be extremely unad-
" vifeable to make any alterations in the fervice of the church;
" unlefs it could be fhewn that fome manifeft impiety or fhock-
" ing abfurdity would follow from continuing it in its prefent
" form. And therefore the virulent declamations of peevifh or
" opinionated men, on topicks fo often refuted, and of which the
" preface to the liturgy is itfelf, a perpetual refutation, can be
" calculated for no other purpofe, than merely to difturb the
" confciences, and poifon the minds of the people."

I ALMOST

I ALMOST suspect that this passage is borrowed from some old Thirtieth of January sermon. It would certainly suit such a place far better than a grave dispassionate treatise on the laws of England. There is one circumstance, however, that looks more like the *lawyer* than the *divine*. A mere divine would hardly have been so far off his guard, as to give so plain a hint of the weakness of the *reasons* and *arguments* in support of the church of England, as Dr. Blackstone has, unawares, done, in saying, that it has been *the terror of penal laws* that has proved the *principal means* of preserving the purity, as well as decency of the national worship.

ADMITTING, what is far from being true, that, for political reasons, it were extremely unadviseable to make any alteration in the service of the church ; and admitting, also, what is as far from the truth, that there is no manifest impiety or shocking absurdity in the present forms of the church of England ; why may I not speak in *derogation* of the book of common-prayer, or even in *contempt* of it, if I really think it a *defective*, and *contemptible* performance ? Where is the great crime if, insulted as the Dissenters have always been, with the malice, and nonsense of high churchmen, they should, now and then, speak, or even write in their own vindication : if it were only to convince those who have been deluded by the lies and the sophistry of their adversaries, that Dissenters are men like themselves, with hands, heads, and understandings like other men ; and that they have no tails, or cloven feet; a notion which some well-meaning people have been almost made to believe ? And how is it possible to vindicate our conduct as Dissenters, that is, our not using the common-prayer book, without speaking *in derogation* of it. If the motive be not *laudable*, it is surely *innocent* and *pardonable*, which is quite sufficient for our vindication.

Semper ego auditor tantum, nunquamne reponam, Vexatus toties—

JUVENAL.

WITHOUT

WITHOUT troubling ourfelves about the eftablifhed church (though it be our indifpenfible duty to endeavour to enlighten the minds of all men, as far as we have opportunity) we muft, now and then, be allowed to write fomething in order to confirm the wavering of our own perfuafion, efpecially confidering that all the influence of this world bears againft us ; fo that, with every advantage of argument, our intereft rather lofes ground ; and what can we fay, that is better adapted to purfuade Diffen- ters to continue in their prefent fituation, than to fhew them how much worfe they would be by the change ? It is not denied, that the laws permit us to *write*. Is it not hard then, not to be allowed to write in our beft manner, and make ufe of our beft arguments ? To me this appears to be a duty of indifpenfible ob- ligation, on a perfon who has the caufe of religion at heart, and is defirous of preferving it free from the corruptions that have been elfewhere introduced into it ; and yet for this difcharge of my duty, I muft forfeit all my goods and chattels, and even be imprifoned for life, and this cool lawyer will ftand by, and deem the fentence *not too fevere* and *intolerant ;* becaufe, according to his cafuiftry, forfooth, it is impoffible my motive fhould be a *laud- able* one. But will this author ferioufly maintain, that confifca- tion of goods and imprifonment for life, is not too fevere a punifh- ment for all actions, the motives of which are merely *not laudable?* Doth this writer himfelf do nothing but what is, ftrictly fpeaking, meritorious and worthy of praife? Doth he never wafh his hands, change his clothes, or pare his nails?

CONSCIENTIOUS, however, as I think myfelf in what I do, and fatisfied as I am, that my motives in writing in defence of the diffenting intereft, if not *laudable*, are *juft* and *reafonable*, this au- thor infifts upon it, that fuch writings as mine can be calculated for no other purpofe, than merely *to difturb the confciences and poifon the minds of the people.* If this be not *the virulent declamation of a pee- vifh and opinionated man*, I do not know what is. It does not feem to be in the power of words to give a clearer indication of it. That any man fhould ever *mean* nothing (and if this be not the fenfe

B   of of the word *calculated*, it has no meaning at all, that is in the least degree to this purpofe in this place) but to diflurb the confciences and poifon the minds of his fellow creatures, I truft I fhall always think fo well of my fpecies, and of its author, as to deem impoffible. I even queftion whether the moft depraved of all beings be capable of doing evil *for it's own fake*. The paragraph I am animadverting upon, is calculated to do as much mifchief as moft things I have ever read, tending to inflame the animofity of a party, and to increafe our unhappy divifions ; but I charitably think this author *meant* fomething elfe, though his paffions have fadly bewildered his judgment.

As this writer has no objection to making *alterations* in the new editions of his works, I will beg leave to fuggeft an emendation of this ftrange paragraph ; and propofe that, inftead of the *virulent declamations of peevifh and opinionated men*, he would write *the calm reafonings of fober and confcientious men* (and I hope he is not fo much a churchman, as not to allow, that fome Diffenters, though perhaps not myfelf, may be confcientious and calm in difcuffing matters of religion) and then it will be no difficult ftep to advance in his argument, if he fuppofe, that calm and confcientious men may have a *true zeal* for reforming what appears to them, a corrupt religion ; and the next, and final ftep in this argument is ftill more eafy, namely, that a confcientious man, influenced by true zeal, is juftified before God and his own confcience (which is all that he is folicitous about) if he do *derogate* from what he thinks to be a corrupt mode of religion, in order to bring about a reformation of it, notwithftanding every *political* reafon that may be alledged to the contrary. Thofe who have the caufe of religion at heart, and are chiefly influenced by a regard to a *future world*, are not very apt to enter into political reafons, and confiderations by which they may pleafe men.

Let us fee, however, if it be only to fatisfy our curiofity, what are thofe deep *political reafons*, that render it fo exremely unad-

unadviseable to make any alteration in the church of England, or its liturgy ; and for this purpose let us follow our author's referrence to vol. 1. p. 98, of this elaborate work, in which we are informed that we shall find them *sufficiently intimated.*

HERE let my reader stop, and cover with his hand what immediately follows, and if I were to adopt the style of my country, I might lay him a very unequal wager, that he would not in many times, guess what this great reason is. I say *reason,* in the singular number, for in the place referred to, I find only *one* mentioned, though I was led to expect *more.* It here follows :

" AN alteration in the constitution or liturgy of the church of
" England would be an infringement of the fundamental and
" essential conditions" Of what ? " of the union betwixt Eng-
" land and Scotland, and would greatly endanger that union."

I REALLY have not read the *Free and candid disquisitions,* but I am pretty confident, that this of Dr. Blackstone's is an objection to their proposed emendations of the liturgy, that never once occurred to any of them. But they ought to have had a *lawyer* among them. There is nothing like uniting the two professions of Law and Divinity ; and the one is very defective without the other.

I THINK, indeed, the reasoning of this author himself, and of the bishop of Gloucester, whom he quotes in a note upon this curious passage (added in the second edition of this work) might have allayed his fears from such an infringement of the union as this. " For" he says, " it may justly be doubted, whether an
" infringement of the fundamental and necessary conditions of
" the union (though a manifest breach of good faith, unless done
" upon the most pressing necessity) would consequentially dis-
" solve it. For the bare idea of a state, without a power, some-
" where vested, to alter every part of its laws, is the height of po-
" litical absurdity. The truth seems to be, that as such an *incor-*
                    B 2   " *porate*

" *porate union* (which is well diftinguifhed by a very learned pre-
" late from a *fœderate alliance*, where fuch an infringment
" would certainly refcind the compact) the two contracting ftates
" are totally annihilated, without any power of revival ; and a
" third arifes from their conjunction, in which all the rights
" of fovereignty, and particularly that of legiflation, muft of ne-
" ceffity refide. (See Dr. Warburton's Alliance, p. 195.) But
" the imprudent exertion of this right would probably raife a
" very alarming ferment in the minds of individuals ; and there-
" fore, it is hinted above, that fuch an attempt might endan-
" ger (though not certainly deftroy) the union."

Though I am of opinion that both thefe learned Doctors
argue very weakly, and upon principles by which they might
quibble away all the natural rights of man, when once he is entered into fociety ; it will ferve my purpofe, as an argument *ad
hominem.* It feems, then, that the *right* to make alterations in
the liturgy is allowed, and all that is neceffary to be obferved
is *prudence* in the ufe of it ; and this I doubt not, will be applied, whenever the reformation of the church is undertaken.

The articles of the union do feem to confirm the different
eftablifhments of England and Scotland, as they then ftood ;
but a man muft be ftrangely wrong-headed, not to perceive, that
this was only intended to bar all encroachments of the one upon
the other. It could never be underftood that the two nations
meant to take that opportunity of binding themfelves from making any improvements in their refpective religious conftitutions,
if they themfelves, feparately taken, fhould think proper. The
fuppofition is abfurd. Should the Scotch nation, in fome future time, (and who knows what the revolutions of time
and the operations of political men and meafures may bring
about) become defirous to adopt the Englifh hierarchy and liturgy, would Dr. Blackftone, ferioufly object either in parliament,
or at the bar, this article of the union againft fo glorious an improvement of the kirk ? Or would he really think it an infringe-

ment

ment of the union? Suppose the church of England should be reformed by an act of the English parliament, is it likely that such a measure would raise any *alarming ferment* in the minds of the Scots? Would they think themselves injured, and complain of a breach of the articles of the union? If they *should* object, would they not be thought very unreasonable, and to pervert the plain meaning of the articles? Certainly the Scots think themselves at liberty to improve their church discipline, or mode of worship, without consulting us, and therefore could not take umbrage at the English doing the same for themselves.

THIS is one, among a number of instances, in which a regard to the punctilio's of law (in minds whose sphere of comprehension has been narrowed by an attention to such minute objects) gets the better of the plainest dictates of common sense. Suppose this happy union had taken place before the reformation, and the Scots had been Mahometans at that time; a person of Dr. Blackstone's principles would certainly have opposed the present establishment of the church of England upon maxims of law; and would have challenged any christian missionaries, who should have thought of going into Scotland, with the articles of the union betwixt the two nations.

BUT with such men as Dr. Blackstone and Dr. Warburton, religion must be governed by the maxims of civil policy; and I am sorry to observe, even for the honour of the church of England, that, according to their new principles of church-authority, (which would have been disavowed by the founders of it) the mode of vindication, which her champions have lately chosen, seems to arise, not out of her proper foundation, *christianity*, but out of those abutments which the policy of men have erected for her support; by means whereof she hath contracted not only an *alliance* with, but a striking *resemblance* of the kingdoms of this world. What effects this new measure may produce on the minds of unbelievers, or of her own serious and considerate sons, I pretend

I pretend not to pronounce : only this I know, that it by no means serves to promote a veneration for her in the minds of thoughtful Diffenters ; who, whatever others may do, confider themfelves as fubjected, in all matters of religion, to an authority much fuperior to human ; obliged by laws which will fupport themfelves without human aid or alliance, and remain in force when the laws of England, and all the commentaries on them, will have no more than an hiftorical exiftence ; and therefore think themfelves bound by the duty they owe to their mafter and lord, Chrift Jefus, to obferve carefully both parts of that injunction he delivered to them, and to proteft earneftly againft the attempts of political men to confound and thereby fubvert it : *Render unto Cæfar the things that are Cæfar's, and unto God the things that are God's.*

THIS writer fpeaks in a very contemptuous manner of the *virulent declamations of peevifh and opinionated men, on topicks that have been often refuted ;* and, as he may not be a logician, we muft give him a little indulgence with refpect to the ftrict meaning of his terms, and fuppofe that by the refutation of *topicks*, he means, by a metonymy, the refutation of *arguments* on thofe topicks ; alfo, as he does not profeffedly enter into thefe topicks, he is at liberty to fay any thing he pleafes about them, and in as dogmatical a manner as he thinks proper ; but as he mentions *the preface to the liturgy*, as being itfelf, a perpetual refutation of our topicks, (that is, of our arguments) I was induced to make fome enquiry about that preface (for, my own copy of the common-prayer book wanting it, I really did not know before, that there was any fuch thing in being) but I own that, after repeated perufals of it, I cannot fix upon any one paragraph, or fentence, in that preface, that I can imagine to have been intended to be a refutation of any thing ; nor can I conjecture what it is this author meant by mentioning it in this light. If this preface was *originally* intended to be a ftanding refutation of the reafonings of Diffenters ; it is pity that the authors were not a little more explicit, and that care fhould not have been taken to have it prefixed

fixed to every copy ; for it is impoſſible to ſay what this book
may have ſuffered by going ſo frequently, and ſo preſumptuouſly
without its intended guard.   This preface appears to me to be,
upon the whole, a decent and modeſt compoſition, recommend-
ing improvements rather than diſcouraging them ; and, together with a deal of good ſenſe, contains a little of the aſperity
and peeviſhneſs that ſavour of the times in which it was written ; without which, indeed, it is even yet impoſſible for high
churchmen to ſpeak of, or even allude to Diſſenters ; and which
(that they may ſeem not to be the aggreſſors) they are generally
very ready to aſcribe to the Diſſenters.

S<small>ECTION</small>

Section II.

THE comparison which this author draws between the principles and practices of the Papists and Dissenters, and his observations on the laws of England, concerning them, are not a little remarkable. " Both Papists and Protestant Dissenters," he says, p. 52. " were supposed to be equally schismaticks in de-
" parting from the national church, with this difference, that
" the Papists divide from us upon material, though erroneous
" reasons, but many of the Dissenters upon matters of indiffer-
" ence, or in other words, upon no reason at all. The tenets
" of the Papists are, undoubtedly, calculated for the introducti-
" on of all slavery, both civil and religious, but it may with jus-
" tice be questioned, whether the spirit, the doctrine and the
" practices of the sectaries, are better calculated to make men
" good subjects. One thing is obvious to observe, that these
" have once within the compass of the last century, effected the
" ruin of our church and monarchy ;* which the Papists have
" attempted indeed, but have never yet been able to execute."

WOULD not any person, unacquainted with the history of christianity, imagine, from reading this paragraph, that the church of England was the oldest christian church in the world ; and that, in some remote period of time, both the Papists and Dissenters broke off from it ? Would he not also imagine, from what this author says of *the disciples of Rome and Geneva having united, with the utmost bitterness, in inveighing against the English liturgy,* that the Papists and Dissenters were very good friends, and had entered into a brotherly league to distress their common enemy ?

* It is observable, that the writer is careful to mention the *church* before the *king,* a circumstance which strengthens my suspicion of these paragraphs of his work, being extracts from some Thirtieth of January sermon.

enemy? What mifreprefentations will bigotry ftick at, in order to favour her malignant purpofes, purpofes to which hiftorical truth will'not be fubfervient. Calumnies and infinuations, fo palpably falfe and malicious as thefe, need no refutation. I think however, the Papifts ought to wait upon Dr. Blackftone, with their moft refpectful compliments, for the tendernefs with which he has treated them ; but he has not ufed the Diffenters as *fo much their brethren*, that they can join with the Papifts upon this occafion.

THE *Papifts*, he fays, *divide from us upon material, tho' erroneous reafons, but many of the Diffenters upon matters of indifference, or in other words, upon no reafon at all.* Very cavalierly, and very wittily fpoken, for a man of your gravity, Dr. Blackftone, but *gratis dictum* all. Who thofe Diffenters that you refer to are, you have not been pleafed to diftinguifh; but as you do not fay that they have *all* been fo abfurd and unreafonable, as to divide from the church of England *upon no reafon at all*, you leave room to fuppofe, that there are *fome* Diffenters who differ from the church of England upon material, though erroneous reafons, as well as the Papifts ? and therefore that their feparation is equally juftifiable. For my own part, I think that *one* of my reafons againft the church of England, is as ftrong as any that the Englifh reformers ever had, or pretended to have, againft the church of Rome*. And there are no Diffenters that I have ever heard or read of,

C   but

---

* I do not recollect what the firft reformers could object againft the fyftem of popery, as more contrary to true religion and common fenfe, than the *idolatrous fervice of the Mafs.* And I cannot help confidering the eftablifhed church of England, the eftablifhed church of Scotland, and every other eftablifhed church in the world to be *idolatrous alfo*, in which fupreme worfhip is paid to any other than *the one God and father of all*, even *the God and father of our Lord Jefus Chrift.* Let it be obferved, however, that I am far from confidering thofe perfons as guilty of the *fin* of idolatry, who really think that the Athanafian doctrine of the trinity is confiftent with the belief of the divine unity ; that I am ftill farther from thinking, that becaufe all chriftian eftablifhments agree in this great error, that they are therefore equal in all other refpects; and

fartheft

but alledge this objection to the church of England, that she usurps a power in the church of Christ, which its only master has not invested in any man or body of men upon earth, viz. a power of making that necessary to christian communion which he has left indifferent; and also of deciding concerning articles of faith, for, in the twentieth of the thirty-nine articles, she not only claims a *power to decree rites and ceremonies*, but also *authority in matters of faith*. But this Dr. Blackstone thinks to be *no reason at all*. For the future, I would advise him to leave this business of religious controversy to his friend Dr. Warburton, whose *Alliance* he quotes with so much respect, and who is much more dexterous in the management of these things than himself.

FROM the latter part of the paragraph I last quoted, one would think that Dr. Blackstone had been so intent upon the study of the *laws*, that he had given but little attention to the *history* of England; for every article of this account is notoriously false from beginning to end. This writer has, indeed, given proofs of a minute acquaintance with *some parts* of the history of England, particularly in his excellent *Law Tracts*. It is, therefore, possible, that he may have just ideas of this part of the history; but I choose to ascribe his mistakes to want of knowledge, because it is the most favourable construction I can put upon them. The naked facts are these.

THE family of the Stuarts, worthy members of the church of England, but having an unfortunate bias on the side of popery*,
uniformly

farthest of all am I from thinking, that *involuntary errors*, of any kind, will be imputed to any set of men whatever, and that the favour of Almighty God will be denied even to Papists, Mahometans, or Heathens, as such. May I relinquish every thing most dear to me, rather than give up this great foundation of *universal charity*.

* James I. however, was so zealous a presbyterian, originally, that he used to call the English liturgy *an ill said Mass*; and had no opinion of bishops till he found how convenient they were to his system of arbitrary power.

uniformly afferted an abfolute power, and made repeated attempts to enflave this nation. The effays of James I. in this favourite road, were undifguifed, but foolifh and impotent. Thofe of his fon Charles I. aided by the deepeft hypocrify, were bold but rafh and unfuccefsful. The *nation*, not the Diffenters only, afferted their natural and civil rights. They bravely oppofed force to force, juftice to injuftice, and at length prevailed.

H A D the king, fupported by all the high-churchmen and Papifts, prevailed, no man can fay that the civil conftitution of this kingdom would not have been entirely overturned, and an abfolute defpotifm have taken place, at leaft as much of it as has taken place in France or Spain; that is, as much as the fpirit of the people of Europe can poffibly bear. I alfo appeal to any intelligent and moderate churchman, whether, if the fchemes of Laud had been put in execution (and he had, in every thing, the concurrence of the court) the ecclefiaftical conftitution of this country would not have been changed too, in favour of fomething much nearer the grofs, abject, and impious fuperftition of the church of Rome.

A F T E R the termination of the war, the greateft part of thofe who before had been Diffenters were ftill friends to monarchy : and, together with them who began the oppofition, would have fpared their fovereign (who, if he had had a thoufand lives had

C 2

forfeited

I am at a lofs to know what this writer means by faying, p. 429. " On the " acceffion of King James I. no new degree of " royal power was added to, or " exercifed by him." Rapin fays, " It is certain that James's chief care af- " ter his acceffion, was to maintain the prerogative royal in its utmoft extent, " nay to carry it higher than any of his predeceffors. He muft, at the time I " am now fpeaking of, have conceived a larger notion, than had been hitherto " formed, of the power of an Englifh King ; fince when he came to Newark, " he ordered a cut purfe to be hanged by his fole warrant, and without trial. " It cannot be denied, that this was beyond the lawful power of a king of Eng- " land, and contrary to the privileges of the Englifh nation." Perhaps Dr. Blackftone may not have read Rapin, or may think him an hiftorian of no credit.

forfeited them all to the juſtice of his injured country, and whoſe memory nothing but a violent death could have ſaved from general execration) but the leaders of the *army*, which will neceſſarily give law to the ſtate in all convulſions of this nature, happened to be independents and republicans; and though they had but few adherents out of the army, they could not be prevented from cutting off the king.

THE death of the king, and the ſubverſion of the monarchy, were not the effect of any *religious* principles of the Diſſenters, as ſuch. Had the army conſiſted of Mahometans, the event would have been the ſame; and if none of their commanders had had power enough to uſurp the empire immediately, ſomething like a republic would have been formed by them.

AFTER this event, the independents made no proper eſtabliſhment in religion. The Preſbyterians, indeed, would have made a moſt intolerant one, ſimilar to that of the church of England in thoſe days, but they were happily over-ruled; and, the friends of the lately eſtabliſhed church would have dwindled into one of the moſt inconſiderable ſects, had not the hierarchy been reſtored with Charles II.

THIS prince was firſt a concealed, and then an avowed Papiſt; always an admirer, and generally, a penſioner of France. His uniform aim was to eſtabliſh Popery and arbitrary power in this kingdom; and his brother and ſucceſſor James II. (always an avowed Papiſt, and a Jeſuit too) had very nearly ſuccceeded in both theſe deteſtible ſchemes; when divine providence raiſed up for our deliverence, king William III. of glorious and immortal memory.

THIS excellent prince to whom, under God, we owe all our liberties, was a Preſbyterian, and he found all of that name, and the Diſſenters in general, his beſt friends in this iſland. The
fame

fame have the princes of the houfe of Hanover* always found them. Very few Scotch Prefbyterians, who were not fubject to the flavery of the late hereditable jurifdictions, and not one Eng-lifh Diffenter of any denomination, that I ever heard of, were in either of the two rebellions†; but numbers of Papifts and high-churchmen (who, at that time, were generally Tories and Jaco-bites) were engaged in both. And I appeal to all perfons who know the Diffenters (for as to Dr. Blackftone, it is plain he knows no more about them, than he does about the Patagonians, or the inhabitants of the Solomon ifles) whether they be not, al-moft *to a man* (I may add, *woman* and *child* too) the firm and in-trepid friends of the liberties of this country, and of its conftitu-tion, as a *monarchy* ; notwithftanding the *republican principles*, with which we are generally and ignorantly charged.

T<small>his</small> writer has alfo given a very falfe account of what he is pleafed to call *the rebellion*, and of the confequences of it in the reign of Charles I. in the laft chapter of this work, which I fhall, therefore, briefly animadvert, or *comment* upon in this place. After enumerating the grievances of thofe times, he owns that the king had behaved in fuch a manner, that " there were " grounds moft amply fufficient for feeking redrefs in a legal " conftitutional way;" and, confequently, as I fhould think, in

any

---

* The princes of this family were *Lutherans*, as is the family of our prefent Queen (to whom Dr. Blackftone is Solicitor) and it is well known, that this mode of the Proteftant religion is fo unlike that of the church of England, and fo like that of the Prefbyterians; that the members of our eftablifhed church will not admit the validity of ordination in either of them; whereas they admit, without fcruple, thofe who are ordained in the church of Rome. As to the members of the *reformed* church in Holland, they are as much the difciples of Geneva as any Diffenters in England.

† In the rebellion of 1715, Mr. Wood, the diffenting minifter at Chowbent in Lancafhire, at the head of his congregation, joined the king's forces, and, under the commander in chief, defended the bridge at the battle of Prefton. In confequence of which he was, as long as he lived, and is to this day, always mentioned by the name of *General Wood*.

any *other* way, if it could not be obtained in what is here called a *legal* one; as was prefently found to be the cafe. " This re- " drefs, when fought, was alfo conftitutionally given." I fhould rather fay it was extorted, and never intended to be acquiefced in. Dr. Blackftone owns that it was not done " with fo good " a grace, as to conciliate the confidence of the people." Indeed, upon this, and feveral other occafions, wefeem to have *the fame ideas*, though we chufeto exprefs them in a different manner. So two painters might chufe to lay different colours on the fame drawing.

" UNFORTUNATELY, cither by his own mifmanagement, or " by the arts of his enemies,the king had loft the reputation " of fincerity, which is the greateft unhappinefs that can befall a " prince." A great misfortune and unhappinefs truly! But I hope the *piety* of this prince was equal to his trials, and I doubt not he bore the *afflicftion* with proper refignation, as the *acft of God*.

" THOUGH he had formerly ftrained his prerogative,not only " beyond what the genius of the prefent times would bear, but " alfo, beyond the examples of former ages, he had now confent- " ed to reduce it to a lower ebb than was confiftent with monar- " chical government. A conducft fo oppofite to his temper and " principles, joined with fome rafh acftions, and unguarded ex- " preffions, made the people fufpecft that this condefcenfion was " merely temporary." If the cafe was as Dr. Blackftone here reprefents it, who can wonder that they entertained thofe fufpi- cions; unlefs it be afferted that the word of a king, though it have been proftituted in the moft fhamelefs manner, ought to be received without the leaft miftruft by any fubjecft if it be *publickly* given; notwithftanding it be contradicfted, not only by other *ex- preffions*, fpoken to his friends, when he was off his guard (fuch as are generally allowed to be moft to be depended upon in deter- mining a man's real intentions) but alfo by *acftions*. Dr. Blackftone, I fuppofe, would have been that *good fubjecft*. I fhould not have had fo much faith, or loyalty.

" FLUSHED

" FLUSHED therefore, with the fuccefs they had gained,
" fired with refentment for paft oppreffions, and dreading the
" confequences if the king fhould regain his power, the popular
" leaders (who in all ages have called themfelves the people)
" began to grow infolent and ungovernable." At this time the
popular leaders, moft certainly, fpake the fentiments, and were
actuated by the fpirit of the people in general (or elfe, according
to this writer's own reprefentation of their grievances,they muft
have had no fpirit at all)and if they did *begin to grow infolent and
ungovernable*, it was becaufe they perceived that the king, notwithftanding all his pretended conceffions, was actually prepar-
ing to levy war againft his people, and therefore they were
obliged to ftand upon their defence. " Their infolence render-
" ed them defperate," and the king, finding that the people
would be cajoled no longer, grew defperate too. Speaking of
the fame popular leaders, he goes on, " and joining with a fet of
" military hypocrites, and enthufiafts" (though but children in
hypocrify, compared with the king and his minifters) " they
" overturned the church and monarchy ; and proceeded, with
" deliberate folemnity, to the trial and murder of their fo-
" vereign."

ACCORDING to this writer, then, all thefe horrid acts
were committed by the *fame popular leaders* who firft oppofed the
king. It is alfo naturally inferred, from the turn of his fentence,
that thefe popular leaders joined the military hypocrites and enthufiafts, *with a view* to the perpetration of this murder. That
there is not the leaft colour of truth in the affertion, or the infinuation, I appeal to any thing that was ever called *a hiftory of
England*. I will even reft it upon the evidence of Carte, Guthrie,
Hume, or any other Jacobite hiftorian this writer fhall name.

WHAT would the glorious Hampden, Pym, and many
others, who figured at the opening of the long parliament (men
whofe names will be immortal, fo long as the principles of integrity,

grity, a love of liberty, or even loyalty, fhall be held in efteem) fay
were they to hear fuch a relation as Dr. Blackftone hath given of
their views and conduct. They would certainly conclude, that all
the authentic memorials, of their time, were perifhed; and could
have no idea of any man's having the affurance to give fo palpably falfe and injurious an account of thofe tranfactions, within
little more than a century after they happened; when there
was fuch a redundance of evidence, that it was eafy for any man
of common fenfe and honefty, to come at the truth of the facts.

Mr. Hume, whofe evidence may well be allowed in this
cafe, has given a very different account of thefe heroes. He alfo
acknowledges, that whatever civil liberty we now enjoy in
Great-Britain, is owing to our anceftors, the Puritans; and I
truft that every wife and virtuous miniftry, who have the liberties and natural rights of their fellow citizens at heart, will always have reafon to depend upon the Diffenters; and that only
a wicked, tyrannical, and profligate adminiftration, who are intent upon making a tool of the king, and thereby grafping all
the power of the ftate to themfelves, will ever entertain any jealoufy of them. A wife, juft, and moderate prince will value fuch
fubjects; though a prince of different character, may rather chufe
to be without them.

If the fpirit and the doctrines of the fectaries in England are
not calculated to make men good fubjects, I think it is incumbent upon this writer to prove his affertion by the hiftory of other
difciples of Geneva. Since the principle is the fame, its influence
may be expected to be uniform. Do the Proteftant cantons of
Switzerland, in the neighbourhood of this Geneva, contain no
good fubjects? As to Geneva itfelf, the fource of all this mifchief, it can be nothing elfe than a den of lawlefs banditti. Are
the French proteftants univerfally bad fubjects? Are the Proteftants in Holland bad fubjects? Or, to come nearer home, will
this gentleman fay that the Prefbyterians in Scotland are bad
fubjects;

subjects; if these *disciples of Geneva* had not given recent and ample proofs of their loyalty, to the entire satisfaction of the most obsequious courtier, they have taken a great deal of pains to very little purpose, and I shall be at a loss to know what test of loyalty will be deemed sufficient. However, let any other be proposed. Every fair test should be required, and refused, before this universal charge against the disciples of Geneva can be fully admitted.

I cannot say that I have ever heard of any material difference between the principles of the Lutherans, and those of the disciples of Geneva (or, as they are called abroad, *the reformed churches*) with respect to their political influence. If, therefore, Dr. Blackstone's charge against the disciples of Geneva be just, I should not expect that the disciples of Luther were entirely innocent; but I do not recollect any thing in the history of Germany, Prussia, Sweden, Denmark, or Norway, that is favourable to this hypothesis. The truth is, that Protestants, of every denomination, have proved disaffected, and sometimes rebellious, when they have been oppressed; but this resistance to government is not to be ascribed to the spirit of their *religion*, but to their spirit as *men*. So great is this writer's antipathy to us, deluded and desperate sectaries, and so much doth the horror he conceives for our opinions engross his thoughts, that the most natural and common actions of our lives will, I suppose, be ascribed by him to our peculiar principles. I shall hardly be able to eat to satisfy my hunger, even though it be not in Lent, but he will fancy it to be a gratification of a schismatical appetite.

However, I am far from denying that religious principles have influence upon mankind as members of civil society, tho' I should not ascribe so much to them as Dr. Blackstone, in the violence of party rage, is disposed to do; but, according to my idea, of *good subjects*, the tendency of the religious principles of the Dissenters in England is to make men truly such. If, indeed,

by

by *good fubjects* this author means *fubjects of defpotifm*, I agree with him, that the fpirit, the doctrines, and the practice of thefe fectaries are not extremely well calculated to make men good fubjects. I am apprehenfive that thefe fectaries would prove a little untractable in fuch a fituation. But, for that very reafon, in a *free*, and *equal government*, a government which leaves men a reafonable fhare of their natural rights, fuch men are, of all others, the beft fubjects. They find themfelves at eafe in fuch a ftate, and will, therefore, endeavour to make others eafy in it. In this light, the Diffenters regard the conftitution of Great Britain. There are no fubjects of the realm who are, from principle and intereft, more attached to their king and country than they are, and every infinuation to the contrary is malicious and abfurd.

IF Dr. Blackftone wants a doctrine calculated to make men good fubjects *on any terms*, I would refer him to the *univerfal maxim* I have animadverted on in Dr. Balguy (in which he fays, the fcriptures are clear and explicit) viz. that *authority, once eftablifhed, muft be obeyed*. I preach no fuch doctrine.

AS to the *church*, that is, the eftablifhed church of England, God knows we cannot, without hypocrify, pretend to be very *cordial friends* to her, becaufe it is well known, fhe has not been the beft, or tendereft of mothers to us. But notwithftanding this, we are far from being fuch *deadly enemies* to her as Dr. Blackftone feems to imagine. We can *fmile* among ourfelves at fome things that appear rather ftrange and whimfical in her; but truly, we are very little difpofed to moleft her ; and upon the whole, we think, that we bear with her *infirmities*, full as well as could be expected, all things confidered.

I CANNOT help thinking, that the regret which this author feels for the fubverfion of *fuch a church* and *fuch a monarchy* as were fubverted within the compafs of the laft century, is fo extreme, that he charges it indifcriminately, upon all who were prefent at the tranfaction; though many of them were

were fo far from being aiders and abettors in it, that they did all they could to prevent it. Thus a tender mother, feeing her beloved child get a dangerous fall, beats even the ground it fell upon.

DR. BLACKSTONE feems to think the prefent laws of England bear too hard upon the Papifts, and I agree with him in it. I think that that antichriftian power feems to be in its old age; that her malice is now impotent; and, fince nothing but felf-defence will juftify hoftilities, that in this cafe, perfecution would be an *unneceffary evil*. Befides, it is cowardly to kick an old and dying lion. But why fhould not this good Doctor think the Diffenters entitled to as much indulgence, and that fome of our laws, not yet formally repealed, bear rather too hard upon us? We think we are, at leaft, as gentle, as inoffenfive, and as well difpofed as the Papifts; and we doubt not that all who are reafonable, generous, and liberal minded, and all who are acquainted with us, will think fo too.

IT is evident that we have no *foreign head*, to whom we fwear allegiance, as the Papifts have. Though it is not impoffible but that Dr. Blackftone (knowing very little about the Diffenters) may be ignorant of this circumftance; and indeed, as he mentions *the difciples of Rome and Geneva* in the fame connection, and in the fame turn of phrafe, he may imagine that the fupreme head of *our* religion refides at Geneva, juft as the fupreme head of the Papifts lives at Rome. And fince he talks of *an union between the difciples of Rome and Geneva*, he may fuppofe, that thefe two heads of the different fects, which *divided from* the church of England, when they left this country, being upon very good terms, chofe to take up their refidence in the fame neighbourhood; where they live together, in as friendly a manner as the two kings of Brentford.

THANKS to God, and a fenfible adminiftration (not to Dr. Blackftone) that the penal laws againft the Diffenters are as ob-

folete

folete as thofe againſt the Papiſts, nor will any friend of religion, or of his country, attempt to revive them. Indeed, I cannot help thinking, there would be ſome difficulty in enforcing one of our admirable ſtatutes to prevent heretical opinions, quoted with approbation by this author, p. 50. It is that of William III. againſt thofe " who either deny any one of the perſons of the Holy Tri-" nity to be God, or maintain that there are more gods than " one." If I have any ideas to theſe words, this ſtatute condemns all mankind: for every man muſt hold one opinion or the other, ſince the one affirms, and the other denies the very ſame thing.

S E C T I O N

SECTION. III.

DR. BLACKSTONE, I doubt not, will deem some parts of my answer to his invective to be *a reviling of the ordinances of the church*, which, he says, p. 50. *is a crime of a much grosser nature than mere non-conformity.* By the way, I did not know that mere *non-conformity* was any *crime* at all in the laws of England (whatever it may be in his Commentaries on them) since the act of Toleration. It is certain there is no *penalty* annexed to it; but with Dr. Blackstone, who can both make and aggravate crimes, according to his own convenience, mere non-conformity it seems, is not only a crime, but a crime of a *gross nature*, though reviling the ordinances of the church be a crime of a *grosser* nature.

THE reasons this author gives for considering this latter offence as more aggravated than the former, are worth our notice. " Reviling the ordinances of the church," p. 50. " is a " crime of a much grosser nature than mere non-conformity, " since it carries with it the utmost indecency, arrogance and " ingratitude; indecency, by setting up private judgment in " opposition to the public; arrogance, by treating with con- " tempt and rudeness that which has, at least, a better chance " to be right than the singular notions of any particular " man; and ingratitude, by denying that indulgence and li- " berty of conscience to the members of the national church, " which the retainers to every petty conventicle enjoy."

I AM so unhappy as not to be able to see the least connection between any of the two ideas which Dr. Blackstone here links together. If setting up private judgment in opposition to that of the public be *an indecency*, then, certainly, Wickliffe, Luther, Mr.

Mr. Locke, and Sir Isaac Newton, were very indecent men; and yet, if history says true, the last of them, at least, was remarkably *modest*. They were, likewise, guilty of great *arrogance*, because they ought to have considered, that the prevailing opinions, which they called in question, had at least a greater chance to be right than their *singular* notions. But, well versed as Newton was in the *doctrine of chances*, he had not, it seems, attended to its use in ascertaining the truth of theological opinions. He might possibly think, with me, that, if this new standard of truth were admitted, no new opinion must ever be indulged, unless it should happen, by an extraordinary concurrence of circumstances, to jump into the heads of the greatest part of the world at the same instant of time. Nay, if this should happen, none of them must venture to publish his opinion, because he could not know but it might be a singular one. This new use of the doctrine of chances, brings to my mind a story I have heard of two school-boys, who were disputing which of them was the better scholar; when one of them proposed to determine it by the tossing up of a half-penny.

But to go on with this author to his last mentioned consequence of reviling public opinions, viz. the *ingratitude* of this conduct. If I had not quoted the whole paragraph relating to this subject, I might have taken another opportunity of putting my reader upon guessing, by what medium of proof this admirable logician could possibly connect his two propositions. For that a man, who reviles the opinions of another, doth thereby deny him liberty of conscience, is to me utterly incomprehensible. If my friend entertain a foolish and absurd opinion, cannot I endeavour to laugh him out of it, without denying him his *right* to hold it. Then every man that laughs is a persecutor. Besides, how do *the retainers to our petty conventicles* (as this excellent writer very elegantly, and respectfully expresses himself) enjoy any liberty of conscience at all, if it be in the power of those who *revile* them to deny it them? If this were the case, this great privilege would be lost every day, especially on a Thirtieth

tieth of January, and could never furvive the publication of this fourth volume of Dr. Blackftone's Commentaries.

THIS whole paragraph is, I think, an unparallelled piece of elegance and reafoning. But *retainers to petty conventicles*, muft be guilty of *indeeency*, *arrogance*, and *ingratitude*, and fuch proofs, of the charge as thefe of Dr. Blackftone's are eafily found. Whether the water run from the lamb to the wolf, or from the wolf to the lamb, the weaker muft be guilty. I wonder, indeed, that this author, whofe invention is fo fertile, fhould not have added a few more articles to this black lift ; fince he could have found no peculiar difficulty in increafing it to a hundred, unlefs terms of reproach in the Englifh language fhould have failed him.

I ALSO cannot help wondering, that it fhould never feem to have occurred to Dr. Blackftone, that every thing he has advanced about Diffenters would have come with much more propriety from the mouth of a Papift, in a remonftrance againft the conduct of the firft reformers. Every argument he has urged would then have had double force. If, for example, it be *indecent*, *arrogant*, and *ungrateful* in us to think differently from the church of England, which is, as it were, but a thing of yefterday; much more indecent, arrogant, and ungrateful muft it have been for Wickliffe, Luther, Calvin, Cranmer, &c. to have prefumed to think differently from a church fo antient and venerable as that of Rome. The Papifts, with far more plaufibility, alledge, that the firft reformers could be actuated by no *laudable motive*, and that their labours were *calculated for no other purpofe*, *than merely to difturb the confciences and poifon the minds of men*. And as to *political reafons*, for *one* that Dr. Blackftone can alledge in his caufe the Papifts might have alledged *twenty*.

IF the revilers of the Diffenters find themfelves incommoded by their own arguments being thus retorted upon them, let them learn, for the future, to profit by the advice of our Lord, Matt. vii. 1. *Judge*

vii. 1. *Judge not that ye be not judged; for with what judgment ye judge, ye shall be judged; and with what measure ye mete, it shall be measured to you again.*

WITH perfect coolness I now close my remarks on the offensive paragraphs I have quoted in Dr. Blackstone's Commentaries, from the value of which I am by no means disposed to detract. Every *Englishman* is under obligation to this writer, for the pains he has taken to render the laws of his country intelligible, and the *philosopher* will thank him for rendering the study of them easy and engaging : but the *man* cannot help regretting that there should be any thing *servile* or *illiberal* in a work of so much excellence; and the *christian* will weep over every symptom of groundless rancour, and unmerited abuse that occurs in it; and lament, that this teacher of *human laws*, should have imbibed so little of that candid and benevolent spirit which distinguishes *the laws of christianity*, and which should influence every person who acknowledges their obligation, whatever station in life he fills, and in whatever field he chuses to employ himself for the public good.

INSULTED as I conceive myself to have been, in the injurious representation this writer has made of the principles and and practices of the Dissenters, I may, in return, have expressed my resentment of it with too much acrimony. Seeing, in a strong point of light, the weakness and folly of his censures, I may have treated them with more contempt and ridicule than a mere by-stander will altogether enter into, and consequently approve. But I hope that I have committed no offence, in either of these respects, that a truly impartial by-stander, who considers the provocation will think yenial. There is no man who is not formed sensible both to affronts, and to ridicule; and it is with difficulty that an ingenuous mind, restrains the natural expressions of its real feelings. I also am a man, and claim the privilege of humanity.

IN

In order to make my apology to Dr. Blackſtone in particular, let him ſuppoſe, if ſo great a misfortune can be ſuppoſed,
that himſelf and not I, had been the ſectary, and myſelf not he,
the great lawyer and able writer; that his father and grand-
father, mother and grandmother, having been Preſbyterians,
he had no more idea of *the crime of mere non-conformity*, than I ſuppoſe he now has of *the virtue of flagellation*, or any other volun-
tary penance of the church of Rome, notwithſtanding the good
he might receive from thoſe wholeſome ſeverities, and notwithſtanding his good inclinations to the poor flagellants:

Let him ſuppoſe, that his deluded parents had been ſo fatally
attentive to his education (and that he had in conſequence of it,
ſo deeply imbibed the *principles*, and been ſo long enured to the
practices of the ſectaries,) that all his reading and thinking afterwards did but tend the more to confirm him in them; that,
though he frequently went to the eſtabliſhed church, and was
much better acquainted with the method in which public worſhip is conducted there, than he now is with what paſſes in *petty
conventicles;* he was, neverthelefs, ſo abſurd, as really to prefer the extemporaneous effuſions of a miſerable enthuſiaſt, to
the *excellent doctrines*, and *methodical compoſition* of the Engliſh liturgy:

Let him ſuppoſe, that though, like me, he had been particularly fond of going, with his neighbours, to the *chriſtian ſervice* of the Thirtieth of January, he was ſo far from entering into the pious deſign of that religious inſtitution (the excellence of
which has preſerved it from corruption or abuſe for more than a
century) that it was rather to amuſe himſelf upon the occaſion,
with ſeeing exemplified the prudent care of the bees, in beſlim-
ing and encruſting the carcaſe of a mouſe, or other noxious ani-
mal, the ſtench of which was in danger of proving offenſive to
them; and that though he was far from entertaining any veneration for the *military hypocrites and enthuſiaſts*, who conferred

E the

the honour of martyrdom on the bleffed Charles; yet, rather than pay devotion at his fhrine, he would have gloried in being defcended from the man, who, on the fcaffold, wifhed to be tranfmitted to pofterity as one *who had a hand and a heart in the death of that tyrant :*

WITH this character, and thefe fentiments, let him fuppofe that I, the great lawyer and able writer, Solicitor-general to the Queen, and in connection with the prefent Britifh miniftry, (whofe adminiftration is likely to make fo great a figure in the future annals of this renowned country) had written his excellent *Commentaries on the Laws of England*, a work that would neceffarily go into the hands of all the youth of the Britifh nation, and could not fail to make them hate and defpife the *fect* to which he belonged, and to which (how unreafonably foever) he was fo firmly attached : In this cafe, I cannot help thinking that, if he, like me, had learnt a little Englifh of his mother, as well as a fmattering of Latin and Greek at a public grammar fchool, he would, in order as far as in him lay, to prevent the impending mifchief, or at leaft to fhow his own fenfe of the injury and infult, have written fome fuch a pamphlet as this, which, with all deference and refpect, I now prefent to the public, and to Dr. Blackftone.

LEEDS, JULY, 1769.

F I N I S.

A REPLY

TO

Dr. *PRIESTLEY*'s

REMARKS

ON THE

FOURTH VOLUME

OF THE

COMMENTARIES

ON THE

LAWS OF ENGLAND.

BY THE
AUTHOR OF THE COMMENTARIES.

AMERICA:

PRINTED FOR THE SUBSCRIBERS,
By ROBERT BELL, at the late UNION LIBRARY, in *Third-street*
PHILADELPHIA, MDCCLXXIII.

A REPLY

TO

Dr. *PRIESTLEY's*

REMARKS, *&c.*

D R. *Priestley* having publifhed, in a very angry Pamphlet, his *Remarks on fome paragraphs in the fourth volume of my Commentaries*, I find myfelf called upon to take fome notice of a performance, to which an author, of reputation in the literary world, has very fairly fubfcribed his name.

T H E method, which I have hitherto obferved, with regard to the numerous ftrictures which my Commentaries have excited, has been to neglect them intirely, if I thought them miftaken or trifling: But, if founded in juftice, from whatever quarter they came, I have availed myfelf of the truths they imparted, and have endeavoured to correct my own miftakes in fome fubfequent impreffion of the book: So true is Dr. *Priestley's* obfervation*, that I have " no objection to making alterations in the new editions " of my works". For I have always thought it more honourable to retract, than to perfevere in an error; and have neither
leifure

* Page 10.

leisure, inclination, nor ability, to dip myself in controversy of any kind, much less theological controversy. But I have departed this once from my usual rule, not with an intention to enter into personal altercation with Dr. *Priestley* (in which I am by no means a match for him) but principally to explain my own sentiments with respect to *religious liberty*, which that gentleman hath taken an handle very greatly to mis-represent.

BEFORE I descend to particulars, I must first of all correct a mistake, which Dr. *Priestley* seems to have fallen into*, by fancying that the offensive passages in my book were *personally* levelled at *him*. Let me assure him, that they were written above fifteen years ago, before I believe, he had ever appeared as an author: And let me add, that, till his present Remarks, I never read any of his productions, excepting his history of electricity ; from whence I conceived a very favourable impression of his talents as a *candid* and *ingenious* writer. How greatly my opinion, with respect to the first of those qualities, has been altered by his late publication, I leave to himself to imagine.

HE supposes me, throughout his performance, to be a bigotted high-church-man, and of a persecuting spirit in matters of religious differences: and to support the opinion, which he has thus unaccountably taken up, he observes†, that I quote *with approbation* the statutes of king *William* against *Arians*, and strongly intimates, that I wish for a revival of the penal laws against the Dissenters.

TO the first charge I answer, that I have barely recited that statute, without either approving or disapproving it. To refute the second, I need only refer to the very pages‡ from whence this author has cited the Paragraph, with which he is principally displeased. The Reader will there find it laid down, " that " our ancestors were certainly mistaken in their plans of compul-
" sion

---

* Page 9, 10, 32, &c.   † Page 28.   ‡ Comm. p. 52, 53.

" fion and intolerance:—that the fin of fchifm, as fuch, is by no
" means the object of temporal coercion and punifhment:—that
" if men quarrel with the ecclefiaftical eftablifhment, the civil
" magiftrate has nothing to do with it, unlefs their tenets and
" practice are fuch as threaten ruin or difturbance to the ftate:—
" that all perfecution for diverfity of opinions is contrary to eve-
" ry principle of found policy and civil freedom;—that, in par-
" ticular, the laws of queen Elizabeth and king Charles II. a-
" gainft the Diffenters, were fuch as I fhould not undertake to
" juftify:—and that the fubfequent indulgence fhewn by the
" toleration-act arofe from a fpirit of true magnanimity in the
" legiflature."

I HAVE indeed illuftrated this doctrine with a few hiftorical
remarks to fhew the motives of originally enacting thofe penal
laws, which are now fufpended by the toleration-act, and in
which I have declared that our anceftors were certainly miftaken.
I have deduced them from the turbulent difpofition which the
Diffenters had fhewn *in former times*; and which I believe no moderate Diffenter will deny to have *formerly* exifted among many of
the feparation, though perhaps he may think it was excited by
the haughtinefs and rigour of the churchmen. I have faid, that
both Papifts and Proteftant Diffenters *were efteemed* by the laws
enacted fince the reformation (not that *I at prefent efteem them*)
to *offend* through a miftaken or perverfe zeal; that they *were
fuppofed* (not that I *fuppofe* them) to be equally fchifmatics, &c. as
in the paffage cited by Dr. *Prieftley**. And then follow thefe
words, " Yet certainly our anceftors were miftaken in their plans
" of compulfion and intolerance;" together with the reft of the
fentiments, which I have juft now quoted, and which alone were
intended to be delivered as my own opinion. But Dr. *Prieftley*
hath atributed to me the adoption of thofe principles, which I
only meant to mention hiftorically, as the caufes of the laws
which I condemn.

I SHALL

* Page 16.

I SHALL own very frankly, that (on reviewing this paſſage) I am convinced, that it is ſomewhat incorrect and confuſed ; and might lead a willing critic to conclude, that a general reflection was intended on the ſpirit, the doctrines, and the practice of the body of our *modern* Diſſenters. A reflection which I totally diſapprove: being perſuaded, that by far the greater part of thoſe, who have now the misfortune to differ from us in their notions of eccleſiaſtical government and public worſhip, have notwithſtanding a proper and decent reſpect for the church eſtabliſhed by law ; deteſt all outrageous attacks on its miniſters, liturgy, and doctrines ; and are zealous in ſupporting thoſe two great objects of every good citizen's care, and which are not ſo incompatible as ſome perſons ſeem to imagine, the *civil liberties* and the *peace* of their country. And ſo far am I from wiſhing to perpetuate or widen our unhappy differences, that I ſhall make it my care, in every ſubſequent edition of this volume, ſo to rectify the clauſe in queſtion, as to render it more expreſſive of that meaning which I here avow ; and which, if read with a due degree of candour, might before have been eaſily diſcerned.

BUT, after having made this ſacrifice to the ſpirit of truth and moderation, I muſt beg leave to inform Dr. *Prieſtley*, ſince it ſeems he is yet to learn it[*], that *non-conformity* is ſtill a crime by the laws of *England*, and has heavy penalties annexed to it, notwithſtanding the act of toleration (nay, expreſsly reſerved by that act[†]) in all ſuch as do not comply with the conditions thereby enjoined. In caſe the legiſlature had intended to aboliſh both the crime and the penalty, it would at once have repealed all the penal laws enacted againſt nonconformiſts. But it keeps them expreſsly in force againſt all Papiſts, oppugners of the trinity, and perſons of no religion at all : and only exempts from their rigour ſuch ſerious, ſober minded Diſſenters, as ſhall have taken the oaths and ſubſcribed the declaration at the ſeſſions, and ſhall regularly repair

---

* Page 29,   † Sect. 16.

repair to fome licenfed place of religious worſhip. But, though theſe ſtatutes oblige me to confider nonconformity as a breach of the law, yet, (notwithſtanding Dr. *Prieſtley*'s ſtrictures) I ſhall ſtill continue to think, that *reviling the ordinances of the church* is a crime of a much groſſer nature than the other of mere *nonconformity.*

F A R be it from me to wiſh any reſtraint to be laid on rational and difpationate enquiries into the rectitude and propriety of our national mode of worſhip. What I have cenſured (and indeed not I, but the law) is not, as Dr. *Prieſtley* moſt unwarrantably fuppoſes*, the *thinking differently from the church of England*;— but the *treating it with contempt and rudeneſs,* the *inveighing with bitterneſs againſt the Engliſh liturgy,* and the *virulent declamations of peeviſh or opinionated men,* in oppoſition to the eccleſiaſtical eſtabliſhment. If Dr. *Prieſtley* is guilty of theſe practices, (though, whether he is fo or not, I profeſs myſelf intirely ignorant, unleſs from his preſent publication) he falls within the danger of the laws; if otherwiſe, he is totally unconcerned in the cenſure.

B u t why, let me aſk, does Dr. *Prieſtley* apply theſe characters, to the body of our preſent Diſſenters? I have not applied them to any, but a few of their anceſtors *in the infancy of our preſent eſtabliſhment,* and to ſuch modern writers of all denominations (not confining them to Proteſtant Diſſenters) as have trodden too cloſely in their ſteps. If I were weak enough to apply them in general to the Diſſenters of the preſent times, and if he were hardy enough to deny the indecent behaviour of fome antient polemical Puritans, we ſhould both of us offend againſt the truth. He will not, I am perſuaded, maintain, that all proteſtant Diſſenters are virulent declaimers againſt the liturgy ; or that none will fall under that deſcription but proteſtant Diſſenters only. I have mentioned the Papiſts as guilty of the very ſame practice : I may alſo add the Infidels and Deiſts. The mentioning theſe oppoſites

F   together,

* Page 30.

together, and involving them in one and the same censure, for one and the same offence, has greatly offended Dr. *Priestley**. But, if men of better principles will be found in bad company upon such an occasion, the law makes no distinction of persons. It indulges them with full liberty of conscience in every other instance, but that of railing at the national establishment. And I should think the same practice would be equally unjustifiable, if directed against the Presbyterian church of *Scotland*, by any Episcopalian there : both churches, since the union, deriving from the law of the land an equal claim to protection and *perpetual* security.

Dr. PRIESTLEY seems astonished†, that I can possibly consider (as I certainly have done) any alteration in the constitution of the churches of *England* or *Scotland*, or in the liturgy of the former, as an infringement of the fundamental and essential conditions of the *British* union. If this doctrine be new to the reader as well as to Dr. *Priestley*, let me only recommend to his perusal the statute, 5 *Ann.* c. 5. which, in order " that the doctrine, " worship, discipline, and government of the church of *England* " may be effectually and *unalterably* secured," confirms and *perpetuates* all acts then in force for its establishment ; particularly the acts of uniformity, of which the book of common-prayer is a part;—enjoins an oath to be taken by every sovereign at his coronation, for preserving *inviolably* the said doctrine, worship, discipline, and government;— and declares that the said act shall forever be holden and adjudged a fundamental and essential part of any treaty of union with *Scotland*, shall be inserted at length in any act of parliament, that shall ratify such treaty of union, and be therein declared an essential and fundamental part thereof. Let him consult a similar act of the *Scotch* parliament, whereby the like precautions are taken " for securing the Presbyterian " church-government and discipline in that kingdom, with the " form

" form and purity of worſhip preſently in uſe within the ſame."
Let him then peruſe the ſtatute 5 *Ann.* c. 8. which ratifies the
articles of union, and declares thoſe two acts to be *fundamental
and eſſential conditions* thereof. And, when he has done this, let
him judge for himſelf, whether any alterations in the conſtitution
or liturgy of the church of *England,* would or would not be in-
fringements of thoſe fundamental conditions : or whether, according to Dr. *Prieſtley**, the articles of union only " *ſeem* to
" confirm the different eſtabliſhments of *England* and *Scotland* as
" they then ſtood, with liberty to make any improvements in
" their reſpective conſtitutions,if they themſelves *ſeparately tak-*
" *en,* ſhould think proper." Indeed, without diſſolving the union, I do not ſee, how the ſenſe of either nation could now be *ſeparately taken ;* how the *Scots* peers or commoners could be prevented from voting either *for* or *againſt* the repeal of the acts of
uniformity, in caſe it were moved in either houſe? or how, without ſuſpending the parliament of *Great Britain,* Dr. *Prieſtley*
would now procure " an act of the *Engliſh parliament,* for reforming the church of *England*†."

A N D, however new or ſurpriſing my conſtruction of this national treaty may appear to Dr. *Prieſtley,* it is certainly conſonant
to the ideas entertained by both nations at the time of the union;
who imagined that they had obtained the moſt ſolemn and ſacred ſecurity that human polity could poſſibly give, that the government and mode of worſhip of their reſpective churches
ſhould for ever remain inviolable. For which I may appeal to
the teſtimony not only of biſhop *Burnet,* the hiſtorian of thoſe
times, and a very active inſtrument in promoting the progreſs of
the union, but alſo of the late Duke of *Argyle* and lord chancellor
Cowper, two of the commiſſioners who negotiated that important
treaty.

THE bishop gives the following account of the opposition that was raised in *Scotland*, by those who wished ill to that measure*. " They insisted most vehemently on the danger that the " constitution of the church would be in, when all should be " under the power of a *British* parliament.—To allay this heat, " an act was prepared for securing the Presbyterian government ; " by which it was declared to be the only government of that " church *unalterable in all succeeding times ;* and the maintaining " of it was declared to be a fundamental and essential article and " condition of the union: And this act was to be made a part of " the act for the union, &c.—By this means the act was carried " as far as any human law could go for their security. For by " this they had not only all the security that their own parlia- " ment could give them, but they were to have the *faith* and *au-* " *thority* of the parliament of *England*; it being, *in the stipulation,* " made an *essential condition* of the union."

HE afterwards gives the history of the rise and progress of the *English* act of parliament; and concludes with exactly the same sentiments (with respect to the *power* of alteration, which must nevertheless still reside in the supreme legislature of the united kingdoms) as I have borrowed and adopted from the bishop of *Glocester ;* and for which his lordship is pronounced by Dr. *Priestley*[†] to be as *weak a quibbler* as myself. " The archbishop of *Canterbury*" (says Dr. *Burnet*[‡]) " moved that a bill might be " brought in for securing the church of *England*. By it all acts " passed in favour of our church were declared to be in full " force *for ever :* and this was made a fundamental and essential " part of the union. Some exceptions were taken to the words " of the bill, as not so strong as the act passed in *Scotland* seemed " to be, since the *government* of it was not declared *unalterable.* " But they were judged more proper; since, where a supreme " legislature is once acknowledged, nothing can be *unalterable.*"

THE

* Hist. of his own Times, ii. 461.   † Page 12, 13.   ‡ Burnet *ibid.* 463.

THE opinions of the other two noble lords were publiskly declared in the debates on the debates on the ftatutes 5 *Geo.* I. *c.* 4. as they may be found in the periodical pamphlets of the times, and as they are fince collected in volumes*. As that bill was originally con-ftructed, it contained not only a repeal of the acts againft *occafi-onal Conformity* and *Schifm*, which had been enacted *fince* the uni-on, but alfo of fome claufes in the *Teft* and *Corporation* acts, which were confirmed and perpetuated by that treaty. In the debates during the progrefs of that bill, the late duke of *Argyle* (at that time Earl of *Ilay*) faid: " that every body knew he was educated
" in a different way from the church of *England*: but neverthe-
" lefs he could not but be againft this bill; becaufe, in his opi-
" nion, it broke the *Pacta Conventa* of the treaty of union, by
" which the bounds both of the church of *England* and of the
" church of *Scotland*, were fixed and fettled: And his lordfhip
" was apprehenfive, that if the articles of the union were broke
" with refpect to one church, it might afterwards be a prece-
" dent to break them with refpect to the other."

LORD COWPER had faid juft before, " that tho' he had always
" a tender regard for the Diffenters, yet he could not but op-
" pofe that part of the bill then before the houfe, whereby part
" of the *Teft* and *Corporation* acts were effectually repealed with
" relation to Diffenters; becaufe he looked upon thefe acts as
" the *main bulwarks* of our excellent conftitution in church and
" ftate, and therefore to be inviolably preferved." And, upon the reafons thus offered in this debate, it was agreed to leave out all the claufes that affected the laws ratified by the union: and to pafs the act as it now ftands, containing merely a repeal of the two ftatutes of Queen *Anne* againft *Schifm* and *occafional Conformi-ty*, and a provifion that no magiftrate fhould appear with the En-figns of his office at a meeting-houfe.

AFTER

* Hiftorical Regifter, *A.D.* 1719, pag. 57, 58. Timberland's Debates of the Houfe of Lords, iii. 99. 101. 110.

AFTER this hiftorical deduction, and contemporary expofition of thefe laws, I think it is not altogether certain, that either nation would fully acquiefce in Dr. *Prieftley*'s conftruction
of the treaty of union : And, if they fhould not, the refcinding
of any part of its fundamental and effential conditions, would be
very *unadvifeable* and *dangerous*.   Indeed I have allowed that the
power of new-modelling the churches both of *England* and *Scotland*(however *dangerous* its exertion might be) ftill refides in the
parliament of *Great-Britain*; and have conceded that, in cafe the
fervice of the church of *England* be *manifeftly impious* or *fhockingly
abfurd*, all dangers fhould be encountered to reform it.   Dr.
Prieftley very roundly afferts*, that it is *manifeftly impious*, is
fhockingly abfurd, nay,that it is even *idolatrous*. Here then we meet
upon fair ground.   Let its *Idolatry*, *Impiety*, or *fhocking abfurdity*
be proved to the fatisfaction of the legiflature ; and my *political*
objections are at an end. But, till that can be done, I fhall continue to think it too hazardous, to move fo momentous a queftion as the ftability of the *Britifh* union, for the fake of fome fan-
cied improvements in matters either trivial or indifferent. And,
confidering the fubject in this light, any *bitter invective*, or *virulent declamation* againft the mode of our national worfhip, is at
leaft unavailing, and can *anfwer* no laudable end. Perhaps it was
going too far to fay it could be *calculated* for none. I am willing
to hope, that whenever fuch things have appeared, they have a-
rifen from miftake, or ignorance, or from the overflowings of a
well-meant zeal, but not regulated according to knowledge.

WITH regard to the want of logical and hiftorical knowledge which Dr. *Prieftley* has difcovered in *the Commentaries*, and
his perfonal reflections on the author's political connections†, I
fhall leave him in full poffeffion of them : remarking only, that
this is not an age in which a man who thinks for himfelf, and
who endeavours to think with moderation, can expect to meet
with quarter from any fide, amid the rage of contending parties.
If, in a matter of mere hiftory and fpeculation, he condemns the
conduct

* Page 8. 17.   † Page 6. and 34.

conduct of the elder *Charles*, but difapproves of the tragical extremes to which his opponents proceeded, he is a friend to Popery and arbitrary power ; whatever proofs to the contrary may
abound in the reft of his writings. If, after a concurrence of
many years together in moft of their political meafures, he differs from his friends in one great conftitutional point, in confequence of the moft diligent enquiry and mature reflection he becomes immediately *connected with*, and *poffeffes the confidence* of a
miniftry, to which he has fcarce the honour to be known, and
from which he holds himfelf totally detatched. If he argues for
toleration and indulgence to Diffenters of every denomination,
but cenfures with fome warmth all indecent attacks upon the
eftablifhment, he commences a bigot and a perfecutor. In this
temper of the times, I am fenfible that all apologies are idle, and
all vindications ufelefs. Yet I thought it a duty to myfelf
thus publickly to declare, that my notions, in refpect to religious indulgence, are not quite fo intolerant as Dr. *Prieftley* has endeavoured to reprefent them; efpecially as fome expreffions of
my own, (not fufficiently attended to, when the work was re-
vifed for the prefs) may have countenanced fuch an opinion in a
fuperficial or captious reader. But, when thus fet to rights and
explained, I truft they will give no offence to any moderate
and confcientious Diffenter; and that Dr. *Prieftley* himfelf, when
he comes to re-confider his remarks, will wifh they had been
written lefs haftily, and had of courfe been more agreeable to
juftice as well as to common civility.

Wallingford, Sep. 2, 1769.

F I N I S.

A N

A N S W E R

T O

Dr. *BLACKSTONE's*

R E P L Y

T O

R E M A R K S

ON THE

FOURTH VOLUME

OF THE

C O M M E N T A R I E S

ON THE

L A W S OF E N G L A N D.

By JOSEPH PRIESTLEY, LL. D. F. R. S.

o

A M E R I C A:

PRINTED FOR THE SUBSCRIBERS,

By ROBERT BELL, at the late UNION LIBRARY, in *Third-ſtreet,*

PHILADELPHIA. M DCC LXXIII.

AN

ANSWER

TO

Dr. *BLACKSTONE*'s

REPLY, *&c.*

SIR,

I HAVE juſt received your *Reply* to my *Remarks on ſome paragraphs in the Fourth Volume of your Commentaries*; and I ſin-
cerely thank and eſteem you for it. It is a genteel and liberal
anſwer to a pamphlet written, as you candidly and juſtly conjecture, in great haſte; and which, I frankly acknowledge, is
not, in all reſpects, ſuch as I now wiſh it had been. You will
give me leave, however, to obſerve, that I have not treſpaſſed
upon civility ſo far as you have repreſented, when you ſay,
page 44, that I call you *a weak quibbler*. I only ſaid you *argued
weakly, and upon principles by which you might quibble away all the
natural rights of man*. I did not even ſay that *you had quibbled*
(indeed you have not touched upon that ſubject) much leſs did I

call

call you a *quibbler*. And I apprehend that, in point of decorum, there is an evident gradation in those expressions, and that the first which I have used, is not, by many degrees, so offensive as the last, which you have ascribed to me. With respect to my charging you with *the want of logical and historical knowledge*, the very turn of my sentences shews that I was not serious.

As angry as my pamphlet appears to you, I do assure you, Sir, it never entered into my head, that any thing in your Commentaries was personally levelled at me; nor, till I saw your pamphlet, could I have imagined, that such a construction could have been put upon my words. Fifteen years ago, when you say your Commentaries were written, I was so far from having *appeared as an author*, that I could hardly be deemed capable of writing at all; but I conceived myself to be insulted in the injurious representations you had given of the principles and practices of the *Dissenters in general;* and so long as I am capable of writing, as well as of feeling, I cannot promise, that I shall always be able to let things of such a nature, coming from persons of reputation and influence, pass without notice. The resentment I shewed was at your own insinuation, that *the spirit, the doctrine, and the practices of Dissenters, as such, were not calculated to make men good subjects;* a reflection that could not but deeply affect a large body of men, who consider themselves, and who imagined they had been considered by others, as most zealously attached to the constitution of this country, as a limited monarchy ; to be foremost in their zeal for the settlement of the crown on the house of Hanover; and, indeed, to be most nearly interested in it.

If I mistook your meaning, in supposing that your reflections were intended for the *modern* Dissenters, I can assure you, that superficial and captious as you take me to be, I was far from being singular in that mistake. It was the construction that every person that I have yet conversed with upon the subject, put upon them; and the paragraphs I have animadverted upon were
actually

actually confidered by many perfons, as a notification to Diffen-ters, in what light they were confidered by thofe who are now in power. They even gave great offence to many worthy and diftinguifhed members of the eftablifhed church; and affected fome of them, who could not be called *willing critics*, with as much indignation as they did me. But the generous manner in which you promife to correct thofe offenfive paragraphs, does you the greateft honour, and more than cancels all that is paft.

THOUGH, after your example, I compofed and delivered a courfe of lectures on the conftitution and laws of England (a fyllabus of which is printed in my *Effay on a courfe of liberal educa-tion for civil and active life*).I profefs to be no more than a very fu-perficial lawyer; I am even afhamed to touch upon a fubject of this kind, in writing to a man of your diftinguifhed abilities in this way, and I fhall not choofe to debate the matter with you; yet I muft own, that you have not convinced me that *mere noncon-formity* is any crime in the laws of England. I apprehend it to have been no offence at common law, and that fince all penalties in-flicted by particular acts of parliament, are declared by the *act of toleration*, not to extend to thofe who comply with the terms of that act, that fuch perfons are in no fenfe criminal. The church of England has no authority but what it derives from the fancti-on of parliament, fo that our privileges ftand exactly upon the fame ground. *Some Nonconformifts*, it is acknowledged, are guilty of a crime in the eye of the law, and fo are *fome men*; but is it therefore proper to fay, that *mere humanity* is criminal?

ADMITTING mere nonconformity to be a crime, I fhould readily have agreed with you, that *reviling the ordinances of the church was a crime of a groffer nature*. I only objected to the *rea-fons* you gave for afferting it to be a crime fo aggravated, namely, *its carrying with it the utmoft indecency, arrogance, and ingratitude*; and ftill more, to the *manner* in which you prove it to be inde-cent, arrogant, and ungrateful.

I MUST

I MUST also beg leave still to dissent from you, with respect to the perpetuity of the ecclesiastical establishments of England and Scotland being intended to be provided for by the *act of union*. I still think that all that those persons, who framed it, really meant, was to bar all encroachments of the one upon the other. Were any man now living to tell me he was going to prepare an instrument, whereby he should bind himself, and his heirs for ever, from changing their opinions, or from acting in consequence of any change in them, I should not easily believe him ; and that the representatives of two great and wise nations should seriously act in this manner is, to me, altogether incredible. If the fact be otherwise, it is such as, in my opinion, throws the greatest reflection on the founders of both establishments, and also on the establishments themselves. But it appears to me, from the paragraph you have quoted from bishop Burnet, page 44, " that the reason of the act of a Scottish parliament, intended to secure the Presbyterian government, previous to the union, was nothing else than the danger, they apprehended the constitution of their church to be in, from the power of a British parliament." The same principle also influenced the duke of Argyle, as you have represented his conduct, page 45.

I SHOULD also be disposed to infer from the passage you have quoted from Bishop Burnet, page 44, that our legislators, at the time of the union, expressly disapproved of the Scots having declared their church establishment to be unalterable ; since, where there is a supreme legislature, nothing can be so. This is the construction put upon those very words by the ingenious author of " Occasional remarks on some late strictures on the Confession- " al, part II. page 45." which I had not seen when I wrote my Remarks.

You say, Page 47, " that you condemn the conduct of the elder Charles, but disapprove of the tragical extremes to which his opponents proceeded." I also sincerely say the same ; for, though

though I go one ſtep farther than you do, having no idea of exempting from puniſhment any perſon placed in an office of truſt, how great and important ſoever; yet I neither approve of the uſurpation of Cromwell, nor of the attempts that were made to eſtabliſh a republic in this nation.

Y o u ſay, Page 31, " that you have barely recited the ſtatute againſt Arians, without approving or diſapproving it." I was led to think you approved of it, by the whole tenor of the paragraph in which it is introduced. The words that immediately precede it are theſe: " Under theſe reſtrictions, it ſeems neceſſary, for the ſupport of the national religion, that the officers of the church ſhould have power to cenſure heretics, but not to exterminate or deſtroy them. It has alſo been thought proper for the civil magiſtrate again to interpoſe, with regard to one ſpecies of hereſy, very prevalent in modern times; for ſtatute, &c." This I think, will be ſome apology for my miſtaking your meaning.

Y o u r ſaying that *many Diſſenters divided from the eſtabliſhed church upon no reaſon at all*, tempted me to mention the ſtrongeſt reaſon that I had for my own diſſent, relating to the proper unity of God; but the ſevere cenſure I paſſed on the oppoſite opinion, namely, the impiety of it, I at the ſame time, declared to be by no means applicable to thoſe perſons who are conſcientious in their belief. Important however as I conceive this doctrine to be, affecting what is moſt fundamental in both natural and revealed religion, and conſequently in all the eſtabliſhments of it, I do not think it my buſineſs, as you hint to me, to addreſs the legiſlature upon the ſubject, conceiving, that as a teacher of chriſtianity, I have nothing to do with men as magiſtrates, but only as individuals.

I s h a l l think myſelf very happy if by means of this letter I be able in any meaſure to recover my character for candour

with

with a perfon of whofe abilities, as a writer, I have formed, and in the height of my refentment expreffed, fo high an opinion. Many perfons however of tafte, and liberality of fentiment, and perfons no way connected with me in religious perfuafion, friendfhip, or even acquaintance, acquit me in this refpect; and I believe, that confidering the provocation, the world in general will acquit me, but I do not acquit myfelf; and had I been convinced that I had done you injuftice on any other refpect, I fhould have acknowledged it with the fame franknefs.

My pamphlet, if it be the occafion of making the flighteft improvement in a work fo valuable as yours, will not be without its merit to the public. It was literally the creature of a day, and, figuratively fpeaking, its exiftence cannot be of much longer duration; whereas your Commentaries on the laws of England will probably laft as long as the laws themfelves.

I am not fo indifferent to reputation with men of fenfe, eminence, and worth, as lightly to incur the difpleafure of a perfon of your character. Nothing would have induced me to rifque it, but the fuperior regard I conceived to be due to the caufe of truth and that refpectable part of the community to which I belong, the proteftant Diffenters; men, who notwithftanding their misfortune with refpect to their religious fentiments, have, in the opinion of thofe whom we think impartial, and liberal minded, great merit with their fellow citizens, and are equal friends to the peace as well as to the liberties of this country.

I am, Sir, yours, &c.

Leeds, Octo. 2, 1769.

JOSEPH PRIESTLEY,

F I N I S.

THE
CASE

OF THE

LATE ELECTION

FOR THE

COUNTY of MIDDLESEX,

CONSIDERED

On the Principles of the Conftitution,

AND THE

AUTHORITIES OF LAW.

By the AUTHOR of
COMMENTARIES ON THE LAWS OF ENGLAND.

AMERICA:
PRINTED FOR THE SUBSCRIBERS,
By ROBERT BELL, at the late UNION LIBRARY, in *Third-ftreet*,
PHILADELPHIA. MDCCLXXIII.

THE

C A S E

Of the late ELECTION, &c.

THERE is a crisis, when, on certain subjects, the sober remonstrances of truth and reason, are of little avail against the misguided impetuosity of public prejudice.

HAPPILY, however, an intemperance of this kind is generally as transient as it is violent; and, as its rage abates, the minds of the people become open to conviction.

THERE is a regard due even to the misapprehensions of the public: And no prudent administration will be inattentive to what is called popular clamour.

INDEED the public opinion is seldom erroneous, when founded on just information : But removed, as the far greater part are, from the source of true intelligence, how easy is it for those who have an interest in imposing on the public, to mislead them by false representations, and alarm them with vain apprehensions ?

IMPELLED by such mistaken motives, how frequently have the people concurred in measures, which tended to defeat the

H 2

very

very ends they had in view, and which were ultimately deſtructive of their own good?

B u t there is that juſtice and generoſity in the public, not
always to be found in individuals. When the people, by candid
and temperate arguments, are perſuaded that their opinions and
apprehenſions are groundleſs, they are ready to renounce them
and to turn their reſentment againſt thoſe who have deceived
and miſled them.

L a t e r times ſcarce afford a ſtronger inſtance of miſappre-
henſion, than that which poſſeſſes the minds of ſome perſons,
with reſpect to the late important determination of the election
for the county of Middleſex.

A s few are acquainted with the true ſtate of this great conſtitutional queſtion, the writer of theſe ſheets, who has taken ſome
pains to inveſtigate it, thinks it the duty of a good citizen, to
ſubmit thoſe reaſons and authorities to the judgment of the public, which have brought conviction to his own mind.

T o this end, he propoſes to ſhew from the records of parliament, and the authorities of law, that the houſe of commons is
legally inveſted with the power they have exerciſed with reſpect
to the late determination of the election for Middleſex.

F a r t h e r, that, on the general principles of reaſon and
conſtitutional policy, they ought to have ſuch a power: And
that, in the inſtance in queſtion, they have exerciſed their power
in a juſt and conſtitutional manner, not only according to the
law and uſage of parliament, but in ſtrict conformity with the
abjudications in the court of Weſtminſter, on ſimilar occaſions.

T h a t the reader may be the better able to judge of the arguments tending to prove theſe propoſitions, it will be neceſſary
previouſly to ſtate the proceedings of the houſe this ſeſſion, with
                                                            reſpect

respect to Mr. *Wilkes*; more especially as the mistakes and misapprehensions, which possess the minds of some, arise from the want of being acquainted with these proceedings, or of considering them with due attention and accuracy.

Mr. WILKES, in the last parliament, was expelled from the house of commons. Being, moreover, by the verdicts of his country, convicted of crimes, for which infamous punishments have not unfrequently been inflicted, he thought proper to abscond; so that sentence could not then be passed upon him: Whereupon he was outlawed.

On the eve of the general election he neverthelefs appeared in public; and though an outlaw, was elected one of the knights of the shire for the county of Middlefex. His outlawry however was afterwards reversed, and sentence was passed upon him; in pursuance of which, he was committed *in execution*, to the prison of the king's bench.

Being in this situation, he himself brought the consideration of his particular circumstances before the house, by his own petition; which occasioned them to call for the records of the king's bench, whereby the several convictions against him, and the sentence passed thereon, appeared before the house.

His petition having been heard and determined, he was afterwards charged with a new offence; that of writing a preface to a letter which had been printed in the public papers: And in the beginning of February last, being at the bar of the house of commons, he confessed himself the author and publisher of the preface under consideration; which the house then resolved to be an insolent, scandalous, and seditious libel: And afterwards came to the following resolution;

" RESOLVED,

" RESOLVED,

" THAT John Wilkes, Efq; a member of this houfe, who
" hath, at the bar of this houfe, confeffed himfelf to be the au-
" thor and publifher of what this houfe has refolved to be an info-
" lent, fcandalous, and feditious libel: And who has been con-
" victed in the court of king's bench, of having printed and pub-
" lifhed a feditious libel, and three obfcene and impious libels,
" and by the judgment of the faid court, has been fentenced to
" undergo twenty-two months imprifonment, and is *now in exe-*
" *cution* under the faid judgment, be expelled this houfe."

Whereupon it was

" ORDERED,

" THAT Mr. Speaker do iffue his warrant to the Clerk of the
" crown, to make out a new writ for the electing a knight of the
" fhire to ferve in this prefent parliament, for the county of Mid-
" dlefex, in the room of John Wilkes, Efq; expelled this houfe."

MR. WILKES, however, being neverthelefs returned, the
Houfe, on the 17th of February 1769, came to the following
refolution ;

" RESOLVED,

" THAT John Wilkes, Efq; having been, in this feffion of
" parliament, expelled this houfe, WAS, and IS, *incapable of being*
" *elected* a member to ferve in this *prefent parliament.*"

IT appearing to the houfe, that there was no other candidate
at the laft election, it was refolved, farther, That it was a void
election: And it was

" ORDERED,

" THAT Mr. Speaker do iffue his warrant to the clerk of the
" crown to make out a new writ, for the electing a knight of the
" fhire

" fhire to ferve in this prefent parliament, for the county of Mid-
" dlefex, in the room of John Wilkes, Efq; who is ADJUDGED
" *incapable of being* elected a member to ferve in *this prefent par-*
" *liament,* and whofe election for the faid county has been de-
" clared void."

A GREAT part of the freeholders of Middlefex, however,
being influenced by a miftaken bias, obftinately perfifted in their
choice, and Mr. Wilkes was again returned. Whereupon the
houfe *refolved* the *election* and *return* of Mr. Wilkes to be null and
void ; and, no other candidate appearing to the houfe, they ordered a new writ.

A T the next election, Mr. Wilkes, notwithftanding the refolutions of the houfe, was again named as a candidate and returned.

WHEREUPON the houfe again refolved the election of Mr.
Wilkes to be null and void. But, it appearing to the houfe
that there were other candidates, they ordered the poll to be
brought before them; and it appearing on the face of the poll,
that, of the candidates capable of being elected, Mr. *Lutterell* had
the majority, they *refolved,* that Mr. *Lutterell* ought to have
been returned, and ordered the return to be amended, by inferting his name in the room of Mr. *Wilkes :* At the fame time they
allowed the ufual liberty for any party to petition on the merits
of the election.

I N confequence of this, fifteen freeholders did prefer a petition ; and on hearing the merits of that petition, the houfe *refolved*
that Mr. *Lutterell* was duly elected.

I N order to fhew that the houfe of commons is legally invefted
with the power they have exercifed on this occafion it will be
neceffary to explain the nature and extent of the powers conftitutionally vefted in that houfe.

T q

To preserve the equal poise, which the jealoufy of our conftitution has endeavoured to fettle, the three orders of the ftate are invefted with feparate, as well as conjunct powers.

The power of legiflation is joint ; and there can be no act of *legiflation*, which has not received the confent of the *three eftates :* But befides their *legiflative* power, each houfe has a *judicial* capacity, for the maintenance, among other purpofes of its own authority and independence. The peers, in their houfe, as lord *Coke* fays, have power of judicature, and the commons, in their houfe alfo have power of judicature : And farther, as he adds, both houfes together, have power of judicature *; and for this, he refers to the records of both houfes.

The rule, and only rule, by which their power of judicature is directed, is the *law of parliament :* which, as will appear, is part of *the law of the land.*

As every court of juftice, fays lord *Coke*†, hath laws and cuftoms for its direction, fome by the common law, fome by the civil and canon law, fome by peculiar laws and cuftoms, &c. fo the *high court of parliament fubfifts by its own proper laws and cuftoms.*

It is declared by the records of parliament, that all weighty matters moved concerning the peers of the realm, ought to be determined, *adjudged* and difcuffed by the *courfe of parliament*, and not by the civil law, nor yet by the common laws of the land ufed in other courts of the realm‡.

The fame declaration, for the like reafon, fays lord Coke, refpects the *commons*, for any thing done or moved in their houfe : And this is the reafon, he adds, why the *judges ought not to give any opinion of a matter of parliament, becaufe it is not to be decided by the common law, but according to the law and cuftom of parliament ;*

---

* 4 Inft. 23. † 4 Inft. 14. ‡ 11 R. 2. n. 7.

liament ; *and so the judges* (he concludes) *in divers parliaments have confessed**.

THUS it appears not only from the several declarations of the judges of the land, at different times, but from the authority of the records themfelves†, that there is a *law of parliament* which, in matters thereby cognizable, is diftinct from, and independent of all other laws ; but is, neverthelefs, a branch of the *law of the land*.

THE *law of parliament* is as much the *law of the land,* as the *common law*, or any other branch of the *general law,* which governs in this realm. Lord *Coke*, enumerating the feveral branches of which the law of the realm confifts, mentions the *law of parliament* as fecond in order.

COOPER, afterwards *lord Cooper*, in his fpeech in the cafe of *Afhby and White*, fays the *law and cuftom of parliament is a part of the law of the land*, and, *as fuch*, OUGHT TO BE TAKEN NOTICE OF BY ALL PERSONS.

LORD Chief Juftice *Holt*, in his argument concerning the granting of a *habeas corpus* to the *Ailefbury men*, fays, " *We are* " *bound to take notice of the cuftoms of parliament*, for they are a part " of the *law of the land*; and there are the fame methods of know- " ing it, as of knowing the law in Weftminfter-hall."—In another place he fays, The *law and cuftom of parliament, is as much the law of the land as any other law*.

THE fame language is held by *Hale,Petyt,Whitlocke,&c.*and will be found, in the courfe of thefe fheets, to have been pronounced

I   from

---

* By the record of parliament 31 H. 6. n. 27. the judges being confulted concerning the releafe of fome members of the commons, who had been imprifoned in the vacation, they anfwered, " That it was not their part to judge " of the parliament, which was judge of the law."

† The records of parliament, as lord Coke obferves, are the trueft hiftories.

from time to time, by the courts of juftice. In fhort, all who have ever written, or fpoken on this fubject, have treated the *law of parliament*, as part of the *law of the land*, and as a law which all perfons are bound to take notice of.

IT is by this law, and by this only, that the houfe of commons regulate their proceedings, with refpect to the various fubjects of the jurifdiction they exercife.

THE *law of parliament* may be confidered as compofed of two branches: 1. The rules, orders, cuftoms and courfe of the houfe, with their expofitions of, and decifions upon the law, with refpect to matters within their jurifdiction.

THE cuftoms, courfe, and common judicial proceedings of a court, are the *law of the court*, of which the common law takes notice, without alledging or pleading any ufage or prefcription to warrant them*.

THAT the courfe of any particular court is a law, and that the determinations of a court make part of the law of the land has been held from the earlieft times, fo far back even as the year book of 11 E. 42 b.

THUS the rules, orders, and courfe of the *houfe of commons*, with their expofition and decifions on matters cognizable before them, are as much the law of the land, as the rules and orders of the court of *king's bench*, or any other court, with *their* determinations are the law of the land. Nay, fuch proceedings and decifions of the houfe of commons, are in truth more binding than thofe of the courts at Weftminfter, becaufe from the former there lies no appeal, and it is effential, as will be fhewn, to the prefervation of public liberty, that no appeal fhould lie.

2. THE

* 2 Rep. 53.

2. THE second branch, compofing the law of parliament, confifts of the *ftatute law* of the realm, fo far as the fame regards the houfe of commons, or the jurifdiction thereof.

IT will not be material, on the prefent occafion, to enquire into the various fubjects over which the jurifdiction of the houfe of commons extends. It will be fufficient, with regard to the queftion now under confideration, to fhew not only from the authorities of the moft antient and refpectable lawyers but from the records of parliament*, that the houfe of commons—

1. HAVE the fole and exclufive power of punifhing their own members, *as fuch*; either by commitment, fufpenfion, expulfion, or otherwife.

2. THAT they have the fole and exclufive power of examining and determining the rights and qualifications of electors and elected, together with the returns of writs for the election of members, and in fhort all matters incidental to fuch elections.

1. As to their power of punifhing their own members, by commitment, *fufpenfion†*, or *expulfion‡*, &c. the inftances of the

I 2

exercife

---

* The journals of the houfe of commons are records, and mentioned as fuch 6 H. 8. c. 16.

† MEMBERS SUSPENDED.

Mr. Payne, For an offenfive fpeech: and complained of as a purveyor, &c. Sufpended the 3d of April 1604, till the doubt be cleared, whether he might ferve.

Mr. Barber, For granting warrants for billeting foldiers.—Sufpended the 9th of April 1628, during pleafure.

Sir Jo. Jacob, For monopoly.—Sufpended the 21ft of Nov. 1640, till his caufe be heard.

Mr. Hollis, For offenfive words—Sufpended the 26th of April 1641, during that feffion of parliament.

Mr.

exercife of thofe powers are innumerable, and the occafions on which it has been exercifed are various.

W ith regard to commitments, their power will not be dif-puted : but with refpect to *fufpenfions* and *expulfions*, more efpe-cially the latter, fome, with what reafon will be feen hereafter, have affected to call it in queftion.

It

Mr. Philips, For fitting in the pretended high court of juftice, &c.—Sufpend-ed the 27th of June 1661, till committee report, and houfe give judgment.

Mr. Love, For not communicating—Sufpended the 3d of July 1661, till he bring certificate of having communicated.

Sir Wm. Penn, For fraud and embezzlement.—Sufpended the 21ft of April 1668, while impeachment depending againft him.

Sir John Prettiman, For impofing on the houfe, with regard to the pro-tection of his fervant, Robert Humes—Sufpended the 8th of April 1670, till he fhall produce Robert Humes.

Mr. Culliford, For feveral mifdemeanors—Sufpended the 8th of March 1692, till he attend to anfwer.

‡ MEMBERS EXPELLED.

Arthur Hall, For a flanderous libel, derogatory to the authority of the houfe, &c. 14th Feb. 1580.

Sir John Bennet, For bribery, 23d April 1621.

William Sandys, Sir Jo. Jacob, and Thomas Webb, For monopoly, 21ft Jan. 1640.

Mr. Taylor, For words impeaching the juftice of the houfe, 27th May 1641.

Mr. Benfon, For felling protections, 2d Nov. 1641.

Mr. Afhburnham, For receiving 500l. from French merchants, 22d Nov. 1677.

Mr. Sackville, For afperfing the King. 25th March 1679.

Sir Francis Wythers, For prefenting an addrefs to his Majefty, expreffing an abhorency to petition his Majefty for calling parliaments, 29th Oct. 1680.

Sir Robert Beyton, For fecret negotiation with the duke of York, 14th Dec. 1680.

Sir Henry Furnefe, For breach of duty, as truftee for circulating exchequer bills under the 5 and 6 W. and M. 19th Feb. 1700.

Mr. Afgill, For being the author of a book, containing many *profane and blafphemous* expreffions, 18th Dec. 1707-8.

Mr.

I T appears from the lift in the note underneath, that the houfe have fufpended their members, fometimes during plea-fure, fometimes till the member fufpended does a certain act, or till fomething depending be determined ; and, at other times, during that particular feffion of parliament ; and the caufes of thefe fufpenfions, it is feen, are as well for offences committed without the houfe, as within it.

W I T H refpect to expulfions, they are much more numerous than fufpenfions. In the earlier times, before the parliamentary ftile had acquired that accuracy which it has fince attained, we find this fentence varioufly expreffed. Sometimes it is that the member be fevered and cut off; fometimes, that he be removed ; at other times, that he be difcharged, and at other times that he be put out; which are only fo many fynonimous expreffions fig-nifying expulfion :—and the word *expelled*, has for more than a century paft been conftantly ufed on thefe occafions.

F R O M the note in this and the foregoing page, the reader will perceive the various caufes for which this fentence has from time to time been inflicted. Sometimes for offences againft *re-ligion* fometimes for offences againft the *ftate*, fometimes for offences againft *morality*, and at other times for offences againft the *houfe* merely.

B U T

Mr. Ridge, For fraud as a contractor, 15th Feb. 1710.

Mr. Walpole, For breach of truft and corruption, 17th Jan. 1711.

Mr. Steel, For a *fcandalous and feditious libel*, 18th March 1713.

Mr. Pryfe, For a contempt of the houfe, 23d March 1715.

For other inftances, the reader may refer to the journals of 10 May 1571, 3d March 1620, 21 Jan. 1628, 21 Jan. 1640, 2 Feb. 1640, 27 May 1641, 30 Oct. 1641, 9 Dec. 1641, 2 Feb. 1641, 9 March 1641, 12 May 1642, 10 Aug. 1642, 11 June 1660, 21 April 1668, 1 Feb. 1677, 25 March 1679, 28 Oct. 1680, 13 May 1689, 12 arch 1694, 26 March 1695, 1 Feb. 1697, 20 Feb. 1698, 22 Feb. 1698, 16 April 1701, 1 Feb. 1702, 19 Feb. 1711, 10 Jan. 1715, 22 Jan. 1716, 23 Jan. 1720, 28 Jan. 1720, 8 March 1720, and many others.

BUT however various the caufes of expulfion may have been, the effect of it is conftantly the fame: For the *neceſſary* confequence of expulfion is, that the perfon expelled fhall be incapable of being elected again to ferve in the fame houfe of commons that expelled him. This incapacity is implied in the very meaning of the word itfelf. Should any man of plain fenfe, nay fhould any young academecian or fchool-boy even, be afked what was underftood by expelling a man from any fociety, they would certainly anfwer, " The meaning is, that he fhall never be a mem-" ber of *that* club, or of *that* college, or of *that* fchool any more."

EXPULSION clearly, *ex vi termini*, fignifies a total, and not a partial, exclufion from the fociety or parliament from whence he is removed. If a member is excluded during pleafure, or for a certain time only, that is, properly fpeaking, a SUSPENSION, and not an EXPULSION: And the Houfe themfelves, as has been fhewn, have made the diftinction in many cafes, by making ufe of the word *fufpended*, where they meant the exclufion to be temporary ; that is, either during pleafure, or for that feffion, or till fome end be attained. But when a member is *expelled*, he is not excluded from the meeting of that day, or of that feffion, but from *that* parliament ; that is, from that body of which he is a member.

No one, acquainted with the conftitution and practice of parliament, will deny that the houfe have a right to expel their own members. Indeed their right is eftablifhed by fuch immemorial ufage, and has been exercifed in fuch a vaft multiplicity of inftances, that it is impoffible to difpute it.

IT is not only evident from precedents, that the houfe have a power of expulfion, but it is clear from the reafon of the thing that they ought to have fuch a power. Otherwife the moft unworthy and unfit reprefentatives may fit in parliament, to the difgrace and detriment of the nation. Since it is not pretended that any fuch power is, or can be, lodged any where elfe.

BUT

BUT to admit their right of expelling, and argue that the member expelled may be re-elected that parliament, is to contend for the grossest absurdity imaginable; it would expose the judicature of the house of commons to the most flagrant insult and contempt; it would render the determination of the house of commons, totally nugatory, if the member whom they expelled to-day, should be forced upon them again to-morrow. Should such an extravagant absurdity be once admitted, the determinations of the *house* of *commons*, which is a court of judicature, from whence there lies no appeal, would in fact become of less weight and authority than the lowest court now existing.

NO man therefore who means to argue seriously and candidly will contend that a member expelled to-day, is capable of being elected the next day. For by whom is he expelled? Why by the people of Great-Britain assembled by their representatives.—And shall a part of the people, shall the electors of a particular county say,—We will not be bound by the judgment of the majority —We will elect no other to represent us than the person expelled? Shall *they* be at liberty to restore him, who had no power to expel him? Certainly not.

SUPPOSE, for the sake of argument, that the people instead of being assembled by their representatives, had been personally convened. Though in such case every man would have a right of being present at an assembly where his own interest, among that of others, is in agitation, yet will any one say that he may not forfeit that right by indecorum, by treachery, by immorality, &c? And are not the majority of the assembly the sole judges of his fitness to continue a member? If they judge him incapable, may they not expel him? and can he ever acquire a seat in that assembly again, against the sense of the majority?

IT is the same where a member is expelled by the representative body. They whom he represents have no power of obtruding him into the national assembly again, against the sense of the majority.

majority. For it is to be obferved, that though every member is chofen by a particular county or borough, yet, as is juftly obferved by lord Coke and others, when in parliament, he ferves for the whole nation. Confequently he ought not to fit in parliament, againft the fenfe of the majority in that nation, expreffed by their reprefentatives.

I f, for want of proper information, or due confideration of the nature of the offence, the caufe of expulfion fhould not in the apprehenfion of the electors, be fufficient to warrant fuch a punifhment, yet they are neverthelefs bound by the determination of the majority in the reprefentative body, to whom they have refigned their right of private judgment in this inftance, and who are, and, as will be fhewn, ought to be the fole judges in fuch cafes.

Though the houfe cannot, and God forbid they ever fhould, fay whom the electors fhall choofe, yet they may declare who by law are *not to be chofen:* And by expelling a member, they declare, without faying more, that he is incapable of being elected for that parliament.

There cannot be a ftronger inftance that, in the general fenfe of mankind, fuch incapacity is the neceffary effect of expulfion, than that of there having never been any attempt made to re-elect one in the fame parliament, out of the very many who have been expelled, except in the fingle inftance of *Robert Walpole*, Efq; and then the houfe, as will be feen, declared the effect of their vote of expulfion.

This cafe however has been cited on the other fide, in order to deftroy the inference, that the incapacity contended for is the neceffary effect of expulfion,

But

BUT, from the bare ftate of this cafe, it will manifeftly appear that it proves the direct contrary of the propofition it is cited to eftablifh.

ROBERT WALPOLE, Efq; after having been expelled, was re-elected: Upon which the houfe

" RESOLVED,

" THAT Robert Walpole, Efq; having been that feffion of
" parliament, expelled the houfe, *was*, and is incapable of being
" elected a member to ferve in that prefent parliament."

Now, fay they, the expulfion did not of itfelf render him incapable of being re-elected: If it had, there would have been no occafion for fuch a refolution.

BUT they who advance this argument muft certainly have read the refolution inconfiderately, or they muft argue againft conviction. The very words of the refolution, if they attend to them, clearly import that the incapacity was *created* by the *expulfion* itfelf. For what does the refolution fay? not fimply that he *is* incapable of being elected, but that he WAS, and IS incapable, &c. Was incapable! By what, and when? Why, by the operation of the former vote of expulfion, and from that time when that refolution paffed. The fubfequent refolution does not *create* the incapacity, but (by the word *was*) refers to the incapacity already created, and (by the word *is*) declares that incapacity ftill to have continuance. So that the laft refolution, not being confined to the time prefent, but referring to the time paft, does thereby only explain and expound the meaning and *effect* of the former refolution. Nothing therefore can be more abfurd than to urge an opinion from *implication* only, contrary to that which is declared in *exprefs* words.

K   STILL,

STILL, however, it is said that the incapacity of being elected is not a necessary consequence of expulsion: And to support this strange proposition, they cite another case of one Richard Woolaston, who was expelled 20 February 1698, and was afterwards re-elected, and served in that parliament.

BUT this case, when it is examined, will by no means prove what it is cited to establish. For though the house, somewhat *inaccurately*, used the word expelled, yet when the cause of his *amotion* is considered, it will appear that his incapacity was of a temporary nature.

THE question put at that time was, " That Richard Woolas
" ton, Esq; being a member of the house of commons, and hav
" ing since been concerned and acted as a receiver of the duties
" upon houses, and also upon births, &c. contrary to the act
" made in the fifth and sixth years of his majesty's reign, &c. be
" expelled this house." Which, upon a division of 184 against
133, was carried in the affirmative.

THUS it appears, from the words of the resolution itself, that the cause of disqualification in this case was merely *temporary*; and the fact is, as appears upon record, that, at the time of his re-election, he no longer held that office : So that he was then unquestionably eligible.

INDEED the house could never be presumed to intend that the effect of their vote should be *permanent*, when the cause, as declared by themselves, was only *temporary:* For the cause of disqualification ceasing, the effect must cease of course. But where the cause of expulsion is permanent, there the effect is permanent likewise, and must operate to exclude him from the body whence he has been expelled, so long as that body exists. No one therefore can pretend that this case is, in any respect, similar to the principal case under consideration.

As

As little will the cafe of *Sawyer*, which has been mentioned on the other fide, ferve to maintain the doctrine which it is cited to prove; that is, That a member expelled is elegible again in *that* parliament. For, in truth, Sawyer, was expelled juft before the diffolution of the parliament, and he was not in fact elected again till the *fubfequent* parliament.

Upon the whole therefore, whether we confider the obvious and common acceptation of the word expulfion, or the natural inference to be drawn from the common ufage and courfe of parliament, in fuch cafes, it is manifeft that the incapacity of being re-elected, is, and has always been confidered as, a neceffary effect of expulfion.

As there is no reafon however to fear the force of any argument which can be urged againft the proceedings of the houfe in this cafe, let it be admitted for a while that expulfion does not of itfelf create an incapacity of being re-elected, yet ftill it will appear that the houfe of commons, not only as expofitors of their own refolutions, but as expofitors of the *common* and *ftatute* law of the land, in cafes where their jurifdiction is competent, have a right to declare who are, and who are not eligible as members of parliament. This leads to the confideration of the next propofition ; which is—

2d, That they have the fole and exclufive power of examining and determining the rights and qualifications of electors and elected, together with the returns of writs, and all matters incidental to elections.

These rights they have afferted and exercifed from time immemorial, and have, with a firmnefs to which we owe the liberties we now enjoy, withftood and repelled all attempts made either by the crown, the peers, or the courts of law, to ufurp, or in any degree encroach upon, thefe great and conftitutional points of jurifdiction.

K 2   ATTEMPTS

ATTEMPTS of this kind have been made in various shapes; some, openly and directly; others in a covert and collateral manner. But that the reader may judge for himself on a subject of such importance, I will state the most material contests relative to matters of jurisdiction, in a full and perspicuous point of view, according to the order in which they occur.

THE first time I shall take notice of when the commons had occasion to assert their right of jurisdiction, was in the *Norfolk* case, the 29 Eliz. 1586, which is stated in *Carew*, but more satisfactorily in *D'Ewes*'s journal of the house of commons, and which was shortly thus:

THE sheriff of Norfolk received a writ, for the election of two knights, but two days before the next county day. By reason of the shortness of time, he could neither summon many freeholders, nor make due proclamation in the county, any one day before the election. The sheriff, notwithstanding on the county day, proceeded to the execution of the writ, and Mr. Farmer and Mr. Gresham were duly chosen. After this a second and new writ, was delivered to the sheriff for a new election, which was executed likewise, without any colour of misfeasance; and thereby Mr. Heydon and Mr. Gresham were duly chosen: And the indenture of their election, with the writ, were delivered to the clerk of the crown, together with the writ and indenture of the former election.

THE lord chancellor and the judges, at a meeting held on the subject of these elections, held, that the first writ was well executed; that the first election was good, and the second absolutely void. Of this their resolution they gave notice to the house of commons:

WHEREUPON the following points were resolved by the whole body of the house of commons:

1. THAT

1. THAT the firft writ was duly executed, and the election good, and the fecond election abfolutely void.

2. THAT it was a moft perilous precedent, that after two knights of a county were duly elected, any new writ fhould if-fue for a fecond election, *without order of the houfe of commons itfelf.*

3. THAT the difcuffing and ADJUDGING *this*, and the *like dif-ferences*, ONLY, *belonged to the faid houfe.*

4. THAT though the lord chancellor and judges were com-petent judges in their proper courts, yet *they were not* in par-liament.

5. THAT it fhould be entered in the very journal book of the houfe, that the firft election was approved to be good, and that the knights then chofen had been *received and* ALLOWED *as mem-bers* of the houfe, *not out of any refpect the faid houfe had, or gave to the refolution of the lord chancellor and judges* therein paffed, *but merely by reafon of the refolution of the houfe itfelf,* by which the faid election had been approved.

6. THAT there fhould be no meffage fent to the lord chan-cellor, not fo much as to know what he had done therein, *becaufe it was conceived to be a matter derogatory* to the *power* and *privilege* of the faid houfe.

THUS we find that the houfe of commons, even in thefe early days, were fo juftly jealous of their jurifdiction in thefe re-fpects, that they refolutely and explicitly afferted their *fole right* of *adjudging this and the like differences:* And though they concur-red with the chancellor and the judges, in their decifion on the merits of this cafe, yet they were fcrupuloufly careful to have it entered opon record, that they received and *allowed* the knights as members, not out of any regard to the refolution of the chan-cellor and the judges, but folely from their *own refolution.*

THE

THE firm and spirited conduct which the house of commons displayed on this occasion, is the more remarkable, as during that reign, the dignity and privileges of that house, were not always regarded with due consideration.

ANOTHER attempt was made on the jurisdiction of the commons in *Goodwin*'s case, 1 James I, printed in the journals of the house, and the 7th vol. of State Trials. This case was re-printed in the year 1704, by order of the house of commons, on occasion of the famous debate on the *Ailesbury* election ; which will be taken notice of in its order. The case of *Goodwin* was as follows:

SIR FRANCIS GOODWIN was elected knight of the shire of the county of Bucks? but the return of his election being made it was refused by the clerk of the crown: And the return of Sir John Fortescue, who had been elected upon a second writ was entered. Whereupon the question was put, after long debate, " Whether Sir Francis Goodwin were lawfully elected and re-" turned? which was resolved in the affirmative."

THREE days after, the lords sent a message to the commons, that there might be a conference about Goodwin's election : To which the commons answered, " That they did con-" ceive it did not stand in *honour* and *order* of the house, to give " account of any of their proceedings and doings."

THE lords replied, that the king having been acquainted with what had passed in Goodwin's case, thought himself engaged in honour to have the affair debated again, and had ordered them to confer with the commons upon it. Whereupon the commons, by their speaker, gave their reasons to the king, why they could not admit of this innovation. But all they could obtain was, that, instead of a conference with the lords, the king commanded them to confer with the judges.

THIS

THIS mandate, to which the houfe were extremely averfe produced very warm debates. One member, with becoming fpirit, obferved, " That by this courfe the free election of the " country was taken away, and none would be chofen but fuch " as pleafed the king and council. Let us therefore," fays he, " with fortitude, underftanding and fincerity, feek to maintain " our *privilege*; which cannot be conftrued any contempt in us, " but *merely a maintenance of our* COMMON RIGHT, which our an- " ceftors have left us, and it is juft and fit for us to tranfmit to " our pofterity."

ANOTHER member faid, boldly, " This may be called a " *quo warranto* to feize our liberties.—Our hands were never " fought to be clofed before. It opens a gap to thruft us all in- " to the petty bag. A chancellor may call a parliament of what " perfons he will by this courfe. Any fuggeftion may be caufe " of fending a new writ. Judges cannot take notice of private " cuftoms or privileges : *But we have a privilege which ftands* " *with the law.*"

AT length, the queftion being put, Whether they fhould confer with the judges ? It was carried in the negative, by a ge- neral voice, *No conference.*

IN the end, a committee was appointed to prepare anfwers in writing, to the four objections which the king had made to the reafons urged by the fpeaker. As the third and fourth objecti- ons do not apply to the prefent purpofe, it will be fufficient to take notice of the firft two.

OBJECTION I. " That we affume to ourfelves power of examining of the elections and returns of knights and burgeffes, which belongeth to your majefty's chancery, and not to us : For, that all returns of writs were examinable in the courts wherein they were returnable ; and the parliament writs being returna- able

able into *chancery*, the returns of them muſt needs be there examined, and not with us.

OUR humble anſwer is, that until the 7th year of king Henry the 4th, all parliament writs were returnable into parliament, as appeareth by many precedents of record, and conſequently the returns there examinable.

ALTHOUGH the form of the writ be ſomewhat altered by this ſtatute, yet *the power of the parliament to examine and* DETERMINE *of elections* remaineth; for ſo the ſtatute hath been always expounded ever ſithence, by uſe to this day : And for that purpoſe, both the clerk of the crown hath always uſed to attend all the parliament time, upon the commons houſe, with the writs and returns : And alſo, the commons, in the beginning of every parliament, have ever uſed to appoint ſpecial committees, all the parliament time, for examining controverſies concerning elections and returns of knights and burgeſſes; during which time the writs and indentures remain with the clerk of the crown ; and after the parliament ended, and not before, are delivered to the clerk of the petty bag in chancery, to be kept there : which is warranted by *reaſon* and *precedents*. By *reaſon:* for that it is fit that the *return ſhould be in that place examined, where the appearance and ſervice of the writ is appointed* : By *precedents;* of which they cited many, too tedious to be here enumerated, and then conclude, that,—" Uſe, reaſon and precedents do concur to prove the *chancery* to be a place appointed to receive the returns, as to keep them for the parliament, but not to judge of them : And the inconvenience might be great, if the *chancery* might, upon ſuggeſtion, or ſheriff's returns, ſend writs for new elections, and thoſe *not ſubject to examination in parliament* : For, ſo, when fit men were choſen by the counties and boroughs, *the lord chancellor or the ſheriffs might diſplace them, and ſend out new writs, until ſome were choſen to their liking.*

OBJECTION 2.

OBJECTION 2. That we dealt in the caufe with too much precipitation, not feemly for a council of gravity, and without refpect to your moft excellent majefty, who had defired the writ to be made: And being but half a body, and no court of record alone, refufed conference with the lords, the other half, notwith-ftanding they prayed it of us.

OUR humble anfwer is, to the precipitation, That we enter-ed into this caufe, as in other parliaments of like cafes hath been accuftomed ; calling to us the clerk of the crown, and viewing both the writs, and both the returns; which hath been warrant-ed by continual ufage among us.

CONCERNING our refufing conference with the lords, there was none defired, until after our fentence paffed ; and then we thought, That, *in a matter private to our own houfe,* which by rules of order, might not be by us revoked, we might, without any imputation, refufe to confer. Yet, underftanding by their lord-fhips, that your majefty had been informed againft us, we made hafte to lay open to your Majefty, the whole manner of our pro-ceedings; *not doubting, though we were but part of a body, as to* MAKE NEW LAWS, *yet for any matter of privileges of our houfe, we* ARE AND EVER HAVE BEEN, A COURT OF OURSELVES, *of fufficient power,* " *to difcern and* DETERMINE, *without their lordfhips, as* " *their lordfhips have ufed always to do for theirs, without us.*"

IN return to this, the king replied, that he had feen and con-fidered of the manner and the matter : He had heard his *judges* and his *council*; and that he was now *diftracted in judgment.* Therefore, for his farther fatisfaction, he defired and command-ed, *as an abfolute king,* that there might be a conference between the houfe and the judges.

THIS unexpected meffage occafioned great amazement in the houfe, but, at length, it was propofed to petition the king, that

L   he

he would be pleafed to be prefent at the conference himfelf. **This** difputatious monarch gladly accepted the propofal, and faid that he would be prefident himfelf.

A t this conference, the king acknowledged, that the *houfe of commons* was a court of record, and a judge of returns. At length this conference produced a kind of compromize. It was agreed that both the members fhould be excluded, and that a new writ fhould iffue ; to which the commons with difficulty confented, at *Goodwin's own particular defire*, expreffed in a letter from him to the *fpeaker* which was read before the queftion was put, and wherein he preffed the houfe to confent to the propofition, chuf-ing rather to wave his right than be the occafion of a quarrel between the king and the commons.

N e v e r t h e l e s s, many members were greatly diffatisfied even with this conceffion. It was faid by one,—" We lofe more " at a parliament, than we gain by a battle. The authority of the " committee was only to fortify what was agreed on by the " houfe for anfwer, and they had no authority to confent."

I t was further urged by another, in thefe terms ;——" We " fhould proceed to take away our diffention, and preferve our " liberties: We have exceeded our commiffion, and drawn up-" on ourfelves, a note of inconftancy and levity."

T h u s we fee, that, even in thefe fpiritlefs days, when the fo-vereign exerted himfelf in the higheft tone of prerogative, the commons boldly afferted the right of jurifdiction ; and the king perceived, by the temper and arguments of the houfe, that he had no profpect of becoming, as he intended, mafter of elections.

R a p i n very juftly reprefents this attempt of the king's, as an evidence of his aiming at abfolute power : And it may be added, that had he fucceeded to his wifh in this attempt, it would have
enabled

enabled him to aſſume that *abſolute* power in *fact*, which he arrogated in *words*.

No veſtige, from this time, I believe, appears, where the excluſive juriſdiction of the houſe of commons, with reſpect to elections and matters incidental thereto, came in queſtion, till juſt before the reſtoration, in the caſe of *Nevil* againſt *Stroud*;* which was an action on the caſe brought in the common pleas, againſt the Defendant, as ſheriff of *Berkſhire*, for a falſe return. The record was delivered into parliament, and was afterwards, by order of parliament, adjourned into the exchequer chamber†, but was never determined. It was nevertheleſs ſtrongly urged in this caſe, " *That as it concerned parliamentary privilege, the common* " *law could not intermeddle with it.*"

I the rather mention this, becauſe the courts of law adopted this opinion in caſes I ſhall hereafter take notice of.

In the year 1672, the commons were again under the neceſſity of aſſerting their juriſdiction. When the Earl of *Shaftſbury* was lord chancellor, writs iſſued, during a prorogation of parliament, for electing members in the room of thoſe that were dead : The king himſelf was ſo cautious, as to the regulating of this proceeding, and had ſo much regard to the privileges of the houſe of commons, that, at the next ſeſſion of parliament, 5th of February 1672, he ſpoke to the houſe of commons from the throne in theſe words:

" One thing I forgot to mention, which happened during this prorogation ; I did give orders for the iſſuing ſome writs for the election of members, inſtead of thoſe that are dead; that the houſe might be full at their meeting: And I am miſtaken, if this be not according to former precedents. But I deſire you will not

L 2   fall

---

* 2 Sid. 168.

† It was uſual, about this time, for committees of the houſe of commons to meet in the exchequer chamber.

fall to other bufinefs, till you have examined that particular ; and, I doubt not, but precedents will juftify what is done: I am as careful of all your privileges as of my own prerogative."

T H E 6th of February 1672, the houfe of commons took the matter into confideration; and feveral precedents being cited, and the matter at large debated, and the general fenfe and opi- on of the houfe being, that, during the continuance of the high court of parliament, the right and power of iffuing writs for e- lecting members to ferve in this houfe, in fuch places as are va- cant, is in this houfe, who are the proper judges alfo of elections and returns of their members.

T H E R E U P O N it was *Refolved*, " That all elections, upon the " writs iffued fince the laft feffion, are void: And that Mr. " Speaker do iffue his warrant to the clerk of the crown, to make " out new writs for thofe places." Which was done accordingly.

N O T many years after, that is, in the 26 Car. 2. an attempt was made to encroach on the exclufive privilege of the houfe in matters of election, by endeavouring to eftablifh a concurrent jurifdiction, in the cafe of *Barnardiftan* againft *Soame*＊.

T H I S was an action on the cafe brought in the *king's-bench* a- gainft the defendant, as fheriff of Suffolk, for a double return. The election of the plaintiff had, upon examination in parlia- ment, been judged good, and they had committed the defendant for making this double return. Neverthelefs the jury found a verdict for the plaintiff, with 800*l.* damages.

I T was moved however in arreft of judgment, that the action did not lie ; and, among other reafons, it was urged, " *That the* " *falfity or verity of the return was only examinable in the houfe of com-* " *mons,*

* 2 Lev. 114. Pollex 470. 2 Keb. 365, 369, 389, 664. 7 St. Tr. 428.

" *mons*, who *are the* SOLE JUDGES, and will punifh fuch falfities,
" as they have done in the prefent cafe."

JUDGMENT however was given for the plaintiff.

LORD chief juftice *Hale*, in this cafe bid all perfons about
him take notice, that, *they did not determine the right of election for
the* JUDGMENT *in that cafe belonged to parliament*; but, he faid,
*fince the houfe of commons have determined the right, he thought they
might follow their judgment, to repair the plaintiff in* damages.

THIS judgment, neverthelefs, was afterwards reverfed in the
exchequer chamber, by the opinion of chief juftice *North*, and
five other judges againft two; the chief, with the five other judges, holding, that the action did not lie: And this judgment of
reverfal was afterwards affirmed in the houfe of lords*.

AFTER fuch a folemn reverfal of the judgment. of the *king's-
bench*, and an affirmative of that reverfal in the houfe of lords, it
might have been expected that this point would never be
moved again. Yet in the 33 Car. 2. it came again in difpute in
the cafe of *Onflow* againft *Rapley*†, which was an action on the cafe
brought againft the defendant as returning officer, for a double
return, and a verdict thereupon for the plaintiff. But, upon
motion in arreft of judgment, it was held clearly by the whole
court, that the action did not lie. They were unanimous *that
they had no jurifdiction of this matter ;* and went fo far as to fay,
" That it would be great prefumption in the court to meddle
" with elections to parliament, before the matter hath been de-
" termined in parliament."

SOMETIME after the refolution, in the 12 Wm. 3, ‡ a farther attempt was made, in a cafe fomewhat different from the
laft

---

* 1 Lutw. 89.   † 3 Lev. 29. 2 Vent. 37.

‡ I take no notice of the cafe of *Norris* againft *Mawdit*, as that was an action
for a falfe return, grounded on the ftat. 23 A. 6. c. 15. and does not apply to
the queftion under confideration. See 5 Mod. 511. Comb. 430.

laſt, to give the courts of law a concurrent juriſdiction with the houſe of commons.

Tʜɪs was in an action on the caſe brought in the *common pleas,* by *Prideaux* againſt *Morrice**, for a *falſe* return, before a determination in parliament, and the court were clearly of opinion that ſuch an action did not lie.

Iɴ this caſe, chief juſtice Trevor delivered the opinion of the court in the following words:

" Tʜᴀᴛ this action would not lie before the election was de-
" termined in parliament *which was the proper court to determine*
" *this matter.* If it ſhould lie, this inconvenience might follow,
" viz. The verdict might find contrary to what the parliament
" might hereafter determine, which is not to be allowed; for it
" is plain that, *if the parliament had determined againſt the plain-*
" *tiff, could never afterwards have this action."*

" Iᴛ is true, in courts which have concurrent juriſdictions,
" there cannot be different judgments in one and the ſame caſe,
" becauſe the determination muſt be in that court, which
" was firſt poſſeſſed of the cauſe, for if an action is brought for
" the ſame matter in one court, the party may plead in the a-
" batement, that it is depending in another : and if judgment
" is given in the firſt action, then he may plead it in bar to the
" laſt."

Bᴜᴛ, *in this caſe, there may be different judgments,* ʙᴇᴄᴀᴜsᴇ ᴛʜᴇ ᴄᴏᴜʀᴛ ᴏғ ᴘᴀʀʟɪᴀᴍᴇɴᴛ ʜᴀᴠᴇ ᴀ sᴜᴘᴇʀɪᴏʀ ᴊᴜʀɪsᴅɪᴄᴛɪ-ᴏɴ ɪɴ ᴛʜɪs ᴍᴀᴛᴛᴇʀ†.

A.

---

* 1 Lu't. 82. Nelſ. Lutw. 31. Salk. 502. Holt. 523. 8 St. Tr. 9.

† The report of this caſe in the French edition of Lutw. 89. is to the ſame effect : But the chief juſtice is there made to ſay further, " *That the houſe are* " *proper judges."*

A writ of error was brought upon this judgment in the court of *king's-bench*, and the judgment was there affirmed.

Nevertheless, such is the contentious spirit which has at all times attended the elections, and such the animosity with which each party opposes the other, that the exclusive right of jurisdiction of the commons, in these matters, did not long remain uncontroverted, but came again in question, in the famous case of *Ashby* against *White*, and others*, in the 2d Ann.

This was an action upon the case brought against the defendants as constables of *Ailesbury* for refusing to receive his vote in the election of two burgesses for that borough. A verdict was found for the plaintiff, and it was afterwards moved in arrest of judgment, that the action was not maintainable; and it was held, by the opinion of three judges, against *Holt*, chief justice, that the action did not lie.

In the end, however, this judgment was reversed, upon an appeal to the house of lords; and the judgment was given for the plaintiff.

But the commons warmly resented this attempt to destroy their independence†, and such violent disputes arose between the two houses, that it was judged proper to put an end to them by proroguing the parliament.

The highest reverence, no doubt, is due to the judgment of that supreme court of judicature, the house of lords; but an insatiate appetite for power is natural to all bodies of men; and if the judgment of that august assembly may be presumed to have less authority in one case than another, it must certainly have the
leaft

* Salk. 19. 3 Salk. 17. 6 Mod. 45 Holt. 524. 8 St. Tr. 89.
† They voted it a breach of the privilege, and committed all the parties concerned, lawyers, &c.

leaft weight in this, wherein their judgment directly tended to enlarge their own jurifdiction, and ultimately to give them a manifeft afcendency over the third eftate in the kingdom, and confequently over the liberties of the people of Great-Britain.

I t muft be premifed likewife, that great deference is undoubtedly due to the opinion of that eminent chief juftice, lord *Holt*; at the fame time it muft be acknowledged, that the three judges, from whom he differed, have ever been reputed among the moft learned and able of the profeffion : And perhaps fome of the arguments* of this great man, on this occafion, will be found to depend on thofe hair-breadth diftinctions, which however they may fhew the fubtilty of argumentation, do not always tend to the eftablifhment of truth.

1 t is to be premifed that it was agreed in this cafe that the burgeffes, for whom the plaintiff tendered his vote, were elected. Neverthelefs lord Holt, in giving his opinion, faid, That it was not material, whether the candidate for whom he would have voted, be chofen or not.

I n this however, he feems to lofe fight of the fubftantial merits of the queftion. For what is the *end* for which the *right* in *queftion* was eftablifhed ? No other than this : That certain perfons *being duly qualified*, fhould have the privilege of electing whom they pleafe, *being duly qualified likewife*, to reprefent them in the great council of the nation.

I f therefore the perfon for whom they tendered their vote, be received, the fubftantial *end*, for which the privilege was granted, is obtained ; fo that they cannot alledge any injury ; and though their votes may have been rejected, yet they are not thereby

---

* In truth, the moft material arguments urged by lord *Holt*, in this cafe, were ftrongly preffed before by Sir *Robert Atkins*, and over-ruled in the cafe of *Barnardiftan* againft *Soame*. See 7 St. T. S. 434 & fequent.

thereby deprived of their *right*. They may tender their votes on any other occasion, and there can be no danger, that, by the rejection of their votes by the returning officer at one time, any person, not of their choice, should, at any subsequent election, be chosen their representative: for it is at all times open to them to assert their right by petition to the house of commons, where, if well founded, it will be allowed and confirmed; and their votes, if necessary to give a majority to the candidate of their choice, will be added to the poll.

B u t, says lord Holt, " by refusing the plaintiff's vote he has an injury done him, for which he ought to have a remedy : Want of right and want of remedy are reciprocal. Wherever there is injury, it imports a damage. The parliament cannot judge of this injury, or give damages to the plaintiff.

T h a t the house of commons cannot give damages, *eo nomine*, as damages, may be admitted; but does it therefore follow, that they cannot judge of the injury, and give a remedy?

H i s lordship very properly slights the notion, that there can be no *damage* but a pecuniary one. But is it not equally exceptionable, to contend, that there can be no other kind of *remedy* but a pecuniary one?

U n d o u b t e d l y there may; and the *remedy* is, to petition the house of commons, who will examine and determine the matter of *right*, and thereby judge of the *injury*, and punish the offender.

N o says his lordship ; there can be no petition in this case. " Was ever such a petition heard of in parliament, as that a man " was hindered of giving his vote, and praying them to give " him a remedy ?"

M   To

To this it may be anfwered, That, as his lordfhip very properly obferved, in this cafe, that it was no objection to the bringing the action, that no fuch action was ever brought before, fo it might have been urged, that it could be no objection againft the preferring of fuch a petition, had no fuch petition ever been preferred before.

As the houfe of commons, only, have competent jurifdiction with refpect to the rights of election, fo every invafion of thofe rights muft, at all times, have been cognizable before them : It was urged, as to this point, by a member, in the courfe of the debate in the houfe of commons, that he had known petitions touching elections preferred by very few perfons ; by the fame rule, faid he, a petition may be prefented by *one*: And in truth it appears from the journals of the houfe of commons, of the 31ft of May 1628, that this doctrine was exprefsly laid down.

At that time, there was a queftion with refpect to *Warwick*, whether the election fhould be made by the mayor and common council, or by the commoners in general. And a petition was produced, whereby above 200 commoners difclaimed to have any right of election. But the petition was refufed, and the reafon alledged, was, " becaufe, if *one* commoner appear to fue for his " right, we will hear him."

And in truth feveral petitions have, of later years, been prefented, merely to afcertain the right of voting, where there was no queftion about the merits of the election.

In the year 1711, which was foon after the cafe of *Afhby* againft *White*, a petition was prefented by *William Treene* and others, of the city of *Coventry*, complaining of their being debarred of their undoubted right of voting, and praying that their right of voting may be afcertained to them, and *reparation* made for the *injury* they have fuftained in being denied the fame.

THEY

THEY were heard by their council, and their right was established.

AGAIN, in 1723, a petition was preferred by *Charles Webb*, and others, of the borough of *Calne* in *Wilts*, complaining that their votes were refused at the laft election.

THEY were heard by their council, who *admitted that the fitting members were duly elected, and juftly returned :* fo that the merits of election, it is feen, were not in conteft, but the right of voting in the petitioners was, as an abftract propofition, the only queftion before the houfe. In the end, their right was difallowed.

IN 1724, another petition was prefented from the inhabitants and houfe-keepers of the borough of *Honiton*, in the county of *Devon*, ftating that they had, and enjoyed an undoubted right of voting, till 1711, when the houfe determined the right of election to be in the inhabitants paying fcot and lot only : That there turning officers fince that time, had refufed their votes; That the petitioners would have voted for the then fitting member, *had there been any poll*, and did defire to fign the return, but were refufed as formerly : and prayed relief; which was granted them, by eftablifhing their right.

FROM thefe inftances, it appears that petitions have been preferred to parliament merely to fubftantiate the right of voting in the elector, as an abftract queftion, where there was no difpute whatever about the right of the elected, where there was no conteft about the election, or the return, and, in the laft inftance above ftated, *where there was no poll even*.

THERE is no room therefore for lord *Holt's* apprehenfions, that there may be a right without a remedy : as the right concerns the parliament, fo the remedy is to be had there only. They only can give the *fpecific thing* withheld : For fhould a

court

court of law recognize the right of voting, yet they cannot add the voter's name to the poll. The houfe only can reftore him to the *fpecific right* which has been refufed.

IT is too much to fay that every injury imports damage. There are many cafes where the law only gives the fpecific thing contended for, without damages, as in cafes of *mandamus*, &c. Nay the common law paid fo little attention to damages, that, in feveral inftances, damages were not recoverable upon real actions; and cofts were not recoverable in any cafes whatever at common law.

BESIDES his lordfhip takes for granted the very thing in difpute, when he fays, that by refufing the plaintiff's vote, he has an injury done him. For the *refufal* can be no injury, unlefs the *right* of voting be firft eftablifhed; and that, as has been fhewn, the verdict of a jury cannot do. The houfe of commons only, are the competent judges of the rights of election, and the legality of votes. Their jurifdiction in thefe cafes is part of the law of the land, which has been recognized by feveral acts of parliament*, declaring that " *fuch votes fhall be deemed to be legal which have been fo declared by the laft determination* IN THE HOUSE OF COMMONS, *which laft determination fhall be final.*"

PERHAPS, indeed, after the right of voting has been determined in the houfe of commons, an action at law may, as was hinted by the other judges, be maintainable for the recovery of the cofts, incurred in the profecution of the right. But to contend that an action lies before fuch determination, is to introduce the inconvenience which lord *Trevor* fo ftrongly infifted upon. For fhould an action be brought againft a returning officer for refufing an elector's vote, this would not ftop the proceedings of the houfe of commons upon a petition : And fhould a verdict be found by a jury, with damages againft the returning officer for

the

* 7 & 8 W. 3. c. 7. 2 Geo. 2. c. 24.

the refufal, and judgment be given thereon, the houfe might afterwards determine on the petition, that he had no right of voting, and might punifh the officer for admitting his vote. So
that on one hand, he might be punifhed by the court of law for
refufing the defendant's vote; and he might be punifhed on the
other hand, by the houfe of commons, for admitting it : which
would be fuch a grofs abfurdity, and fuch a fcandal to juftice, as
the laws of no country can be fuppofed to countenance, and
which the laws of this country do not countenance ; for, by the
antient law of the land, recognizable by act of parliament, rights
of this nature can only be determined in the houfe of commons.

A FARTHER attempt to give the courts of law a concurrent jurifdiction with the houfe of commons, with refpect to
elections, was made in the cafe of *Kendal* againft *John*† the 5th
Ann.

THIS was an action in the cafe againft the defendant for a
falfe return : and after a verdict for the plaintiff, it was moved
in arreft of judgment, that the action did not lie ; and the judgment was arrefted, by the unanimous opinion of the court, who
held that no action would lie.

IN this cafe, among other arguments, it was urged, that the
right in queftion was a *parliamentary right*; That the *remedy*
therefore *muft be parliamentary*, and could be had no where elfe
but in parliament.

IT was faid farther that THE COURT WOULD JUDICIALLY
TAKE NOTICE OF THE LAW OF PARLIAMENT: that IT WAS THE
LAW OF THE LAND: and according to lord *Coke*, OUGHT TO
HAVE PRECEDENCY.

ANOTHER reafon affigned why there was no caufe of action
was, *That the plaintiff had had the* EFFECT *of his election*; that
he

---

† Holt. 629, &c. Fortefc. 104: And fee the S. C. by the name of Coundell
againft John, Salk. 504.

he was returned, and had his place; there was nothing remaining wherein he could pretend himself injured, but the costs he had been at in the prosecution, and as to them it ought to be supposed *that the house considered them.*

In short, lord chief justice *Holt* himself, in delivering his opinion, said,—" The proper remedy is in the house of commons; " and we cannot meddle with it; but they can cause returns to " be altered, and then they become the same as if the person was " originally returned."

Thus it appears, from the foregoing historical deduction, that every attempt which has been made to encroach on the exclusive jurisdiction of the house of commons, in matters of election, either with respect to electors or elected, has either dropped of itself, or been resolutely withstood and repelled by the house of commons; who have constantly, as they did in the case of *Goodwin,* asserted and maintained this jurisdiction, as their COMMON RIGHT, which they derived from their ancestors.

As to their right of deciding with respect to the qualifications of the *elected,* that has not, in any of the cases, been disputed. Even Sir *Robert Atkins,* who in the case of *Barnardiston* against *Soame,* contended most strenuously for affirming the judgment, said, " *We know that the house of commons is now possessed of the juris-* " *diction of determining all questions concerning the election of their* " *own members, so far at least, as in order to their being admitted or* " *excluded from sitting there.*"

Nay, in the case of *Ashby,* against *White,* neither lord *Holt,* nor any of the zealous whigs of those days, ventured to dispute that the jurisdiction of the house was fully competent, *as to the seats of their own members.* One of the lords, at a conference said, " We do not meddle with the commons right to determine their " own election; they have a settled possession of it, which is a " right." So that the case of *Ashby* against *White,* though cited on
the

the other fide, concludes ftrongly againft the doctrine they labour to introduce.

NEVERTHELESS they contend, that the right of being elected is a *common law* right, of which no man can be deprived, but by act of parliament.

THIS, in the firft place, is affuming a propofition for granted which may fafely be denied. The right, as was faid, in the cafes above cited, is a *parliamentary right*, to be exercifed only in parliament, and therefore cognizable there only, where the duty is to be executed.

BESIDES, none can fay that, in the prefent inftance, Mr. *Wilkes's* right of being elected is taken away; for in truth it is only *fufpended* during the exiftence of this parliament. When the body which expelled him is diffolved, his capacity of being elected revives. The incapacity is not perpetual, but only temporary. To make it perpetual, is what, in the better opinion perhaps, an act of parliament only can do. But the houfe of themfelves can difqualify any member during that parliament. For let the right be a common law right, or a parliamentary right, yet, like other rights, it may be forfeited by crimes and mifdemeanors, &c. And who fhould judge of thofe caufes of forfeitures, but the body of which he is a member?

INDEED, the right of jurifdiction in the houfe of commons, in this refpect, is fo fully eftablifhed by immemorial ufage, that it cannot be difputed, without controverting the fundamental principles on which the law of the land depends. The houfe, as appears from their journals, have determined with refpect to the qualifications of the *elected*, from time to time, down from the year 1553, to the prefent period : and it is by their *refolutions* only, that perfons of various claffes are at this day difqualified. It is by their refolutions, that—

I. CLERGYMEN

1. CLERGYMEN are not eligible.

THE 12th October 1553, a committee was appointed to enquire about the right of *Alexander Newell* and *John Foster* to fit
in the houfe: and the committee reported that Alexander Newell
being prebendary of Weftminfter, and thereby having a voice in
the convocation houfe, cannot be a member of this houfe : which
was agreed by the houfe, and a writ was directed for another
burgefs in his place.

WE find the like refolutions the 8th of February 1620, and
the 17th January 1661, with refpect to other clergymen.

2. Judges are not eligible.

" THE 28th June 1604 it was moved by Sir Edward Hobbes,
" as a doubt to be refolved, whether if a member of this houfe
" be called to the place of a *judge*, or other *attendance above*, dur-
" ing the time of parliament, he ought to fit here during the
" fame parliament."—We do not find any refolution on this
point, at that time. But on

THE 9th of November 1605, the committee having reported
two members to be attendants as *judges* in the higher houfe, the
queftion was put on the report, Whether they fhould be recalled?
and the houfe *refolved*, That they fhould *not*.

ACCORDINGLY we meet with feveral paffages in the journals, particularly the 11th April 1614, where the exclufion of
the judges is fpoken of as an eftablifhed practice; and we fee by
daily experience, that whenever any members of the houfe of
commons are appointed judges, new writs are iffued for the e-
lection of others in their room : of which the numerous precedents are fo notorious and recent, that it is needlefs to refer to
them.

3. RETURNING

3. *Returning officers* are not eligible.

THE 25th June 1604, upon a motion of Mr. *Moore* to know the opinion of the House, whether the Mayor of a town &c. might lawfully be returned, and serve as a member?

THE House *resolved* and ordered, and the clerk of the House was commanded to enter it accordingly, that from and after the end of this present parliament, no mayor of any city, borough or town corporate, should be elected, returned, or allowed to serve as a member of this House, and if it did appear that any member was returned a burgess, that presently a new writ should be awarded, for the choice of another in the room and place of the said mayor.

THE 14th April 1614, upon a report of the committee, that Mr. *Berry,* bailiff of Ludlow, had returned himself,

THE House *resolved,* That he should be removed, and a new choice made:—And *resolved* farther, That all mayors and bailiffs, in the like case, should be removed.

ACCORDINGLY, 22d May 1621-2, we find, that a mayor being returned, he was removed, and a new writ ordered. And, on

THE 2d June 1685, The House resolved, That no mayor, bailiff, or other officer of a borough, who is the proper officer to whom the precept ought to be directed, is capable of being elected to serve in parliament for the same borough of which he is mayor, bailiff, or officer, at the time of the election.

4. *Aliens* are not eligible.

THE 28th May 1624, *resolved,* upon the question, That the election of Mr. *Walter Stewart,* being no natural born subject is void: and a warrant to go for a new writ for Monmouth.

N

5, THE

5. THE eldeſt ſons of Scotch peers are not eligible.

THE 3d December 1708, A motion being made, and the queſtion put, " That the eldeſt ſons of the peers of *Scotland* were " capable, by the laws of Scotland at the time of the " union, to elect or be elected as commiſſioners for ſhires " or boroughs to the parliament of Scotland, and therefore, " by the treaty of union, are capable to elect or be elected " to repreſent any ſhire or borough in *Scotland*, to ſit in the " houſe of commons in *Great-Britain*."

IT paſſed in the *negative*.

ACCORDINGLY, The 6th December 1708, a new writ was ordered in the room of lord *Haddo*, who, being the eldeſt ſon of a peer of that part of Great-Britain called Scotland, was declared incapable to ſit in the houſe. And,

THE 18th November 1755, a new writ was ordered in the room of *Charles Douglas* Eſq; commonly called lord Douglas, then become the eldeſt ſon of a peer of that part of Great-Britain called Scotland.

BESIDES theſe, which are permanent diſqualifications of particular claſſes, the houſe have, in various other inſtances, determined and adjudged with reſpect to the qualifications of the elected. They have adjudged perſons in *execution* not to be eligible.

THE 24th March 1625, it appearing to the Houſe, that ſir *Thomas Moncke* was in execution before, and at the time of, his election, a writ was ordered to iſſue for a new choice in his room.

THE 22d March 1661, at the election for Leinſter, the *poll was denied* to Mr. *Coningſby*, who was put in nomination for

that

that borough : but he being a prifoner in execution for debt‖, and not *eligible*, it was adjudged, which is very obfervable, that the denying the poll to him *did not avoid the election*; and Mr. *Cornwal* and Mr. *Graham*, the other candidates, were duly elected.

The 15th December 1689, on proof of *bribery* in the election for *Stockbridge*, the houfe *refolved*, that it was a void election : And refolved farther,

" That William Montague, Efq; be difabled from be-
" ing elected a burgefs to ferve, in this prefent parliament,
" for the borough of Stockbridge."

The 10th November 1707, *refolved*, That every perfon who by an act of the firft feffion of the laft parliament, intitled, " An act for the better fecurity of his majefty's perfon and " government, and of the fucceffion of the crown of England " in the Proteftant line," is difabled, from and after the diffolution or determination of the faid parliament, to fit or vote as a member of the houfe of Commons in any parliament to be thereafter holden, is by virtue of the faid act, incapable of fitting or voting as a member of the Houfe of Commons in this prefent parliament.

The 7th December 1708, *refolved*, That *Anthony Hammond*, Efq; being a commiffioner in the navy, and employed in the out-ports, is thereby *incapable of being elected*, or voting as a member of this Houfe.

The 9th June 1733, *refolved*, That the accepting a commiffion of governor or lieutenant-governor of any fort, citadel, or garrifon, upon the military eftablifhmont of his majefty's guards and garrifons of Great-Britain, by any member

of

‖ The reafon why a perfon in *execution* is not eligible, is obvious, becaufe fuch an one is not bailable? confequently he cannot attend to difcharge the duty of a reprefentative : Whereas a perfon arrefted on mefne procefs is admiffible to bail.

member of the houfe, being an officer in the army, does *not* vacate the feat of fuch member.

T H U S, even where the difqualification is by ftatute, the Houfe is the only court where the ftatute can receive an expofition, or where any adjudication can be made.

B U T the following inftance is of itfelf fufficient to prove, that the houfe are, and have been acknowledged to be, the proper and only judges concerning the qualifications of the elected. On

T H E 19th November 1606, not many years after the cafe of Goodwin, the Speaker produced a note fent unto him, as he faid by commandment of the lord chancellor, containing the names of certain members of the houfe, difpofed and employed by his majefty fince the laft feffion in fpecial fervices, with direction TO KNOW THE PLEASURE OF THE HOUSE, *whether the fame members to be continued*, or their places fupplied with others.

I N this lift are the names of Sir Thomas Ridgway, treafurer of war, and Sir Humphrey Winch, chief baron of Ireland, with others. And,

T H E 22d November 1606, upon the report, warrants were ordered for the choice of new members in the places of Sir *Thomas Ridgway, Humphrey Winch,* &c.

T H U S it appears from the foregoing precedents, that the houfe have antient time exercifed the fole right of determining the qualifications of the elected : And that this right has been recognized in one of the moft arbitrary reigns, by *referring to their pleafure*, to determine, whether certain members fhould continue, or their places be fupplied by others.

I T appears likewife, that they have exercifed the right of adjudging and declaring the incapacity of being elected, not only as expofitors of the written or ftatute law, but even *where the*

the law has been silent, they have adjudged persons incapable of being elected, from the particular circumstances of the case, and upon general principles of constitutional policy.

Thus, it has been shewn, that from immemorial usage, recognized and confirmed by the statute law of the realm, the house of commons have the sole right of judicature, in all matters respecting elections; and indeed, it is clear, upon the general principles of reason and the spirit of constitutional policy, that such a power ought to be vested in them, and them only, as essential to the security of public liberty.

The constitution of the British government, being of a mixed nature, the house of commons are the body, whose peculiar duty it is, to vindicate the liberties of the people, against the encroachments either of the sovereign or of the nobles.

The better to secure the popular interest, the commons are elective; and certain people, being qualified as the law directs, have, at stated times, the privilege of electing whom they please, *being likewise qualified by law,* to act as their representatives in parliament.

If any doubt or dispute arises, in respect to the qualification either of electors or the elected, who does the constitution point out as the proper judges to decide in such cases? Most certainly, that body only, who are constituted as the representatives of the people, ought to determine, upon points which are so essential to the preservation of their liberties.

None will be extravagant enough to suppose, that the people at large, can exercise a judicial power of determining the law, with respect to their own qualifications or the qualifications of their representatives: When the electors of a particular county or borough have made their election, they have executed their power; and should any doubt arise, either with respect to their qualifications, or the qualifications of the elected, they then are parties interested in the question,
and

and confequently cannot be judges. The queftion is then between them and the reft of the people; for every member, as has been faid, though chofen for a particular place, ferves for the whole nation.

NOTHING therefore can be more abfurd, than to fuppofe that they fhould be judges in their own caufe, and that their determination, in a matter wherein they are interefted, and may therefore be prefumed partial, fhould bind the whole community.

IT would be as abfurd to contend, that any of the courts of Weftminfter, or any other judicature whatever, fhould be allowed to take cognizance of matters refpecting the qualifications of electors or elected.

SHOULD any other court be admitted to a concurrent right of judicature in fuch cafes, it would neceffarily introduce a clafhing of jurifdiction, and a contrariety of judgment.

BESIDES, as it has been fhewn, that the electors of the particular county or borough, whofe rights are in queftion, cannot judge of the matter in difpute, it would be highly ridiculous to imagine, that any twelve men of thofe electors, fhould have a power of determining in fuch cafe.

To contend for fuch a power in the courts of Weftminfter, is not only abfurd, but it is highly dangerous. For—

As an appeal lies ultimately from the judgments of all the courts at Weftminfter, to the houfe of lords, the *Lords would become the ultimate judges with refpect to the qualifications of electors and elected,* which would apparently give them fuch *an afcendancy* over the commons, as would ruin their independence, overthrow the balance which it has been the provident care of our forefathers to eftablifh, and, in the end, deftroy the rights and liberties of the people.

A s

A s this Power cannot, nor ought to be lodged in any of the courts at Weftminfter, fo neither can it be in the king and council, or any where elfe, without being attended with the fame inconveniencies and dangers: It can therefore only refide in the general body of the people, by their reprefentatives; that is, in the houfe of Commons: Which is, and by the conftitution can only be, the general court of the people.

T H E fatal effects of placing fuch a Power elfewhere, are obvious and certain. Therefore no man, who is not an enemy to the conftitution, would wifh to fee any other judicature interfere with that of the houfe of Commons. On the jurif-diction of that houfe, the liberties of this country depend. Our wife and fpirited anceftors, in their addrefs to *James* the 1ft, declared, that the privileges, liberties and *jurifdiction* of " parliament, where the right and inheritance of the fub-" ject."†

A s it has been fhewn, that the houfe have, and ought to have, the fole jurifdiction over their own members, *as fuch*, that they may punifh them by expulfion, &c. That they may declare and *adjudge*, who are, and who are not, capable of fitting in that Houfe.—It will appear, 3dly, That they have exercifed this right, with refpect to the late election for Mid-dlefex, in a legal and conftitutional manner, not only ftrictly agreeable to the law and ufage of parliament, but conform-ably to the proceedings of the courts of Juftice in Weft-minfter Hall, on fimilar occafions.

I T has been already ftated, by extracts from the votes, that, upon Mr. Wilkes's being returned after his expulfion; the houfe *refolved*, That he *was*, and *is*, *incapable of being elected* to ferve in this prefent parliament.

T H E R E F O R E, admitting that his incapacity was not a *ne-ceffary confequence* of his expulfion, which the Freeholders

were

† See Rufh. col. 53.

were bound to take notice of, yet this *exprefs* declaration of incapacity was fuch as *all the Freeholders of Great-Britain* were bound to take notice of. For this, which is but an expofition of their former refolutions, is the folemn adjudication of a *court of* judicature, on a fubject wherein they have not only a competent, but the *fole jurifdiction*. It is therefore as binding, nay, being without appeal, it is, in its effect, more obligatory than a judgment of any of the courts of Weft-minfter, to which every fubject is bound to fubmit.

N o w it is a known and eftablifhed maxim, that every man is bound to take notice of the law. With what colour then can it be pretended, that the Freeholders of Middlefex had no notice of Mr. Wilkes's incapacity? Ignorance of the fact may, in fome cafes, be pleaded in excufe, but ignorance of the law never can.

I n truth, however, it is notorious, that they were neither ignorant of the law, nor of the fact. The incapacity of the perfon they thought proper to elect, was, with fcrupulous caution, fet forth in the introductory part of the writ, which is always read publickly, previous to the election. Yet, even this caution, which takes away all pretence of want of notice to the freeholders, has been made the foundation of another objection.

I t has been objected, on the authority of Lord *Coke,* that the writ can receive no alteration, but by an act of parliament. No one will difpute this authority. But the clear anfwer to this objection is, that the writ, in reality, was not altered. The body, or directory part of the writ, did not vary a jot from the eftablifhed form; but the introduction, which declares the caufe of vacancy, muft, in the nature of things, be varied according to the different caufes which occafion the vacancy.

I f the vacancy is occafioned by the death of a member, it is faid, in the room of fuch an one deceafed : If it is occafioned by acceptance of an office, it is faid, in the room of fuch an one, he having accepted fuch an office: If it is occafioned

by

by the incapacity of the late member, it fhould fay, *in the room of fuch an one incapable of being elected.* And in like manner with refpect to other caufes of vacancy.

IT is evident, therefore, that the Freeholders of Middlefex could neither be fuppofed ignorant of the fact, or of the law. Having elected a reprefentative again and again, after a legal declaration of his incapacity, in contempt of the jurifdiction of the houfe, and in direct oppofition to the law of the land, no prefumption could be made in their favour. Such a flagrant mifufer of their franchife, at leaft amounted to a non-ufer; their votes muft be confidered as thrown away; and the perfon next upon the poll, having majority of legal votes, could only, in point of reafon and law, be confidered as duly elected.

HAD there been, in this cafe, no line chalked out to direct the determination of the houfe, yet the neceffity of the occafion would have dictated fuch a decifion, in order to maintain their own jurifdiction, on which the liberties of the people depend, againft the contumacy of a fet of miftaken perfons, who were inftigated to betray their own interefts.

BUT though the reafon and neceffity of the cafe would have fufficiently juftified the proceedings of the houfe, yet they did not act without precedent.

ON the 20th of May 1715, in the cafe of the election for the borough of Malden, the poll ftood thus:

| For Serjeant Comyns | 215 | Mr. Tuffnel | 168 |
| Mr. Bramfton | 215 | Sir Will. Jollyffe | 128 |

SERJEANT COMYNS having refufed to take the oath of qualification, they *refolved* that his election was void. But what did they farther in this cafe? why they did not iffue a new writ! But they confidered the votes given for the ferjeant as thrown away: And *refolved*, That Mr. Tuffnel, who had a leffer number of votes than the ferjeant, was duly elected.

O

AGAIN,

AGAIN, on the 14th of February 1727, and 16th of April 1728, in the cafe of the election for the town of Bedford, the poll ftood thus:

| For Mr. Ongley | 465 | Mr. Orlebar | 240 |
| Mr. Metcalfe | 462 | Mr. Brace· | 236 |

IT appearing that Mr. Ongley held an office in the cuftoms, and the 12 and 13 W. 3. c. 10. againft officers in the cuftoms fitting in parliament being read, and no furrender appearing to have been made of the faid office, before the election; the Houfe *refolved*, that Mr. *Ongley* was incapable of claiming to fit in parliament. Therefore, though he had the majority of votes, they confidered thofe votes as thrown away: And *refolved* farther, that Mr. Metcalfe and Mr. Orlebar were duly elected, though Mr. Orlebar had a leffer number of votes than Mr. *Ongley.*

As it is always to be wifhed, that there fhould be a harmony and correfpondence of judgment in the feveral courts of judicature throughout the kingdom, fo, happily in the prefent inftance, the adjudications of the courts of Weftminfter perfectly agree and correfpond with the determinations of the Houfe of Commons.

IN the cafe of the King againft the Mayor and Aldermen of Bath, the 15 Geo. 2. Mr. *Taylor* brought a *mandamus* to be admitted and fworn into the office of one of the Aldermen of the city of *Bath*. To which it was returned, that he was not duly chofen; and upon that iffue being joined, it was tried before Lord Chief Juftice *Lee.*

IT appeared at the trial, that by the charter of the corporation, the Aldermen are to be elected by the Mayor, Recorder and Aldermen, or the major part of them ; but it was agreed that the prefence of the Recorder was not neceffary. It was given in evidence to the jury, that the whole number of electors were *thirty*, of whom *twenty-eight* were lawfully affembled

fembled for the election of an Alderman:—That for this office there were three candidates, Mr. *Bigges,* who had 14
votes, the faid Mr. *Taylor* who had 13, and Mr. *Kingfton,*
who had *one* vote; but that Mr. *Bigges,* was not duly qualified
to be elected into this office, being neither a freeman of the
corporation, nor an inhabitant of the city of *Bath.*

ONE Bifh, and another witnefs, gave evidence that they
made the objection to *Bigges,* at the time of the election; and
that the electors, at the time the candidates were propofed,
difcourfed among themfelves about *Bigges,* as a perfon not
qualified.

ON the other fide, there was one witnefs who was prefent
at the time, and denied that he heard any fuch notice given
by Bifh.

UPON the whole of this cafe, Lord Chief Juftice Lee, one
of the moft cautious judges that ever prefided in a court, and
whofe judgments are held in the higheft efteem, gave the
following direction to the jury.——

THAT if they were fatisfied the electors had notice of this
want of qualification in *Bigges,* that then the 13 votes for
Taylor were to be looked upon as fufficient to determine the
election in his favour; and he told the jury, that if they
thought the 14 had voted for a perfon, *whom they knew to be
unqualified, at the time they voted for him, their votes muft be
confidered as thrown away, and they were to be deemed as not
voting at all,* or as confenting to the election of *Taylor:* For
that their diffent could no way be regarded, becaufe *their
voting for a perfon not qualified, was the fame as if they had
voted for a perfon not exifting or dead:* And therefore *they
could not be confidered as voting againft Mr. Taylor, fince no
man could vote againft another, but by voting for fomebody elfe.*
So that, on the whole, he confidered thefe 14 votes as flung
away, and of no more avail that if they had not voted at all.

UPON this, the jury found a verdict for Taylor; and a
motion was afterwards made for a new trial.

O 2

ON

O n ſhewing cauſe againſt the motion for a new trial, ſeveral laws were cited in ſupport of Lord Lee's direction to the jury. Among others the caſe, of the *Queen* and *Hugh Boſcawen* was cited from a note of Mr. *Werg*'s, which was an information, in the nature of a *quo warranto*, againſt Mr. *Boſcawen*, to ſhew by what authority he exerciſed the office of one of the capital burgeſſes of *Truro*, in the county of Cornwall. It appeared on ſhewing cauſe, that Mr. Boſcawen had 10 votes, and that one Robert D——had 10 likewiſe; but that no perſon was capable of being elected unleſs he was, at the time of the election, an inhabitant of the borough. Mr. Boſcawen had a houſe near the town, but was not an inhabi- tant of the town; and though the court might have granted the information againſt Mr. Boſcawen, on the foundation of an equality of votes, yet lord *Parker*, on making the rule abſolute, ſaid, " *He conſidered thoſe* 10 *votes for the unqualified perſon as thrown away, and that the other perſon was duly elected*;" from which the reſt of the court did not diſſent.

T h e caſe of the *King* and *Withers*, likewiſe the 8th Geo. 2. while that eminent lawyer lord *Hardwicke* was chief juſtice, was cited. This was an information in the nature of a *quo warranto*, againſt one Withers, for taking upon him the office of one of the capital burgeſſes of W——.

I t appeared, on ſhewing cauſe, that by the antient uſage of the borough, whenever there was a vacancy of a capital burgeſs, the Mayor, had a right to nominate two perſons, out of which two perſons, and no other, the Mayor, and burgeſſes choſe one to fill the vacancy.

T h e defendant Withers and another were nominated by the Mayor, purſuant to the cuſtom. The defendant had five votes, and the other perſon nominated by the Mayor had but *one*. But there were ſix other burgeſſes who inſiſted to vote, and did vote, for a perſon not nominated by the Mayor. The Mayor, however, refuſed to take the poll for the perſon not nominated by him.

T h e

THE court held, that *the six votes for the person not nomi-nated by the Mayor were thrown away,* and on that foundati-on discharged the rule.

IN the end, upon the sound reasoning in lord Lee's directi-on, and the authority of these cases, the court were unani-mous in refusing to grant a new trial.

BUT independent of these great authorities, it is clear up-on principles of common sense, that a vote given for a person disqualified cannot be a legal vote. For to constitute a legal vote two requisites are essential:· 1. That there be a capacity in the elector giving the vote; and 2. That there should be a capacity in the candidate receiving it. Mr. Wilkes, there-fore, having no capacity to receive the votes, they were clear-ly illegal, and must be considered as thrown away.

NAY, indeed, it has been admitted on the other side, that they were thrown away: for, on the question whether the foregoing elections of Mr. Wilkes were null and void, they were, without a division, determined to be null and void; which was, in fact, determining that the votes given for him were thrown away.

STILL it is answered, on the other side, that if they were not good votes *for* Mr. *Wilkes,* they were nevertheless good votes *against* Mr. *Lutterell.*

ON any other occasion one might be ashamed to mispend time in answering such futile objections. Did ever any one hear of votes having a *negative* quality? Suppose, on Mr. Lutter-ell's being proposed, a number of electors had cried out, No ! could a *negative* of this kind be considered as a vote against him? Certainly not. There is no way, as was said by lord *Lee,* of voting *against* a person, but by voting *for* some other: and if a number of electors might put a negative upon a can-didate

didate in such a manner, they might keep a seat in parliament vacant as long as they pleased; whereby they might deprive not only their fellow electors, but the state, of the assistance of a member.

IT is contended, however, that admitting these votes not to be good, yet the election should have been declared void, and Mr. Lutterell should not have been received. To prove this, they say, it has been held that the voting for a person under age, who had a majority, did not make the next person elected, who had the minority.

To this it may be answered, That every case must depend on its own circumstances. Where indeed the incapacity is of such a nature as can only be ascertained by evidence, there, tho' the candidate having the majority should appear to have been ineligible, yet perhaps his competitor, having the minority, should not be received; but the election should be declared void. Because it may be presumed, that had the incapacity been previously known, the majority might have made choice of some other person.

THUS, in the case of a minor, if such a candidate be so near being of age, that no man can, upon view of his person, determine whether he be of age or not, and if no certificate, or other proof of his minority, be produced in a case of such uncertainty, it would perhaps be too much to say that the votes for him were thrown away, and that the next candidate should be admitted.

BUT if in this case any certificate, or other good evidence of his minority, be produced, or if a candidate be so young, that his minority is notorious and apparent, in these cases the votes should be considered as thrown away, and the next candidate should be received.

THE true criterion of distinction is, whether the incapacity be or be not notorious of itself, and if not notorious of itself, whether there was, or was not notice of it ? If it be notorious

of

of itfelf, or if it appear that the electors had notice of it, in either cafe it muſt be confidered as an obſtinacy and con- tumacy in the electors, to vote for a difqualified perfon ; their votes, therefore muſt be deemed as thrown away, and then the next candidate ſhould be received.

The houſe of Commons therefore, in ſuch cafes will uſe their difcretion; and if they are fatisfied upon evidence, that the electors had notice of the incapacity of the difqualified perfon at the time they voted for him, they will reject their votes; and if there be any other candidate, though with a leſſer number of votes, they will, as has been done in the cafes above cited, admit him.

But it is faid on the other fide, that in the cafe of Mr. *Walpole*, who was returned after he was expelled, the houſe did not receive Mr. *Taylor*, the other candidate, but declared the election void.

True; but this cafe is by no means applicable to that of the Middlefex election. For though Mr. Walpole was return- ed after expulfion, and though, as has been contended, the incapacity was the neceſſary effect of the expulfion, yet in as much as this was the firſt and only inſtance in which the e- lectors of any county or borough had returned a perfon expel- led to ferve in the fame parliament, and the electors might be prefumed not to have due notice of the effect of expulfion, the Houſe gave them an opportunity to correct their error, by giving exprefs notice, and by refolving, that *he was* there- by *incapable* of being elected, and at the fame time declaring the election void.

It may be faid, indeed, that by their voting for a perfon ineligible, a right attached, by operation of law, in Mr. *Taylor*. But a right of this kind in an individual, ſtanding in competition with the rights of fo many electors, and the law, with regard to the effect of expulfion, having never been be- fore declared, it was proper and juſt in the Houſe to give the
electors,

electors who had voted for an incapable candidate, an opportunity of making a new choice, after the law creating the incapacity had been expounded.

But this their resolution leaves no room to doubt what part they would have taken, if, upon a subsequent re-election of Mr. Walpole, there had been any other candidate in competition with him. For, by their vote, they could have no other intention than to admit such other candidate; otherwise their vote would amount to a resolution that the seat should remain vacant during that parliament.

But how unlike to this is the present case! In the present case, the House, with the same moderation, explained the effect of the expulsion, by declaring that Mr. Wilkes *was* thereby *incapable* of being elected. Still, however, after the fulleſt notice, after he had been again and again declared incapable of being elected, they obstinately persisted in choosing him.

Therefore, as there was not the least colour for presuming that they had not notice of his incapacity, and as Mr. *Lutterell* stood next upon the poll, the House could not, without injustice to him, without betraying their own jurisdiction, without violating the precedents of parliament, and the corresponding determinations of the courts at Westminster; in short, without opposing the principles both of reason and law, they could not act otherwise than they did.

In truth, there was no alternative but to admit Mr. *Lutterell*, or to refuse issuing a new writ. To have rejected Mr. *Lutterell*, after the law in such cases had been expounded, would have been to have denied him his right: To have refused issuing a new writ, would have been a violation of the rights of the Freeholders. By arbitrarily keeping seats vacant, the House may be purged, as in Oliver's time, to any degree a minister thinks proper: And this mode of proceeding, which some pretended patriots affect to prefer, would have been as

has

has been faid not only unjuft with regard to Mr. *Lutterell,* but dangerous and unconftitutional with refpect to the people.

NEVERTHELESS it is pretended on the other fide, that tho' the rejecting the perfon returned, and receiving the other candidate, might have been right, had the perfon rejected been difqualified by act of parliament, yet it is otherwife, as he is difqualified only by the judgment of the Houfe. By this means, they contend, the franchifes of the electors are taken away, which nothing but an act of parliament can do; for that the Houfe, being but one of the three branches of the legiflature, cannot make laws to bind the people; and that though their orders and refolutions are binding upon themfelves, yet they do not operate without doors.

IN anfwer to this, it is to be obferved, that though the houfe of Commons in their *legiflative* capacity, as one only of the three branches of the legiflature, cannot, as has been faid, *make* laws to bind the people, yet it is to be remembered, as was ftated in the beginning, that they have a *judicial,* as well as a *legiflative* capacity, and it is in their *judicial* capacity that they take cognizance of elections. Confidered therefore as a *court of judicature,* their adjudications are as obligatory as the judgment of any other court whatever; nay, more fo, as has been intimated, becaufe they are without appeal.

To fhew, however, that the judgments of parliament are not binding without doors, they are extravagant enough on the other fide, to cite the cafe of the king and queen againft *Knollys*||, commonly called *Lord Banbury's* cafe, which was fhortly thus:

CHARLES KNOLLYS, earl of Banbury, was indicted for the murder of Capt. *Lawfon,* by the name of *Charles Knollys,* Efq; and this indictment was removed into the *King's*

P *Bench,*

|| Salk. 47, 509, 512. 3 Salk. 242. Carth. 297. Comb. 273. Skin. 336, 517. Caf. P. R. 55. Holt 530.

Bench, where the defendant pleaded in abatement, that he was a peer. To which it was replied, that the defendant had *petitioned* the lords in parliament, to be tried by his peers; upon which the lords, by an order of their House, dis-allowed his peerage, and dismissed the petition. To this re-plication there was a demurrer, and a joinder in demurrer. Notwithstanding this order of the Lords, however, judgment was given for the defendant, and the indictment abated.

But the grounds on which the court rested their opinion, as expressed by lord Holt, was that the *order* of the lords was not any determination, for that the cause was not properly be-fore them: It was not properly before them, because the peti-tion was preferred to the lords, in *the first instance*, whereas it should have been preferred to the King, and from his Ma-jesty have been referred to the consideration of the lords: So that the petition to the lords, was *coram non judice*.

This case, therefore, is not applicable to the case in ques-tion in any point whatever. For, in Lord *Banbury's* case, the reason, it is seen, which influenced the court, was, that the proceeding coming irregularly before the house of Lords, their order thereon was not a *judgment* of the House. From whence it is to be inferred, that if, in this case, the lords had acted judicially, in a matter regularly laid before them, the court would, and they certainly must, have taken notice of their *judgment*. But, in the present case, the House of Commons acted as a *court of judicature*, in a cause regularly before them; their declaration therefore was the adjudication of the court; and the adjudication of a court having competent jurisdiction, more especially of a court without appeal, is the *law of the land*.

It has already been observed that there are in this king-dom, as in most others, divers laws for the administration of government.

WILL

WILL any one say, that the *common-law* is not as binding as the ftatute law? that the *cuftoms of particular places* are not of equal force with the ftatute law? And will any one fay, that the *law of parliament* is of lefs force and efficacy than the ftatute law? Are not all equally the *law of the land?* And does not the jurifdiction of the houfe of Commons, in matters of election, ftand upon as firm a footing as the jurifdiction of any other court in the kingdom? nay, has it not been recognized again and again by the ftatute law?

IF it be afked when, and how they acquired this jurifdiction; the anfwer is, That they gained it at the fame time, and by the fame means that they gained their right of impeaching the greateft perfonages in the land; at the fame time, and by the fame means, that they acquired the right they exercife with regard to money bills, and other undoubted privileges. In fhort, their jurifdiction in this refpect, which is confirmed by immemorial ufage, is as antient as the *common law,* and muft be fo deemed, for no written law can be produced which fhews the commencement of the inftitution : It is coeval with the conftitution, and without fuch a jurifdiction the houfe of Commons, as has been fhewn, could not exift as an independent body: And if this jurifdiction is queftioned, all their other privileges may, on as good a foundation; be difputed; fince thefe, *together with many privileges of the other Houfe,* can only be fupported by immemorial ufage.

As to the pretence that the Houfe, by the exercife of this jurifdiction, have taken away the franchifes of the electors, which nothing but an act of parliament can do, this infinuation is altogether fallacious.

Is the prohibiting of them from exercifing their franchife againft law the fame thing as depriving them of it ? Is it not neceffarily underftood in the exercife of every franchife, that it fhall not be ufed contrary to the rules of law !

IN

In the prefent inftance they exercifed it fo clearly contrary to the rules and reafon of the law, that, independent of the declaration of incapacity by the Houfe, the fheriff might, on the authority of the cafe of *Leimfter*, above cited, have even *refufed to have taken any poll* for Mr. *Wilkes*, and even that would not have avoided the election; but any other candidate, having a majority of legal votes, would have been duly elected.

But how does the determination of the Houfe deprive the electors of their franchife? No one difputes their right: All that is contended is, that they have exercifed their *right* IN-EFFECTUALLY. Their right, as has been faid, is to vote for whom they pleafe, *being duly qualified*, to reprefent them. But they have wilfully and obftinately, with their eyes and ears open, voted for one difqualified, and of whofe incapacity they were not only bound by law, to take notice, but of which notice was actually and repeatedly given them.

Their votes therefore, on this occafion, muft be confidered as not given at all. But ftill, though, in ftrictnefs of law perhaps, a wilful mifufer of a franchife is a caufe of forfeiture, yet no one contends that their franchife is hereby forfeited. No one means to take away their franchife: They have ftill the right of voting, on any future occafion for whom they pleafe, being duly qualified. But furely no one will contend that the electors of Middlefex are above the law; and that their will is to overrule the fenfe of the people at large, declared by their reprefentatives.

But it has been faid, and an obfolete act of Hen. the 4th has been cited, which declares, that " all elections fhall be free without being interrupted by the *Pope*, or by *commandment of the King;*" much lefs, fay the objectors, ought elections to be interrupted *by a commandment of the Houfe of Commons*.

One would fufpect, by the levity of fuch arguments, that
they

they who ufe them really meant to betray the caufe which they affect to fupport. That elections fhould be free, no one will difpute; but the freedom here fpoken of is a freedom limited by law.—That the *Pope* fhould interfere with elections we have no reafon to fear: as little reafon have we apprehend, that our fovereign will interrupt the free courfe of elections. Neverthelefs it was provident in our forefathers to declare any commandment of the king to be illegal; for fhould a commandment of that kind be admitted, it would directly tend to deftroy the independence of the houfe of Commons; *fo would the influence of any other power whatever.* But the objectors are to learn, that the *refolution*, or the *commandment*, if they choofe to call it fo, of the Houfe of Commons, is not againft law, but declaratory of the law of the land. They are the proper and fole judicature, entrufted with the expofition of the law in fuch cafes.

WHEN the jurifdiction of the Houfe, however, can no longer be difputed, attempts are made to alarm us with the dreadful confequences, which, as fome affect to apprehend, may enfue from it. At this rate, fay they, the houfe of Commons may declare that no freeholder under 10*l. per annum* fhall vote at an election for a knight of the fhire.

IF they were ferious in this apprehenfion, it migt eafily be removed, by affuring them that the ftat. of Hen. the VIth having fixed the qualification of the freeholders at 40*s. per annum*, it is not in the power of the houfe of Commons, nor of any judicature whatfoever, to alter it: The *legiflature* only can enlarge or diminifh the qualification.

THERE muft, in all cafes, ultimately be a power of judicature fome where, without appeal; and wherever the conftitution has thought proper to veft it, it is not fuppofed that it will, or ever can, be exercifed againft the exprefs letter of the law.

UPON the whole, whether the jurifdiction of the Houfe, with refpect to elections, be examined on the foundation of

par-

parliamentary precedents and authorities of law, or on the general grounds of reason and constitutional policy, it is evident that they have, and ought to have, the sole and exclusive right of judicature in all such cases: that it cannot, consistent with the preservation of public liberty, be lodged any where else; and that, in the instance in question, they have exercised this right not only according to the established law and usage of parliament, but in conformity with the adjudications of the courts of Westminster, on the like occasions.

I T is scarce to be credited, that in these days, which we boast of as enlightened, the public should be so far misled as to question the exercise of a jurisdiction, on which there own welfare and security depends.

B U T what shall be said of those, who have employed every artifice thus to mislead and irritate the minds of the public, and who industriously augment the difficulties of administration, by obliging the ministry to pay that attention to their interested opposition which might be better employed in improvements for the public good!

I F lord *Coke* had reason to lament that " much time was spent in parliament concerning the right of elections, &c. which might be more properly employed for the public good,"* how would he have lamented, had he lived in these days, to have seen *one election* only, consume so considerable a portion of a long session of parliament; and to have known, that this deplorable waste of time was occasioned by the opposition of a party, who laboured to force a member upon parliament *against law*, whom they themselves had caused to be expelled!

W H A T fruits are to be expected from such a flagrant inconsistence of conduct!

H O W E V E R

* 4 Inst. 49.

HOWEVER ftrongly fuch a party may be united at prefent, by a common intereft, the purfuit of profit and power, yet when they come to a diftribution of that power and that profit, how foon would they divide! Their different views, difpofitions and paffions would quickly fet them at variance; new factions would be formed; new difcords would arife; and the public intereft be facrificed to private views and refentments.

THESE confequences are obvious to the difcerning and difpaffionate part of the people, who unhappily for the affairs of mankind feldom compofe a majority.

IT is to be hoped, however, that, before it is too late, the public judgment will be corrected. They will then find, that the perfons whom they have been perfuaded to confider as the invaders of their rights, are in truth the affertors and protectors of thofe rights; and they will then know in what eftimation to hold thofe, who, by every unwarrantable artifice, have laboured to inflame their minds with reprefentations of imaginary grievances, at the very time that, by a felfifh oppofition, they were entailing real mifery upon them and their pofterity.

F I N I S.

LETTERS

To the Honourable

Mr. Justice BLACKSTONE,

CONCERNING

His EXPOSITION of the ACT of TOLERATION,

AND

Some Positions relative to RELIGIOUS LIBERTY,

In his celebrated

COMMENTARIES on the LAWS of ENGLAND.

By PHILIP FURNEAUX, D.D.

The Second Edition with Additions.

AND

An APPENDIX, containing Authentic Copies of the Argument of the late Honourable Mr. Justice Foster in the Court of Judges Delegates, and of the Speech of the Right Honourable Lord Mansfield in the House of Lords, in the Cause between the City of London and the Dissenters.

AMERICA:

PRINTED for the SUBSCRIBERS,
By ROBERT BELL, at the late Union Library, in *Third-street*,
PHILADELPHIA. MDCCLXXIII.

THE

PREFACE

TO THE

SECOND EDITION.

IN publishing the following letters to the Honourable Mr. Justice Blackstone, containing observations on some parts of his Commentaries on the Laws of England, my design was, not only to induce the learned Commentator to reconsider several passages of his celebrated work, which, as I thought, were injurious to the interests of religious liberty; but to promote amongst my readers in general just conceptions of the right of private judgment, and of impartial liberty in matters of conscience; which of all human rights seems to me to be one of the most sacred and unalienable. How far I have succeeded in either of these views, it becomes not me to suggest. The worthy Commentator, indeed, in a new edition of his work, hath made very considerable alterations in the most obnoxious passages on which I had remarked: however, I will not assert, that the conviction which produced these amendments, was owing to my performance, in as much as the honourable gentleman hath not given me authority to assert it. But whether these corrections are to be ascribed solely to his own reflections, or in part at least to the suggestions and reasonings of any other person; in either case they are a noble sacrifice to truth, which whoever doth not greatly admire and applaud, must, I think, be destitute of every spark of ingenuity and candour. I am bound in honour and

justice

juftice to the learned gentleman, to point out diftinctly in this edition of my letters, the particular corrections he hath made, of thofe paffages which I had confidered.   Thus the reader will know, how far we are now agreed, and in what points we ftill differ; and will confider me in the former cafe, as not now writing againft Mr. Juftice Blackftone; but againft any other perfon who may happen to hold, or advance, the fentiments which he before feemed to efpoufe.

THERE are ftill fome material queftions between us; in particular, with refpect to the act of Toleration, as to which I cannot perceive the learned judge hath at all altered his fentiments. I obferved in my firft letter, that I never fhould have argued this point with a perfon of his uncommon acquaintance with the laws of England, if I had not known the opinion I had formed, had been agreeable to the declared fentiments of thofe who either have been, or now are, the ornaments of the higheft ftations in the law; and to the moft folemn judicial decifions. I think myfelf, therefore, fingularly happy in the opportunity of publifhing authentic copies of the argument of the late Mr. Juftice Fofter delivered in the court of Commiffioners Delegates, and of the celebrated fpeech of Lord Mansfield in the Houfe of Lords, in the fheriff's cafe; a fpeech, which in point of arrangement, weight of argument, perfpicuity and energy both of expreffion and fentiment, hath feldom, I believe, been equalled on any occafion, unlefs by the noble lord himfelf. And I here make my moft humble and grateful acknowledgments to that truly great man, for the peculiar honour he hath done me, in permitting me to convey to the world a copy of that admirable model of juridical and fenatorial eloquence.

I MENTIONED in the former edition of my letters having in my poffeffion a copy, which by many very competent judges, who were prefent when the fpeech was delivered, and fome of them members of the fupreme court by which the caufe was determined, was thought to be not inaccurate: an imperfect

tranf-

tranſcript of which having, entirely without my knowledge, appeared in an evening paper, I was deſirous, if I could obtain his lordſhip's permiſſion, to favour the world with a more faithful copy. I accordingly waited on his lordſhip, and had my requeſt in the moſt condeſcending manner granted. Indeed his lordſhip when he delivered that incomparable ſpeech, had no notes, and had afterwards taken no memorandums; but having read the copy, he declared his approbation of it : and it is accordingly printed in the Appendix, by permiſſion.

My learned and worthy friend Mr. Dodſon will likewiſe accept my particular thanks for communicating to me in the moſt obliging manner, the original of his late uncle the Hon. Mr. Juſtice Foſter's very accurate and maſterly argument.

These excellent performances, thus authenticated, may be quoted as authorities: and they are ſuch authorities as will be reſpected by the bench and the bar, as long as ſound reaſon, accurate law, and impartial juſtice ſhall have their proper weight with either.

THE

THE

PREFACE

TO THE

FIRST EDITION.

PERSECUTION is unwarrantable in any caufe; yet it may moft naturally be expected in favour of a bad one. I do not much wonder, therefore, that the church of Rome hath recourfe to it in fupport of her manifold corruptions and ufurpations. But that Proteftants fhould have imitated her in this greateft of all her enormities, and have thereby imprudently given a fanction to her cruel treatment of themfelves, is aftonifhing. Neverthelefs, that it is true, the hiftory of our own country abundantly teftifies.

AT the beginning of the reformation, in the reign of Elizabeth, feveral who had been perfecuted in the preceding reign, the queen herfelf not excepted, difcovered very intolerant principles, and made no fcruple to perfecute thofe who differed from them. Very oppreffive and fanguinary laws were enacted againft the puritans, and all nonconformifts to the ecclefiaftical eftablifhment. In the fubfequent reigns of the male line of Stuart, fuch laws were greatly multiplied, and the moft fevere and violent meafures purfued, to accomplifh that Utopian fcheme, an ecclefiaftical uniformity. Immediately upon the revolution, the great Mr. Locke pleaded with a clearnefs

and

and ſtrength peculiar to himſelf, the cauſe of univerſal and impartial liberty of conſcience in his celebrated letters on Toleration*. Senſible and enlarged minds quickly felt the force of his argument. But it required time for the moſt perſpicuous and cogent reaſonings, to eradicate general prejudices, and to alter the ſentiments and complexion of the public. For not only in the beginning of the reign of our glorious deliverer king William, when the Toleration was enacted, were the views of the legiſlature ſo confined, that it was clogged with exceptions againſt heretics; but upon them, as well as infidels, very ſevere penalties were afterwards inflicted in the ſame reign, by a particular ſtatute. This, I am

per-

---

* The Toleration-act received the Royal Aſſent May 24, 1689, and the 6th of June following Mr. Locke, writing to Mr. Limborch thanks him for ſending over the copies of the Latin letter concerning Toleration, which was printed in Holland: where indeed it had been written during his retirement in the year 1685, as we are informed by the author of his life prefixed to the folio edition of his works; and it was probably now publiſhed with a view to promote the Act of Toleration. The copies which were not bound, he ſaith, were not yet come to hand; and thoſe which were bound, and which were come to hand, were probably intended for preſents, and might arrive time enough to be diſperſed amongſt the principal members of both houſes during their debates upon the Toleration-act; eſpecially as it appears, they had been arrived ſome conſiderable time, by his ſaying, that he underſtood there was a perſon now employed (aliquem Anglum jamjam occupatum intelligo) in tranſlating the letter into Engliſh. I have been the more particular in this account, becauſe it hath been ſaid, that Mr. Locke's letter upon Toleration could not poſſibly have any influence on the Toleration-act; which the form of expreſſion in the next ſentence but one in the former edition implied it might. It is now ſo altered as to be conſiſtent with either ſuppoſition.

Mr. Locke's ſentiments concerning the imperfection of the Act of Toleration he thus elegantly expreſſes in the ſame letter to Mr. Limborch: It is framed, ſaith he, non eâ forſan latudine, quâ tu et tui ſimiles, veri et ſine ambitione vel invidiâ Chriſtiani, optarent. Sed aliquid eſt prodire tenus. His initiis jacta ſpero ſunt libertatis et pacis fundamenta, quibus ſtabilienda olim erit Chriſti eccleſia: not with that latitude perhaps, which you, and ſuch as you, who are genuine Chriſtians void of all ambitious and party views, would wiſh. It is ſomething, however, to advance thus far; for by ſuch beginning thoſe foundations of liberty and peace are, I hope laid, on which the church of Chriſt will come in ſome future time to be eſtabliſhed.

perfuaded, was not at allowing to the king, who feems to have had more generous fentiments of men's religious rights; but to the blind zeal of the times, and to the high principles of fome leading men in convocation and parliament.

HOWEVER, the fentiments and temper of the nation have been fince greatly meliorated, efpecially under the mild administration of the Princes of the houfe of Hanover; to which happy reform no one contributed more than that admirable fecond to Mr. Locke, the late bishop of Winchefter*, by his excellent writings in defence of religious as well as civil liberty. Infomuch that perfecution having been difcouraged by the civil power, and now become a ftranger amongft us, the generality of people, no doubt, imagine, that this hideous monfter hath no more countenance in the laws of their country than in the fpirit of the times. The truth is, the legal ftate of religious liberty in thefe kingdoms is very little underftood. Men naturally prefume, that, in this free and enlightened age, the rights of confcience, efpecially as they fee them poffeffed without reftraint or moleftation, have the fame legal fecurity with their civil right. It will perhaps furprize many of my readers, if they are unacquainted with the laws of their country, or have not read the late excellent Commentaries upon them, to hear that Deifts and Arians, if they declare their fentiments, are by law incapable of holding any offices or places of truft, bringing any action, being guardians, executors, legatees, or purchafers of lands, and are to fuffer three years imprifonment without bail: that to revile, or even openly to fpeak in derogation of the common prayer, renders a man liable to a fine of an hundred marks for the firft offence, to one of four hundred for the fecond, and for the third, to a forfeiture of all his goods and chattels, and imprifonment for life: and that the Toleration-act itfelf is fo limited, that many who are commonly thought to enjoy under it, defervedly, every fecurity which the law can give them, are yet fubject to very fevere and heavy inflictions,

R

to

---

* Dr. Hoadley.

to their utter ruin, as the law now ftands:—And as for thofe comprehended within that act; if according to the opinion of fome lawyers, they are only exempted by it from the penalties of certain laws, and are not reftored to a legal confideration and capacity; upon this idea, I fay, they lie open to fuch inabilities and oppreffions, that, were advantage taken of them, their very enemies would hardly wifh their fituation to be more deplorable. However this confined expofition of the Toleration-act, though ftill maintained, it feems, by fome of the profeffion, hath been happily condemned by moft of the judges, and is inconfiftent with thofe grounds, on which was founded, in a particular cafe, a folemn judgment of the fupreme court of judicature. And under this difcouragement it will never again, I truft, obtain the countenance of any court of law.

However that be, there are feveral perfecuting ftatutes, thofe which I have mentioned and fome others, which I think, were a reproach to the times when they were enacted, and are much more fo to the boafted freedom and liberality of fentiment of the prefent age, which fuffers them to continue unrepealed.

Let me only afk any friend of civil liberty, what, would be his reflections, if he had no fecurity for the poffeffion of his rights and privileges in the laws and conftitution of his country, but held them only through the moderation of his fuperiors, or the fpirit of the times? I believe, he would be extremely uneafy, till they were fixed on a legal bafis; extremely attentive to the fentiments and conduct of thofe who, from their abilities, or their rank and ftation, might probably obftruct or promote fo defirable a fettlement; and thofe who, in any critical juncture, would be likely to act in oppofition to the caufe of liberty, would certainly be the objects of his jealoufy, if not of his averfion. Now let every fuch friend of the civil rights of his country, whatever be his own religious opinions, and however fecure he may himfelf be in his religious profeffion under the protection of
the

the law, confider the cafe of thofe who are obnoxious to fuch penal ftatutes, as being ftill in force, may poffibly be employed (and he can never be fure they will not be employed) as inftruments of prefecution and oppreffion. Every generous mind will make the intereft of others, in fuch cafes, his own; and will be far from palliating or excufing, much more from defending, fuch laws as are incompatible with equity and humanity, and which, by thofe who would be thought friends of religious liberty, fhould never be mentioned but with difapprobation and cenfure. What part the ingenious and learned Commentator on the Laws of England, to whom the following Letters are addreffed, hath taken, when he is confidering fome of thofe ftatutes to which I refer, is not for me to fay: the public, as it is fit it fhould, will judge.

No laws which are unjuft, and inconfiftent with that religious liberty which it is right the inhabitants of thefe kingdoms fhould enjoy, (and I apprehend that which they do enjoy, it is generally thought right they fhould, becaufe they have now enjoyed it for many years unmolefted); I fay, no laws which are indefenfible, and incompatible with the rights of confcience, fhould be fuffered to remain unrepealed. For if it be proper, that fuch rights fhould be poffeffed in the extent in which they are through the lenity of the times, it is proper there fhould be a legal fecurity for the poffeffion of them; that they may not be trampled upon through the poffible caprices of men in power, or fome unaccountable turn in the fentiments of the public. And though I would not be underftood to infinuate, that there is at prefent any likelihood of fuch an infringement; yet the rights of human nature, (and religious liberty in its full extent is one of thefe) fhould never lie at the mercy of any; but on the contrary, fhould have every protection and ground of fecurity, which law, and the policy of free ftates, can give them.

IF any one fay, It is right to keep a rod *in terrorem,*
R 2   though

though it would be injuſtice or inhumanity to uſe it: I ſhall be apt to ſuſpect, that, notwithſtanding his fair pretences, when a proper opportunity offers, he will not fail to uſe it. For I am ſure, if, in the concerns of religion, human *terror* be a proper motive, human *puniſhment* is equally ſo.

A D V E R T I S E M E N T to the FIRST EDITION.

THE following Letters were nearly printed off, before the Gentleman, to whom they are addreſſed, was appointed to the high ſtation which he now fills in the law. This is mentioned as an apology for a form of addreſs which the reader will perceive is not ſuitable to his preſent character.

L E T T E R S

T O

WILLIAM BLACKSTONE, Efq;

L E T T E R I.

S I R,

YOUR candour, I doubt not, will readily excufe an admirer of your excellent Commentaries on the Laws of England; if, from a defire of their being rendered ftill more excellent than they are, he gives you an opportunity of reviewing fome paffages, which, to him at leaft, appear to be exceptionable; and not fo judicious and accurate, as other parts of your truly admirable performance. It were to be wifhed, that a work, fo nearly perfect, were *omnibus numeris abfolutum.*

My profeffion, Sir, is not that of the law; and if it were, it would be with diffidence, at leaft with much deference I fhould make remarks on the compofition of fo great a mafter. The point, however, which I have in view, not only is of great importance to myfelf, amongft others, who diffent from the eftablifhed church; but fome cafes of a public nature; which have come under my obfervation, have given me frequent occafion to confider it with no fmall attention. Neverthelefs, if I had not found my own fentiments authorized and fupported by their congruity to the declared opinion of perfons of the moft accurate and comprehenfive acquaintance with the laws of England, and by thofe general grounds and

reafons,

on which the moſt ſolemn judgments have been given: I
ſhould hardly have preſumed to offer to you, and to the
public, the following obſervations.

I REMEMBER, when ſome years ago, I read your
Analyſis of the Laws of England, and obſerved, that, in the
third chapter of the fourth book, under the head of offences
againſt the eſtabliſhed church, you mentioned " Nonconformity to its worſhip—through Proteſtant diſſenting;" and
added " Penalty: ſuſpended by the toleration-act:" I then
imagined that your ſentiments of the intent and influence of
that act, and of the ſtate and condition of the Diſſenters under it, were confined and narrow. However, I flattered myſelf, that when you came to conſider the matter more thoroughly in your larger work, you would ſee reaſon to repreſent the caſe of the diſſenters ſomewhat differently; and do
it, as I think, more juſtice.

BUT in the fourth volume of your Commentaries, chapter
the fourth, p. 53. I am ſorry to find the following paſſage:
" The penalties (viz. thoſe which are laid upon the Diſ-
" ſenters by abundance of ſtatutes, in particular by * 35 Eliz.
" c. 1. 17. Car. II. c. 2. 22 Car. II. c. 1.) are all of them
" ſuſpended by the ſtatute 1 Will. & Mar, ſtat. 2. c. 18. †,
" commonly called the Toleration-act, which exempts all
" Diſſenters (except Papiſts, and ſuch as deny the Trinity)
" from all penal laws relating to religion, provided they take
" the oaths of allegiance and ſupremacy ‡ and ſubſcribe the
" declaration againſt Popery, and repair to ſome congrega-
" tion, regiſtered in the biſhop's court or at the ſeſſions, the
" the doors whereof muſt be always open: and diſſenting
                                                    teachers

---

* In the new edition is inſerted, " 23 Eliz. c 1." There are ſeveral other ſtatutes, which ſhould have been mentioned; and above all, (for a reaſon which
will be hereafter aſſigned) 1 Eliz. c. 2. §. 2. & 14.

† In the new edition is here added the title of the act; namely, " for exempting
" their Majeſty's proteſtant ſubjects, diſſenting from the church of England, from
" the penalties of certain laws."

‡ Added in the laſt edition (" or make a ſimilar affirmation being quakers,")

" teachers, are alſo to ſubſcribe the thirty-nine articles, ex-
" cept thoſe relating to church government and infant baptiſm.
" Thus are all perſons, who will approve themſelves no Pa-
" piſts or oppugners of the Trinity, left at full liberty to
" act as their conſciences ſhall direct them in the matter of
" religious worſhip.*"

THIS is all you ſay of the toleration act in your Commentaries; and before I make any obſervations upon it, I beg
leave to mention a paſſage in your anſwer to Dr. Prieſtley;
who had obſerved†, that he " did not know that MERE _non-_
" _conformity_ was any crime at all in the laws of England—
" ſince the act of toleration:—You ſay‡, that you " beg
" leave to inform Dr. Prieſtley, ſince it ſeems he is yet to
" learn it, that nonconformity is ſtill a crime by the laws of
" England, and hath ſevere penalties annexed to it, notwith-
" ſtanding the act of toleration, (nay expreſsly reſerved by
" that act) in all ſuch as do not comply with the conditions
" thereby enjoined. In caſe the legiſlature had intended to
" aboliſh both the crime and the penalty, it would at
" once have repealed all the penal laws enacted again,
" nonconformiſts. But it keeps them expreſsly in force
" againſt all Papiſts, oppugners of the Trinity, and per-
" ſons of no religion at all: and only _exempts from_
" _their rigour_ ſuch ſerious, ſober-minded Diſſenters, as
" ſhall have taken the oaths, and ſubſcribed the declara-
" tion at the ſeſſions, and ſhall regularly repair to ſome li-
" cenſed §" (regiſtered) place " of religious worſhip. But,
　　　　　　　　　　　　　　　　　　　　　　　　though

* Added, " And if any perſon ſhall wilfully, maliciouſly, or contemptuouſly
" diſturb any congregation, aſſembled in any church, or permitted meeting-houſe,
" or ſhall miſuſe any preacher or teacher there, he ſhall, (by virtue of the ſame
" ſtatute) be bound over to the ſeſſions of the peace, and forfeit twenty pounds."

† Remarks, p. 29.　　　　　　　‡ Reply, p. 40. 41.

§ _Regiſtered_ is the word in the act. A _licence_, in its common acceptation, implies a power of refuſal : but in the preſent caſe there is no ſuch power : for the
clerk of the peace, or the regiſter of the archdeacon's and biſhop's court, is by
the act _required_ to regiſter ſuch place of meeting, upon its being certified. Ac-
　　　　　　　　　　　　　　　　　　　　　　cordingly

" though thefe ftatutes oblige me to confider nonconformity
" as a breach of the law, yet (notwithftanding Dr. Prieftley's
" ftrictures) I fhall ftill continue to think, that *reviling the*
" *ordinances of the church* is a crime of a much groffer na-
" ture than the other of mere *nonconformity*."

So that, in your opinion, Sir, mere nonconformity is a
crime, though not fo great as fome others; and is fo confidered in the eye of the law, notwithftanding the toleration-
act. The *penalties*, indeed, by that act are SUSPENDED, but
the CRIME fubfifts ftill.

IN fupport of this opinion you remark, that " nonconfor-
" mity is ftill a crime, and hath heavy penalties annexed to it,
" notwithftanding the act of toleration, (nay, exprefsly re-
" ferved by that act) in all fuch, as do not comply with the
" *conditions* thereby enjoined." But thefe *conditions*, in my
opinion improperly fo ftiled, are only a *prefcribed method* in
which Diffenters are to approve themfelves MERE NONCON-
FORMISTS, or in your own words " no Papifts, oppugners
" of the Trinity, or perfons of no religion at all." Your remark then amounts to this, that popery, herefy and infidelity, or irreligion, are ftill crimes in the eye of the law, notwithftanding the toleration act. But can it be inferred from
hence, that there is any crime in MERE *nonconformity*?
You feem to think it may, and to make it plain, you obferve,

cordingly, where this hath been refufed by uninformed juftices and clerks of the
peace, a *mandamus*, upon application, hath been always granted, and it muft
be, to compel their compliance. Yet in the bifhop's court of the diocefe of Win-
chefter (I know not whether in any other) notwithftanding that the toleration-act
requires only that the place of worfhip be *certified*, an *humble petition* is, at leaft,
lately was, infifted upon, to the Right Reverend Father in God, &c. alledging a
variety of particulars in fupport of the petition, and *humbly praying*, that he would
be PLEASED to licence fuch a place of worfhip. To fuch an unwarrantable extent hath the idea of licenfing been carried. But, I hope, this practice is, or will
be difcontinued. If it is not, and fhould be legally queftioned in the courts at
Weftminfter, as perhaps it may, it will be quickly found that it cannot be fupported.

ferve, that " in cafe the legiflature had intended to abolifh both
" the crime and the penalty, it would at once have repealed all
" the penal laws enacted againft nonconformifts; but it hath
" exprefsly kept them in force," you fay, " againft all Papifts,
" oppugners of the Trinity, and perfons of no religion at all."
Your argument I take to be this, that becaufe the legiflature
" hath kept them in force againft all Papifts, oppugners of the
" Trinity, and perfons of no religion at all;" *therefore*, (a
ftrange non-fequitur furely!) it did not intend to repeal them,
and abolifh the crime as well as the penalty, as to thofe who are
NO Papifts, or oppugners of the Trinity, or perfons of no religion at all, but mere nonconformifts to the eftablifhed rites and
modes of worfhip. Thefe ferious fober-minded Diffenters are
only exempted from the RIGOUR *of the penal laws*. They are ftill
criminals it feems, only the *penalties* due to their crime are *fufpended ;* and their nonconformity is ftill a breach of the law.

UPON this principle, the ufe of the term, fufpenfion of penalty, both in your Analyfis and Commentaries with refpect to
the effect of the toleration-act, may be eafily accounted for, and
appears confiftent.

It is true, in your Commentaries, after declaring the penalties to be *fufpended* by the toleration-act, you immediately add,
" which" (toleration-act) " *exempts* all Diffenters (except papifts,
" and fuch as deny the Trinity) from all penal laws relating to
" religion, provided they take the oaths," *&c.* But this feems
to mean nothing more than the fufpenfion which you had juft
fpoken of, and to be only exegetical of that term ; to be an " ex-
" emption (as you exprefs it in your reply to Dr. Prieftley*)
" from the rigour" or penalties " of thofe laws," but not from
the crime on which the penalties were grounded. This I apprehend, to be your real meaning : I fhould be glad to find myfelf miftaken. I think the truth is, that nonconformifts (name-

S   ly,

* Page 40.

ly, to the peculiar rites, difcipline and government of the church
as this word always fignifies) are freed from all the effects of the
penal laws, as to crime as well as penalty ; but thefe ftatutes
remain in force, both as to crime and penalty, with refpect to
thofe who are *more* than mere nonconformifts; who are Arians,
or Papifts, or perfons of no religion at all : and that, not on account of their nonconformity, but of their fuppofed herefy, or
enmity to the government, or infidelity, and irreligion : It is not,
I fay, their " nonconformity which is ftill a crime, and hath heavy penalties annexed to it" as you affert ; but their fuppofed
herefy, or popery, or irreligion : which is very plain ; for, if
they purge themfelves of thefe, and fhew, in the way defcribed
by the toleration-act, that they are no Arians, Popifh recufants,
or infidels, and perfons of no religion, they are immediately,
notwithftanding their nonconformity, unaffected by thefe ftatutes.

T h e queftion then is, whether Nonconformity be a crime in
thofe, who, complying with the toleration-act, have " approved
" themfelves no Papifts, oppugners of the Trinity, or perfons
of no religion at all ?" Or, what is the ftate of Mere Nonconformifts *under that act?* Are they in the eye of the law criminal, though the penalties are fufpended? or are they reftored to
a legal capacity, and to a freedom from all crime as well as penalty, in virtue of the toleration-act ?

I n my opinion, to reprefent nonconformity as a crime, the
penalties of which are merely fufpended, is a defective and erroneous account of the ftate of the Diffenters, under the toleration-act. And to fhew this,

T h e first obfervation I would make is: That *fufpenfion* of
penalty is not the language of that act. The title of the act indeed ufes the phrafe, exemption from penalty : it is ftiled, An
act for exempting their majefties Proteftant fubjects, diffenting
from the church of England, from the penalties of certain
laws*.

laws*.   But the act itself uses a comprehensible and forcible expreſſion, which excludes the *crime* as well as the *penalty* ; it leaves
theſe penal ſtatutes *no operation at all*, with reſpect to the Diſſenters who are under the Toleration-act ; it *repeals* and *annihilates*
thoſe ſtatutes with regard to ſuch Diſſenters.   The words of
the toleration-act are, that thoſe ſtatutes ſhall not be conſtrued
to EXTEND to ſuch perſons.   And if they are not to be conſtrued
to *extend* to them, nothing can be plainer, than that they are
not to be conſtrued to *affect them at all*, either as to crime or
penalty.   Now, if the ſtatute-law doth not make this a crime,
it is certain, it is no crime at all by the *common-law ;* becauſe the
conſtitution of the church, and its peculiar doctrine, worſhip,
diſcipline, and government, are founded wholly upon the ſtatute-
law, and not at all upon the common law†.

S 2   INSTEAD,

---

* It was obſerved by a learned Judge, who differed in opinion from his brethren in the ſheriff's caſe, that the titles of acts of parliament furniſh a very
good clue for explaining them ; and from hence he inferred, that the act of
toleration is *merely* an exemption from the penalties of certain laws.   But I beg
leave to obſerve, that to illuſtrate or *explain* acts of parliament by their titles is
one thing, to reſtrain or *limit* them is another.   Whether they amount to *more*
than their titles expreſs, muſt be determined by the words or clauſes of the act
itſelf.   The teſt-act ſupplies us with a caſe in point, it being entitled, An act for
preventing dangers which may happen from Popiſh recuſants ; and yet every one
knows it is ſo drawn as to comprehend alſo the Proteſtant Diſſenters.   Indeed
numberleſs inſtances might be produced, in which, were we to reſtrain the intention of acts by their titles, we ſhould fall into moſt egregious miſtakes.

† " If it is a crime not to take the ſacrament at church," ſaid a Noble Lord
in a high department of the law, (and by parity of reaſon, if it had been t the
particular purpoſe of his argument at that time, he might have ſaid, If it be a
crime not to go to church, or join in any of its public offices) " it muſt b.
" crime by ſome law ; which muſt be either common or ſtatute-law, th.
" law inforcing it depending wholly upon the ſtatute-law.   Now th.
" law is repealed, as to perſons capable of pleading, that they are f.
" qualified ; and, therefore, the canon law is repealed with regard
" perſons. If it is a crime by common law, it muſt be ſo either by uſage c
" ciple.   There is no uſage or cuſtom, independent of poſitive law, v
                                                                " m.

INSTEAD, therefore, of saying in the Commentaries, that the *penalties* are all of them *suspended by the toleration-act*, which exempts

" makes nonconformity a crime.　The eternal principles of natural religion are
" part of the common law; the essential principles of revealed religion are part
" of the common law; so that any person reviling, subverting, or ridiculing
" them may be prosecuted at common law.　But it cannot be shewn from the
" principles of natural or revealed religion that, independent of positive law,
" temporal punishments ought to be inflicted for mere opinions with respect to
" particular modes of worship.　Persecution for a sincere, though erroneous
" conscience, is not to be deduced from reason or the fitness of things: it can
" only stand upon positive law.　See his Lordship's speech in the Appendix
N°. II.

The act of uniformity 1 Eliz. c. 2. is that positive law upon which rested the obligation to conformity previous to the toleration-act, the acts of uniformity of Edward the Sixth having been repealed by 1 Ma. Seff. 2. c. 2.　But it is expresfly declared by the toleration-act, that the 14th clause of the act of Elizabeth, which enjoined conformity to the church, shall not be construed to *extend* to Protestant Dissenters, that is, it is repealed with regard to such persons; and the acts of the 2d of Edward the Sixth, c. 1. and of the 5th and 6th of Edward the Sixth, c. 1. which were revived by the second clause of the act of uniformity of Elizabeth, are, as far as they require conformity to the church, repealed by section the third of the toleration-act, which frees Dissenters from all ecclesiastical censures, and consequently from those to which they were exposed by the revived acts of Edward the Sixth.　When, therefore, the learned Commentator mentions 23 Eliz. c. 1. 35 Eliz. c. 1. 17 Car. II. c. 2. 22 Car. II. c. 1. as acts from which the Dissenters are exempted by the toleration-act, he ought above all to have mentioned the 14th clause of the act of uniformity, and those ecclesiastical censures to which the Dissenters were liable by the revived acts of Edward the Sixth.　His not having done this may possibly lead some of his readers to conclude, that notwithstanding the subsequent penal laws against Dissenters, are repealed, yet those acts of uniformity on which the original obligation to conformity was founded are still in force with regard to them; and that accordingly they are obliged to conformity de jure, though excused from the penalties of certain laws by which it is enforced; whereas an attention to the repeal of the acts which I have mentioned, in respect to Dissenters, would, I think, clearly shew that they are under no such obligation, and consequently are not criminal in their Nonconformity; and, I hope, therefore, that these plain matters of fact, which are so material to the right decision of the question between us, will not be omitted in any future edition of the Commentaries.

exempts all Diffenters, except Papifts, and fuch as deny the Trinity, from all penal laws, &c. fhould it not have been faid, that all penal laws for nonconformity are *repealed*, with regard to thofe Diffenters, who are qualified as the act directs? And would it not have been proper to mention, that the Diffenters are freed from profecution in the ecclefiaftical courts? And that there is nothing, therefore, in the law of England, which can make mere nonconformity a crime, any more than liable to penalty?

THE SECOND obfervation I would make is this: That both the crime and penalty of mere Proteftant nonconformity are abolifhed by the act of toleration, is evident from the protecting claufes of that act: which, in the words of a great lawyer, " have not only exempted the Diffenters way of worfhip from- " punifhment, but rendered it innocent and lawful; have put it, " not merely under the connivance, but under the protection " of the law, have *eftablifhed* it. For nothing can be plainer, " than that the law protects nothing in that very refpect, in " which it is, at the fame time, in the eye of the law a crime. " Diffenters by the act of toleration, therefore, are reftored to " a legal confideration and capacity." And this is a view of their condition under the toleration-act, of great importance. For many confequences will from hence follow, which are not mentioned in the act; and which would not follow, if the act amounted to nothing more than a fufpenfion of penalty. For inftance, previous to this act, a legacy, left to diffenting minifters and diffenting congregations, was not efteemed a valid one; becaufe the law knew no fuch perfons, and no fuch affemblies; and it was left to what the law called fuperftitious purpofes. But will it be faid in any court in England, that fuch a legacy is not a valid one now? and yet there being nothing faid of this in the toleration-act, it can only follow, confequentially, from the Diffenters being reftored by that act to a legal confideration and capacity, and being no longer criminal in the eye of the law, as they were before that act was enacted.

THE

THE THIRD obfervation which I would make is: That the unanimous judgment of the commiffioners delegates*, and of the Houfe of Lords† affirming that judgment, in the great caufe between the city of London and the Diffenters, concerning the fine inflicted by a by-law of the city on thofe who refufed the office of fheriff, was grounded entirely on this opinion, " That the to- " leration-act removed the crime as well as the penalty of mere " nonconformity."

THE cafe, you know, was this: By the corporation-act no perfon can be placed, chofen, or elected into any office of or belonging to the government of any corporation, who hath not taken the facrament in the church of England within a year preceding the time of fuch election. The defendant ‡ pleaded, That not having received the facrament at church within a year preceding, he was both uneligible and difabled from ferving; and that, being a Diffenter within the defcription of the toleration-act, and thereby freed from all obligation to take the facrament at church, his omitting it was no way criminal; and that, therefore, the difability he had incurred was a lawful plea in bar of this action, to excufe him from the fine impofed upon thofe who refufed the office of fheriff. The city having brought the caufe before the Houfe of Lords by appeal from the commiffioners delegates, who had given judgment for the defendant; the Houfe ordered this queftion to be propofed for the opinion of the judges. How far the defendant might, in the prefent cafe, be allowed to plead his difability in bar of the action brought againft him?

I T

---

* Lord Chief Baron Parker, Mr. Juftice Fofter, Mr. Juftice Bathurft, and Mr. Juftice Wilmot, now Lord Chief Juftice of the Common-pleas. They delivered their opinions *feriatim*, on the 5th of July 1762, after hearing counfel feveral days. Lord Chief Juftice Willes, who was firft in the commiffion, died before judgment given.

† On the 4th February 1767.

‡ Allen Evans, Efq;

I т was allowed on all hands, that if his nonconformity, and his confequent difability, was criminal, he could not plead it.

A n d for this reafon one of the Judges* was of opinion, (contrary to the reft of his brethren), that the defendant's difability, in the prefent cafe, could not be pleaded ; becaufe, as he faid, the toleration-act amounted to *nothing more than an exemption of Proteftant Diffenters from the penalties of certain laws therein particularly mentioned* ; and the corporation-act not being mentioned therein, the toleration-act could have no influence upon it ; and therefore his difability, incurred by his nonconformity in confequence of the corporation-act, was, in his opinion, a culpable one, and rendered him liable to any penalties, to which any others are liable for refufing to ferve the office of fheriff; inafmuch as no man can difable himfelf: but if he refufed to take the facrament according to the rites of the church of England, he difabled himfelf; and the fine impofed was a punifhment upon him for the crime of his nonconformity, from which he could plead no legal exemption.

But all the other Judges † were of a contrary opinion, That the corporation-act exprefsly rendered the Diffenters uneligible, and incapable of ferving ; its defign being to keep them out, as perfons at that time fuppofed to be difaffected to the government : and though the difability arifing from hence could not *then* have been pleaded againft fuch an action as is now brought againft the defendant, nonconformity being *then* in the eye of the law a crime, and no man being allowed to excufe one crime by another ; yet the cafe is different fince the toleration-act was enacted, *that act* amounting to *much more* than a mere exemption

on

* Mr. Baron Perrott.

† Mr. Juftice Hewitt, now Lord Lifford, and Chancellor of Ireland ; Mr. Juftice Afton, Mr. Juftice Gould, Mr. Baron Adams, Mr. Baron Smythe, Mr Juftice Clive. Mr. Juftice Yates was at that time ill, and incapable of being prefent.

on from the penalties of certain laws, and having an influence upon the corporation-act confequentially, though the corporation-act is not mentioned therein ; by freeing the Diffenters from all obligation to take the facrament at church, abolifhing the crime as well as penalties of nonconformity, and allowing and protecting the diffenting worfhip. The defendant's difability, therefore, they faid, was a lawful one, a legal and reafonable, not a criminal excufe ; it was not in the fenfe of the law difableing himfelf ; the meaning of that maxim, " That a man fhall " not difable himfelf," being only this, that no man fhall difable himfelf by his own wilful fault or crime ; and nonconformity being no longer a crime fince the toleration-act was enacted, he is difabled by judgment of parliament, namely, by the corporation-act, without the concurrence or intervention of any crime of his own ; and therefore he may plead this difability in bar of the prefent action.

S o that the arguments of the Judges turned upon this fingle point, That the toleration-act removed the *crime* as well as the *penalties* of nonconformity ; and in this they all, except one, agreed. The whole was fummed up, and the reafoning on the oppofite fide examined and confuted, with his ufual perfpicuity and force of argument, by Lord Mansfield*; and upon this ground the Houfe of Lords affirmed, *nemine contradicente*, the judgment of the commiffioners delegates.

I n ftating, therefore, the cafe of the Diffenters under the toleration-act, fhould not fome notice have been taken of the protecting claufes of that act †, and of their influence and operation upon

---

* See his Lordfhip's fpeech in the appendix No. II.

† In the laft edition of the Commentaries the protecting claufes are mentioned, but no conclufion is drawn from them ; nor is it mentioned, as I before obferved it fhould have been, that Diffenters under this act are exprefsly freed from all ecclefiaftical cenfures; much lefs is it faid, as the refult of the whole, that they are reftored to a legal capacity, and neither punifhable nor criminal on account of their nonconformity.

upon the legal condition and capacity of the Diffenters? Surely the fufpenfion of penalties is not all that this act amounts to.

WHETHER the toleration-act is extenfive enough as to thofe who *fhould be* its objects, is one queftion; what is its meaning and intent, with refpect to thofe who *are* its objects, is another. Mere nonconformifts with refpect to the worfhip, difcipline, and government of the church, are certainly its objects: and I think it ought not to have been limited, as it is, in regard to the doctrinal articles of religion. But ftill, with refpect to thofe perfons whom it does comprehend, that is, the mere nonconformifts to the conftitution and rites of the church, it puts them on a very liberal footing, not on that of *connivance* only but of *protection* alfo. And the more the idea of *legal protection* is examined, the more will it appear to juftify the ftrong expreffion, which the Noble Lord before mentioned ufed concerning the diffenting worfhip, that it is ESTABLISHED. If the juftices of the peace at the quarter-feffions, or the regifter of the bifhop's court fhould refufe to regifter a diffenting place of worfhip, a *mandamus* always is and muft be granted, upon application, in Weftminfter-hall, to compel them to the difcharge of their duty. And is it not abfurd to fuppofe, that a *mandamus* muft iffue in a cafe, which the law regards as criminal? Is not the law to be confidered as giving its *whole fanction*, and exerting its *whole energy*, in refpect to whatever juftifies and requires a *mandamus?* and does not this amount, ftrictly fpeaking, to the idea of the word *eftablifhed?*

WHEN the late incomparable Speaker of the Houfe of Commons, Mr. Onflow, was informed of the expreffion, which the learned and Noble Lord ufed on this occafion, he obferved, in a converfation with which he honoured me, that this was the language he himfelf had always held; that, as far as the authority of the law could go in point of *protection*, the Diffenters were as

T   *truly*

truly eftablifhed as the church of England*; and that an eftablifhed church, as diftinguifhed from their places of worfhip, was
properly fpeaking, only an *endowed church* ; a church, which
the law not only protected, but endowed with temporalities for
its peculiar fupport and encouragement†.

I F it fhould fo happen, after all, that I fhould have miftaken
your meaning, and that your idea of the condition of the Diffenters under the toleration-act is the fame with mine, that they
are freed from the *crime* as well as penalties of their nonconformity ; I apprehend, fome alteration will ftill be neceffary in your
reprefentation of the purport of the toleration-act : which reprefentation, as it now ftands, leads your reader naturally, and al-
moft neceffarily to conclude, that your apprehenfion of the defign of that act is not fo enlarged as, in my humble opinion, it
ought

* The penalties inflicted by the act of toleration on thofe who difturb any
diffenting congregation for divine worfhip, or mifufe the preacher, are precifely
the fame as on thofe who difturb the congregation, or mifufe the preacher, in
any cathedral, parifh church, or chapel ; and diffenting minifters, as well as
the clergy of the church of England, are excufed from all burdenfome offices.

† I fuppofe it is upon this idea, that, fince the toleration, it hath been the invariable practice of our Sovereigns, in their fpeeches to their parliaments, upon
their acceffion, after declaring their affection to the church of England, and refolution to fupport it, to add, That they will maintain the toleration inviolable. When this was done at the commencement of the prefent reign, the Lords
in their addrefs of thanks, paid a juft and expreffive compliment to the toleration, by ftiling it, THAT SUREST CEMENT OF THE PROTESTANT INTEREST
IN THESE KINGDOMS. And this expreffion, in anfwer to that part of the royal
fpeech, which contained a promife of preferving and *ftrengthening* the conftitution in *church* and ftate, was the more appofite, as it conveyed this certain
truth, That the union of Proteftants among themfelves in mutual affection and
efteem, however they may differ in formularies of doctrine or rites of worfhip,
is the beft fupport of their common intereft ; and that the church of England,
in particular, can never be more *ftrengthened*, or placed on a firmer foundation,
than by encouraging the generous principles of *toleration*, and an impartial regard to the right of *private judgment*.

ought to be. And if, upon further reflection, you are convinced of this, I am very sure, from the specimens you have already given of your candor in similar cases, you will take care to guard against any misapprehension of your judgment in future editions of your incomparable book. That openness to conviction, and that consequent disposition to correct mistakes, which you have discovered, does you more honour, in a moral view, than all your intellectual abilities, great as they are; in asmuch as integrity and ingenuity of heart deserve, and will receive from those whose good opinion is worth regarding, much more applause than the acutest discernment, or the profoundest and most accurate judgment. I am,

S I R,

with great esteem,

your obedient humble servant,

P. F.

L E T T E R II.

S I R,

YOU have a difpofition, I am perfuaded, too ingenuous and liberal, to be offended at a candid, though free difcuffion of your fentiments : I fhall make no apology, therefore, for laying before you my remarks on fome other paffagcs, as I have already done on one particular point, in your juftly-admired Commentaries on the laws of England.

WHEN Dr. Prieftley obferved in his Remarks, p. 28. that you qouted with approbation *the ftatute of William the Third, a-gainft " perfons educated in the Chriftian religion, or profef-" fing the fame, who fhall by writing, printing, teaching, or " advifed fpeaking, deny any one of the perfons in the Holy " Trinity to be God, or maintain that there are more gods " than one :" by which ftatute they are made liable to the pains and penalties inflicted by the fame ftatute on apoftacy; that is, " for the firft offence, they are rendered incapable of holding a-" ny office or place of truft ; and for the fecond, are rendered " incapable of bringing any action, being guardian, executor, " legatee, or purchafer of lands ; and are to fuffer three years " imprifonment without bail†:" I fay, when Dr. Prieftley re-marked, that you cited this fevere ftatute with approbation, you difclaimed the imputation in your Reply‡ ; and alledged, that you " barely recited the ftatute, without either approving " or difapproving it." It will furely then, be proper to omit

thefe

---

* Comment. vol. iv. p. 50.

† The Emperor Marcian, in an edict againft the Eutychians and Appollina-rifts, rendered them incapable of difpofing of their eftates, of making a will, or of inheriting any thing by the will of others, or by deed of gift. Concil. tom. 2. p. 678. edit. Hard. Some of the claufes in the act of parliament feem to have been copied from this worthy original.

‡ Reply, p. 38.

thefe words in your Commentaries*, which you will find a little before your citation of this ftatute. " Every thing is now as
" it

---

* Comment. p. 49. This paffage is altered in the new edition in the following manner : " Every thing is now as it fhould be *with refpect to the fpiritual cogni-*
" *zance, and fpiritual punifhment of herefy* ; unlefs perhaps that the crime ought to
" be more ftrictly defined, and no profecution permitted, even in the ecclefiafti-
" cal courts, till the tenets in queftion are by proper authority previoufly de-
" clared to be heretical. Under thefe reftrictions, it feems neceffary for the
" fupport of the national religion, that the officers of the church fhould have
" power to cenfure heretics ; yet *not to harrafs them with temporal penalties, much*
" *lefs* to exterminate or deftroy them." If the worthy author means, that the
cenfures of the church are not to extend to the infliction of any temporal penalties on hereticks, as I muft fuppofe he does. this is an amendment of very great
importance ; tacitiy condemning a power of excommunication accompanied with
any fuch penalties, efpecially when, as in the church of England, that cenfure deprives men of all the privileges of fociety ; of fuing an action, being witneffes, making a will, receiving a legacy, and, after a certain time, renders
them liable to imprifonment ; and confining it, as it ought to be confined, to a
mere exclufion from chriftian communion, which affects the perfon fo cenfured
in none of his civil rights.

But if the author intends, which I can hardly allow myfelf to furmize, that
the cenfures of the church may include temporal penalties, though not in fuch
a degree as to *harrafs* the heretick : then all the arguments which I have urged
againft the infliction of any kind or degree of temporal penalties in fuch cafes,
will be ftill applicable to the paffage as it is now amended.

" The fpiritual cognizance and fpiritual punifhment of herefy;" *fhould* ex vi
termini, exclude all temporal penalty ; but whether in our ecclefiaftical conftitution " all things are as they fhould be" in this refpect, I think, with fubmiffion to the learned gentleman, deferves to be reconfidered. The act for the repeal of the writ de hæretico comburendo, 29 C. II. c. 9. fect. 2. exprefsly provides, that the judges of the ecclefiaftical courts fhall have a power to punifh
herefy by excommunication, (which, as we have feen, includes very *harraffing*
temporal penalties) by deprivation, degradation, and other ecclefiaftical cenfures, only not extending to death : which is the fole exception. When the
learned Commentator therefore grants that hereticks " are not to be harraffed
" with temporal penalties, much lefs to be exterminated or deftroyed," he
feems virtually to deny, what he had juft before too incautioufly affirmed, that
" all things are now as they fhould be," " with refpect to the fpiritual cogni-
" zance and fpiritual punifhment of herefy."

However, on the whole, I am inclined to think, by the conceffion, that hereticks

" it fhould be, unlefs perhaps that herefy ought to be more
" ftrictly defined," &c. This, your readers will be apt to think
amounts to an approbation of all that follows; and particularly
of the act here referred to, which is prefently after quoted as
now in force; and therefore, as one of the things which, you
fay, " are as they fhould be."

TRULY, Sir, it is much to be defired, that you would review this whole paragraph with attention. The only objection
which you make to the intolerant and perfecuting laws now in
force againft herefy is, that " herefy is not defined in them with
fufficient precifion;" and, you think, " no profecution fhould
" be permitted, even in the ecclefiaftical courts, till the tenets
" in queftion are, by proper authority, previoufly declared to
" be heretical." And provided this be done, " every thing is
" then," you fay, " as it fhould be."

So that, in your opinion, it is fit, that herefy fhould be punifhed with temporal penalties; only care fhould be taken, that
what is herefy, be firft fettled by proper authority*. But here
the

reticks are not to be harraffed with temporal penalties, he intended to declare
againft the ufe of any temporal penalties in cafes of herefy. And I only wifh
that he had expreffed his meaning fo precifely, as to exclude all poffibility of the
fevereft critic's putting a lefs favourable conftruction upon his words ; and that
before he had declared his approbation of the prefent ftate of our ecclefiaftical
conftitution, in regard to what he calls the fpiritual cognizance and fpiritual
punifhment of herefy, he had well confidered to what that approbation a-
mounts: whether it does not imply more than any one, who is an enemy to
harraffing hereticks with temporal penalties, will undertake to defend. I fubmit it therefore to the confideration of the learned gentleman himfelf, whether
it is not neceffary to make fome further alteration in this paragraph, in juftice
to the liberality of his own fentiments, and to prevent his authority being produced in fupport of a power vefted in ecclefiaftical governors, of cenfuring and
punifhing hereticks in a manner which he feems to difapprove.

* The nature of herefy, in the fcripture fenfe of the word I think, hath been
very much miftaken. The hereticks, whom, in the New Teftament, we are directed to avoid, were not the humble, modeft, and peaceable, though errone-

ous

the queſtion occurs, What is proper authority? and where is it lodged? I ſuppoſe, Sir, you will place it either with the eccleſiaſtical governors, or with the legiſlature. But in the hands of either, it will certainly amount to nothing more than human authority, the authority of fallible men; which, I apprehend, upon examination, will be found to be no authority at all in the preſent caſe, that is, in defining what is true faith, and what is hereſy, and marking out their reſpective boundaries.

If the ſcripture is to determine for us, the point, I think, is clearly decided. For our bleſſed Saviour hath commanded his diſciples not to be " called maſters; for," ſaith he, " one is your Maſter, even Chriſt, and all ye are brethren†;" and this he ſaid in oppoſition to the authority which the Jewiſh rabbies aſſumed, in deciding queſtions of their law. And the apoſtles, who certainly, if any perſons, might have pretended to authority in matters of faith, declared, " that they had no dominion over " the faith" of Chriſtians; but were " only helpers of their " joy*." They appealed to reaſon and conſcience, and referred the final deciſion to every man's own private judgment : " We " ſpeak as unto wiſe men; judge ye what we ſay‡." The Bereans are commended for " ſearching the ſcriptures" of the Old Teſtament daily, to ſee, " whether the things" which the apoſtles declared to them " were ſo" as they reported§. And it is

___

ous Chriſtians, who adhered to the authority of Chriſt, and deſired to know and do his will; but the proud, pragmatical, turbulent party-men, who diſturbed and divided the church by their impoſitions, and innovations in the terms of brotherly affection and Chriſtian communion, and by aſſuming an authority over their fellow Chriſtians. Hereſy, in the ſenſe of ſcripture, doth not conſiſt in ſimple error; nor were thoſe hereticks, who were anathematized and perſecuted : but only thoſe who anathematized and perſecuted others, refuſing to acknowledge them for true Chriſtians, on account of their ſuppoſed or real miſtakes. Whoſoever carefully and conſcientiouſly conſults the ſacred oracles, with a deſire of knowing and doing the will of Chriſt, cannot be an heretick in the ſcripture-meaning of the expreſſion. See Hallet's Notes and Diſcourſes, vol. 3. diſc. ix. throughout, eſpecially p. 390.

† Matth. xxiii. 8, 10.

* 2 Cor. i. 24.   ‡ 1 Cor. x. 15.   § Acts xvii. 11.

is the duty of every Chriſtian to endeavour, for himſelf, to underſtand the ſacred oracles, as well as he is able, in the uſe of all
the means and helps which divine providence puts in his power†.

Indeed, every man's private perſuaſion or belief, muſt. be
founded upon evidence propoſed to his own mind; and he cannot but believe, according as things appear to HIMSELF, not to
others; to his own underſtanding, not to that of any other
man. Conviction is always produced by the light which is
ſtruck into the mind ; and never by compulſion, or the force of
human authority‡.

But

---

† Human helps and aſſiſtances, while they are only employed to open and inform the underſtanding, are very deſireable and uſeful. But human authority, ſitting in judgment on points of faith, and deciding caſes of hereſy, and
controuling, without enlightening, our underſtandings, is a very different
thing. There is, ſurely, ſufficient room for our receiving inſtruction and aſſiſtance in matters of religion, without being deprived of our right of judging, in
the laſt reſort, for ourſelves. And that we muſt do in oppoſition to all human
authority, in whatſoever hands it be lodged, and with whatſoever venerable
titles it comes recommended ; or elſe we violate our allegiance to Chriſt, the
only lawgiver and king in his church.

‡ If it be urged, that we believe many things upon *human authority* : I admit it,
in caſe by authority we mean *teſtimony*. But there is a manifeſt difference between human teſtimony, as to matters of fact: and human authority, as to matters of opinion, and principles of truth. The former may be, and often is, a
rational ground of belief; the latter is believing upon no evidence, and is a re-
nunciation of reaſon. The authority or teſtimony of the apoſtles, and firſt
teachers of Chriſtianity, was accompanied with divine credentials; and this
rendered it a ſufficient foundation for the belief, both of the facts and doctrines
they revealed. And, indeed, human teſtimony, under the influence of inſpira-
tion, and ſupported by miraculous interpoſition, is *always* a juſt ground of our
belief of religious truth, as well as facts ; but the authoritative decrees and in-
junctions of fallible, uninſpired men, *never*. The former claim an abſolute regard, as being a proof and evidence of a divine miſſion; the latter are no evidences of religious truth, or ground of belief of it all, and therefore deſerve no
regard. And it ſeems very ſtrange, that men ſhould preſume to exact of us,
what God himſelf does not ; the belief and profeſſion of opinions for which we
can perceive no ſort of evidence.

BUT it may be alledged, perhaps, that other men's underftandings are better, and more penetrating and judicious than
ours; or, that great numbers, efpecially of perfons venerable
for their age, as well as for their piety and learning, are more
likely to be in the right, than a few individuals; and that, confequently, it will be *fafer* to be guided by their judgments than
by our own. To this I reply: That a man's own underftanding, be it more or lefs judicious, is the only faculty which God
hath given him to diftinguifh truth from error: and as every
man is accountable only for the ufe of his own underftanding,
not for that of other men's; confequently, his fafety confifts,
not in giving up his own to the direction and controul of others,
but in ufing it himfelf to the beft advantage. And fhould he,
in the careful and confcientious ufe of it, err; that error will
never be imputed to him as a crime: Whereas, if he follows the
judgment of other men, though ever fo wife and learned, contrary to his own fenfe of things; he may perchance *profefs* what
is *right*, but he *does* what is *wrong*, and is highly criminal in the
fight of God. For, the profeffing of any doctrine fhould always
follow conviction of the truth of it; at leaft, a man muft never
profefs what is contrary to his conviction. To embrace, or profefs, any point which he does not believe to be true, in compliment to human authority, is exalting *human* into the place of
divine authority; and faying in one word, That it is better to
obey man than God.

So that for any man, or body of men, whether clergy or laity, to affume an authority, firft, to define what is herefy, and
then to condemn and punifh it by temporal penalties, is the ready way to make men hypocrites; while it can, in no cafe, render them true believers or good men.* But not to infift upon
                              U   this:

---

* Submitting to the decifions of human authority in matters of faith, is *fome-*
times prejudicial to, and even fubverfive of, true religion, where it does not
iffue in downright hypocrify. For, as, on the one hand, by the exercife of our
                                                                      rational

this: what I would principally obferve to you, Sir, who are by profeffion a lawyer, is:

THAT herefy not being fufficiently defined by our laws, feems to be no fmall fecurity, in connection with the lenity of the times, that thofe laws will not be executed; on account of the difficulty of defining what is herefy; and, perhaps, of finding a jury, or even any ecclefiaftical judges, that will be forward in defining it, where the law hath left it doubtful and undefined. What, therefore, you, Sir, imagine a defect in the law, which ought to be fupplied, appears to me to be a circumftance very favourable to the fecure enjoyment of the rights of confcience; and, I hope, criminal profecutions for opinion, either in civil or ecclefiaftical courts, will never be rendered more eafy and feafible, than they are at prefent.

THE next enquiry, on fuppofition herefy is cognizable and punifhable by human authority (as you feem to think) naturally is: What that punifhment fhall be?

You tell us, that " under thefe reftrictions" (namely, that herefy fhould be more ftrictly defined; and no profecution permitted, till the herefy is by proper authority afcertained) " it " feems neceffary, for the fupport of the national religion, that " the officers of the church fhould have power to cenfure here- " ticks, but not to exterminate or deftroy them†." In this affertion is it not plainly fuppofed, that the cenfures of the church

are

rational faculties in fearching after truth, we are not only likely to arrive at it, but to improve in the love of it, in candor, docility, and opennefs to conviction; and are difpofed to fubmit to its influence: fo, on the contrary, in *proportion as we refign ourfelves* to the conduct of human authority, truth lofes it charms and its influence over us; and we become blind to its cleareft evidences, and brighteft characters, and are thus prepared to be led into the moft abfurd fuperftitions, and vileft corruptions of religion. And this is the cafe among all parties, in the degree in which they give up the free exercife of their underftandings, and take human authority for their guide.

† Comment. vol. iv. p 49.

are to be attended with temporal penalties? only not fo as to exterminate or deftroy the heretick.   In the name of humanity, Sir, is this the only exception to the extent and effect of the church's cenfures, that they fhall not reach to utter extermina-nation? Are all other pains and penalties proper, in whatfoever degree they are inflicted, which affect only a man's liberty or property, provided he is not deftroyed thereby? If this be your meaning, (and, I think, you fhould have left no ground for fuf-picion that it is your meaning, if it is not) what more ample fcope could any perfecutor defire for his wanton cruelty, than you al-low; unlefs, like another Bonner, he thirfted for human blood? —Excufe me, Sir, the warmth of my expreffion.   This fentence of yours muft, furely, have dropped from you inadvertently; and can never ferioufly be intended to mean, what it feems to imply.

To examine the point more thoroughly: Is the infliction of temporal penalties upon heretics, really neceffary to the fupport of a national eftablifhment? If fo, how comes it to pafs, that a national eftablifhment is in its nature fo oppofite to the genius of Chriftianity, of that kingdom which is not of this world, and which confifts not in any thing this world can beftow or fecure; but only in righteoufnefs, truth, and peace? Religion is feated in the heart of man, and converfant with the inward principles and temper of the mind; and it cannot therefore, properly fpeak-ing, be eftablifhed by human laws, or enforced by temporal pu-nifhments.   There is nothing in a fine, or a dungeon, or in any other penalty which the magiftrate can inflict, that is calculated to produce conviction.   Truth can only be fupported and pro-pagated by reafon and argument; in conjunction with that mild and perfuafive infinuation, and that opennefs and candor, and apparent benevolence in its advocates, which are fuited to invite men's attention, and difpofe them to examination.   No civil pu-nifhments are adapted to enlighten the underftanding, or to conciliate the affections.   And therefore the " weapons" which

the

the minifters of religion (or, in your ftile, " the officers of the " church") are directed to ufe " are not carnal†," but fpiritual.

For my own part, I believe, it would have fared much bet-. ter with the intereft of true religion, if it had been left to make its way by the force of its own native excellence, and evidence only ; than it hath done fince it hath been incorporated with civil conftitutions, and eftablifhed by human laws. For, even temporal emoluments, (leaving penalties out of the queftion) annexed to the profeffion of any form of religion, in fuch degree as to excite men's avarice and ambition, and difpofe them to mean an unworthy, not to fay wicked compliances to obtain or fecure them ; have done, 1 apprehend, infinite mifchief to the religious and moral characters of multitudes in all ages and countries‡.

But

---

† 2 Cor. x. 4;

‡ The ingenious author of the Free Enquiry into the nature and origin of evil, gives us a very ftrong picture in a different point of view, of the bad effects of religious eftablifhments; namely, of the ill influence which they have, both on the purity of religion and the liberties of mankind. " The moment," faith he, " any religion becomes national, or eftablifhed, its purity muft cer- " tainly be loft, becaufe it is then impoffible to keep it unconnected with men's " interefts; and if connected, it muft inevitably be perverted by them," p. 225. edit. 4. Again, " that very order of men, who are maintained to fupport its " interefts, will facrifice them to their own," p. 225, 226. " By degrees knaves " will join them, fools believe them, and cowards be afraid of them; and " having gained fo confiderable a part of the world to their interefts, they " will erect an independent dominion among themfelves dangerous to the liber- " ties of mankind ; and reprefenting all thofe who oppofe their tyranny, as " God's enemies, teach it to be meritorious in his fight to perfecute them in " this world, and damn them in another. Hence muft arife Hierarchies, In- " quifitions, and Popery ; for Popery is but the confummation of that tyranny " which every religious fyftem in the hands of men is in perpetual purfuit of, " and whofe principles they are all ready to adopt, whenever they are fortu- " nate enough to meet with its fuccefs." See p. 223—230. The freedom of thefe fentiments having " given fome offence", as being fuppofed to con- tain " a reflection upon all national churches, and a perfuafion to fchifm, and " diffention ;"

BUT when such national establishments, besides the rewards
which they bestow upon their church-officers are guarded by
temporal

" dissention ;" the author makes this apology in the preface to his fourth edition, p. 25. " Those," saith he, " who think thus, totally misapprehend the
" tenor of this whole work, which endeavours to prove, that every thing hu-
" man must be attended with evils, which therefore ought to be submitted
" to with patience and resignation ; that many imperfections will adhere to all
" governments and religions in the hands of men ; but that these, unless they
" rise to an intolerable degree, will not justify our resistance to the one, or *our*
" *dissention from the other*." And to make it the more apparent that he is no e-
nemy to establishments, he adds, that were no religion to be established at all,
" it would let in such an inundation of Enthusiasm and contradictory absurdi-
" ties, as must in a short time *destroy not only all religion, but all peace and mora-*
" *lity whatsoever* : of which no one can entertain the least doubt, who is not
" totally unacquainted both with the nature and history of mankind." Though
the author had before painted, in very lively colours, the ill effects of that connection between religion and men's secular interests, which subsists in national
establishments ; he here represents those effects to be of little consequence, in
comparison of that " inundation of enthusiasm and contradictory absurdities,
" which," in his opinion, were there no establishment, would, in a short time,
" destroy not only all religion, but all peace and morality". On the contrary,
I think it would be easy to shew from the history of mankind, that greater
evils have been produced by religious establishments, than either have been, or
are likely, or I think possible to be, by the want of them. The grossest enthusiasm and absurdity have often made a part of them, and have been patronized
and upheld by those who have been most zealous for them, sometimes by persecution and violence, at the expence of every principle of humanity and justice.
But supposing there were no establishments, why must " all religion be destroy-
" ed ?" I rather think the free exercise of the human understanding, without
any byas from interest, would tend very much to promote both the purity and
progress of religion. And I have too high an idea of the strength of its evidence, and the charms of its excellence, and of its interest in the protection of the
great Sovereign of the Universe, to imagine its existence depends upon human
establishments. It is certain, fools will be fools and enthusiasts will be enthusiasts ; nor will establishments prevent their acting agreeably to their real character. If recourse be had to penal laws and to intolerant measures, it will augment and inflame the disease ; and if the caustic is continued till the patient is
destroyed, still enthusiasm and absurdity will spread like an infection ; and not
being tolerated, will perhaps, in some shape or other, take possession of the establishment ;

temporal penalties, inflicted on all who cannot follow the lead of the public wisdom and public conscience; they are then neither better

blishment itself; either under false colours and by the artifice of their votaries, or through the folly of those, who in the wantonness of power and weakness of intellect, frequently bring in, and impose, more extravagant absurdities, and things more destructive of true religion, themselves; than they refuse to tolerate in others. It had been well, if this conduct had been wholly confined to the church of Rome.

Again, why must " all peace and morality be destroyed," if there be no religious establishments? Does the existence of common sense, and a regard to the essential interests of society, wholly depend upon such establishments? Can magistrates do nothing by enacting and executing wholesome laws, to preserve the public peace and order? Will no wise, no good, no public-spirited men, (not to say ministers of religion) promote the same salutary end? or will there be no such persons existing?

But though the evils of establishments are very great and numerous, as the author had represented them, yet he saith, " the imperfections which adhere to " all governments and religions, unless they arise to an intolerable degree, will " not justify our resistance to the one, or *our dissention from the other*." Resistance or force, I own, should not be employed against civil government, except in cases of extreme necessity, and when what is stiled government is no longer government, but tyranny: nor indeed should any attempt be made to overturn a religious government by force, unless its existence is incompatible with the safety or essential rights of others; as indeed it always is, when it will not allow a toleration; and in that case its destruction, in any method suited to accomplish it, is mere self-defence. The Author therefore should have compared with resistance to civil government, not a dissent from an establishment, but an attempt to overthrow an establishment by force; because, though civil government cannot allow or suppose resistance or force to be used against itself (for that as I have said, becomes warrantable only when it ceases to be government); yet that establishment which does not always allow a dissent from itself, is a mere ecclesiastical tyranny: for liberty of religious dissent is a right incident to human nature; and a right, which the legislature of this country hath accordingly recognized by the Toleration; which, nevertheless, this Author strangely compares to an illegal resistance of the civil power.

He further observes, that " from a dissent can accrue no remedy to the evils " of an establishment," p. 26. It must however be admitted, that it serves at least to correct the virulence of the disease, and to retard its progress towards an intire state of corruption, or tyranny; to which, according to his own account, it

better nor worfe than notorious violations of the laws of Chrift, and of his royal prerogative? they are deftructive of the very defign of his religion, which is of no value if the profeffion and practice of it be not a free and reafonable fervice: and are an open invafion of the common rights of humanity.

B u t perhaps you will fay, I am leading you into " a theogical controverfy*." I fhall only refer it, therefore, to your further

it naturally tends. From a flight attention to the hiftory of the church of England from the time of the reformation, we may eafily collect, that the Puritans and Diffenters have had no inconfiderable fhare, efpecially at certain periods, in ftopping the progrefs of ecclefiaftical corruption, and keeping down that exorbitant power, which the Hierarchy otherwife might, and certainly would, if the author's account of its tendency be juft, have long fince attained. And this, I hope he will admit to be no contemptible fervice.

In confequence of fome things I have advanced, it will perhaps be afked, whether I aim at fubverting all ecclefiaftical eftablifhments? The reader may be affured, I am not fo vifionary as to aim at an object, which is wholly out of fight, and not at all to be expected. But I am perfuaded, that fuch eftablifhments are not vindicable de jure, or perfectly compatible with the right every man hath of judging and acting for himfelf in matters of religion; whatever fpecious arguments may be adduced to prove their expedience, or at leaft that they are, as this Author fuppofes, neceffary evils. And if this be our opinion concerning eftablifhments, that they are not ftrictly vindicable on principles of liberty, we fhall eafily perceive, that an eftablifhment without a toleration is deteftible; and that in an eftablifhment with a toleration, it is the toleration which is the moft facred part of the conftitution; that being the affertion of religious liberty which is a natural right, whereas an eftablifhment is always, more or lefs an invafion or infringement of it. And fhould any of thofe who acquiefce in religious eftablifhments, happen to embrace fuch fentiments concerning them, I can fee no worfe confequence likely to arife, than that they would be made more zealous for reducing them to as near a conformity as poffible, with chriftian liberty and chriftian fimplicity: whereas high notions of the authority of ecclefiaftical governors, or of the civil magiftrate, in matters of religion, are apt to teach that " patient refignation" of private conduct to public judgment, which, though this ingenious author feems to think it very commendable, I am glad it is not my tafk to defend.

* See Reply to Dr. Prieftley, p. 38.

ther confideration, whether the *law* cannot fupport the church in all her *rights* and *immunities*, unlefs fhe is invefted likewife with the unwarrantable and dangerous power of *punifhing* thofe who call in queftion, or diffent from her eftablifhed formularies of doctrine or worfhip.

If you only mean, indeed, by the cenfures of the church, her refufing communion to thofe who differ from her in articles of faith which fhe thinks important, without allowing her to in-force thofe cenfures by any temporal penalties; I acknowledge, I have then mifunderftood you. But I appeal to yourfelf, Sir, up-on further reflection, whether that miftake, if it be one, is not owing to your affigning no other limitation to the effects of thofe cenfures, than that they fhould not extend to " utter extermi-" nation and deftruction."

I freely confefs, I am fo far from thinking, that any church hath a right to ufe temporal penalties to bring perfons to her own terms of communion, that, I apprehend, fhe is in-vefted with no authority to make any terms of commu-nion at all, which Chrift hath not made; and thofe which he hath made, are only to be enforced by fpiritual fanctions; by his own authority as head of the church, by the dread of his dif-pleafure, and by the hope of his favour. And a national church I apprehend, will ftand much firmer upon this noble and exten-five foundation of reafon and fcripture, than on the narrow and feeble one of human authority, fenced as much as you pleafe, with all the terrors of pains and penalties.

Perhaps it will be afked, Are we to leave every man at li-berty to propagate what fentiments he pleafes? It is my opinion, I profefs, that truth is fo far from fuffering by free examination, that this is the only method in which fhe can be effectually fup-ported and propagated. But, with this idea I am not fo happy as to be able to reconcile the following fentiment: " I would " not," you fay, " be underftood to derogate from the juft " rights

" rights of the national church, or to encourage a loofe latitude
" of propagating any crude undigefted fentiments in religious
" matters : of propagating, I fay ; for the bare entertaining
" them, without an endeavour to diffufe them, feems hardly
" cognizable by any human authority*."

THAT indeed is very true, if by bare entertaining you mean
merely believing; and a good reafon there is for it, becaufe
the heart of man is infcrutable; becaufe there it *a natural
impoffibility* for any human authority to interfere with the
inward fentiments of the mind, while they are concealed
from outward obfervation. But if by entertaining you intend
(contrary to the ufual fenfe of the word, and not very confiftently with your approving of our prefent laws againft herefy) to
allow the profeffion of fuch fentiments, provided men do not
aim at diffufing them ; yet the moment reafons are offered to
fupport or recommend that profeffion, human authority may
interpofe, it feems; becaufe it is, " one of the juft rights of the
" national church, from which," you fay, " you will by no
" means derogate," to prevent " the propagation of any crude
" undigefted fentiments in religious matters :" that is in reality,
(for to this it amounts) any fentiments different from thofe by
law eftablifhed ; every eftablifhment fuppofing thofe fentiments
to be crude and undigefted, which are contrary to its own principles and practices. A maxim, which will vindicate the exercife of human authority in fupport of every eftablifhment that
ever was, or will be: Mohammedifm at Conftantinople, Popery
at Rome, Epifcopacy in England, Prefbyterianifm at Geneva, or
in Scotland! For all the adherents to thefe feveral perfuafions
think, thofe who differ from them entertain, at leaft, *crude and
undigefted fentiments in religious matters.* Indeed, this principle,
purfued into its genuine confequences, would have precluded the
reformation from Popery, and would even have ftifled in its
birth our holy religion itfelf. If the propagation of truth, or of
fuppofed truth, in matters purely religious, is to be reftrained
by human authority, (whether you call it civil or ecclefiaftical,

W   is

* Comment. vol. iv. p. 49.

is the fame at laft; for they are both alike exercifed by fallible men): in that cafe, the fuccefs of true religion in the world, depends wholly on the power of the magiftrate, or on the majority; either of which may be as likely, at leaft to be on the fide of error as of truth.

FROM this idea, that the fuppreffion of herefy, or the preventing the propagation of it, by temporal penalties, is neceffary to the eftablifhment of truth, or of a church, have been derived all thofe execrable and outrageous perfecutions, which have difgraced not only our religion, but human nature itfelf. For there is a gradation, in this cafe, as natural as it is common; the fame principle which induces men, at firft, to employ what are called moderate penalties, in order to compafs fo good an end as the fuppreffion of error, leading them (in cafe that end cannot *otherwife* be accomplifhed, that end which they think *muſt* be accomplifhed: the very fame principle, I fay, leading them) to the meafures ftill more and more fevere and intolerant, till by degrees they are reconciled to the moft inhuman perfecutions, and bloody maffacres. And in cafe they do not proceed to fuch lengths, to what fhall we afcribe it? to their principle? or to their humanity pleading againft principle?

I AM far, Sir, from infinuating, that you hold all the confequences which flow from the maxim you feem to entertain, namely, that temporal penalties may be employed in promoting truth and fuppreffing error: it is fufficient for me to obferve, that all thofe pofitions muft be erroneous, from which fuch confequences naturally follow.———I am, Sir, *&c.*

LETTER

LETTER III.

SIR,

THOUGH the reasoning in my last letter, may be applied to the case of apostacy, as well as heresy; the case of renouncing Christianity, or professing Deism; yet as you have advanced some particular arguments for inflicting human punishment upon infidels, I shall take the liberty to give what you have offered a distinct consideration; because, I apprehend, it would be dishonourable to the Christian religion to be even suspected to owe its preservation, not to its own excellence and evidence, and the special protection of Providence, but to the terror of penal laws, and the sword of the civil magistrate.

Having premised, that " the loss of life is a heavier penalty " than the crime of apostacy deserves;" you remark that " a- " bout the close of the last century, the civil liberties to which " we were then restored, being used as a cloak of maliciousness, " and the most horrid doctrines, subversive of all religion being " publicly avowed both in discourse and writings, it was found " necessary again" (the punishment of death for this crime being become obsolete) " for the civil power to interpose, by not " admitting these miscreants" (explained in the margin by *mescroyantz*, the French word used in our antient laws for unbelievers) " to the privileges of society, who maintained such prin- " ciples as destroyed all moral obligation." To this end, you say, " it was enacted by a statute 9 and 10 Will. III. c. 32. that " if any person educated in, or having made profession of, the " christian religion, shall, by writing, printing, teaching, or " advised speaking, deny the Christian religion to be true, or " the holy scriptures to be of divine authority, he shall for the " first offence, be rendered incapable to hold any office or " place of trust; and, for the second, be rendered incapable of

W 2

" bringing

" bringing any action, being guardian, executor, legatee, or
" purchaser of lands and shall suffer three years imprisonment
" without bail :" the same penalties, which have been already
mentioned, as by this very statute inflicted on Arianism.—And
you had just before observed, that " all affronts to Christianity,
" or endeavours to depreciate its efficacy, are highly deserving
" of human punishment*."

I have already shewn, that principles or sentiments relating
to religion are not punishable by penal laws. The infliction of
such punishment, even when they are professed, is out of the
magistrate's province; as, when they are concealed, it is out of
his power; for human laws have nothing to do with mere
principles, but only with those overt acts arising from them,
which are contrary to the peace and good order of society.

But

---

* Comment. vol. iv. p. 44. In the new edition this passage is thus altered :
" All affronts to Christianity, or endeavours to depreciate its efficacy, in those
" who have once professed it, are highly deserving of censure." If by *censure*
the author means *blame*, as I think he must when he opposes it to human punishment; this is a very material amendment; which affords ground to suppose, he would have given a different turn to the immediately subsequent words,
if he had considered them with due attention : " But yet," saith he, " the loss
" of life is a heavier penalty than the offence, taken in a civil light deserves."
An observation, which implies, I think, notwithstanding the preceding con-
cession, that human punishment may be inflicted, though it ought not to be capital. And therefore I apprehend, that upon further reflection the worthy Commentator will alter these words, for the same reason that he altered the former;
for I cannot suppose, so candid and respectable a writer, will retain any phrase-
ology which seems evidently to imply, that he will no longer venture to affirm.

If indeed any one should suggest, that the word *censure*, in the connection in
which it stands with the subsequent clause, is designed to convey the same idea
with the exploded phrase, *human punishment* only in a more covert, and therefore less offensive manner; I think it would be an uncandid and indecent reflection upon a gentleman, who doubtless is incapable of aiming to impose upon his readers by studied ambiguity of expression. And therefore, I repeat, that
I have no doubt this passage will, upon another review, be so modelled, as to be
liable to no possible misconstruction.

But it will be said, Hath the magiftrate no concern with thofe principles which " deftroy the foundation of moral obligation ?" that is, if I underftand you right, which have a tendency to introduce immorality and licentioufnefs.

I allow, he may encourage amongft all fects, thofe general principles of religion and morality, on which the happinefs of fociety depends. This he may, and fhould do, as *confervator* of the public weal. But with regard to the belief or difbelief of religious principles, or religious fyftems ; if he prefumes to exercife his *authority* as a *judge*, in fuch cafes, with a view of reftraining and punifhing thofe who embrace and profefs what he diflikes, or diflike and explode what he embraces, on account of the fuppofed ill tendency of their principles ; he goes beyond his province, which is confined to thofe effects of fuch principles, that is, to thofe actions, which affect the peace and good order of fociety ; and every ftep he takes, he is in danger of trampling on the rights of confcience, and of invading the prerogative of the only arbiter of confcience, to whom. alone men are accountable for profeffing or not profeffing, religious fentiments and principles.

For, if the magiftrate be poffeffed of a power to reftrain and punifh any principles relating to religion becaufe of their tendency, and he be the judge of that tendency ; as he muft be, if he be vefted with authority to punifh on that account ; religious liberty is entirely at an end ; or, which is the fame thing, is under the controul, and at the mercy of the magiftrate, according as he fhall think the tenets in queftion affect the foundation of moral obligation, or are favourable or unfavourable to religion and morality. But if the line be drawn between mere religious principle and the tendency of it, on the one hand ; and thofe overt acts which affect the public peace and order, on the other ; and if the latter alone be affigned to the jurifdiction of the magiftrate, as being guardian of the peace of fociety in this world, and the former, as interfering only with a future world, be referred

ferred to a man's own confcience, and to God, the only fovereign Lord of confcience; the boundaries between civil power and liberty, in religious matters, are clearly marked and determined; and the latter will not be wider or narrower, or juft nothing at all according to the magiftrates opinion of the good or bad tendency of principles.

I F it be objected, that when the tendency of principles is unfavourable to the peace and good order of fociety, as it may be, it is the magiftrates duty then, and for that reafon, to reftrain them by penal laws: I reply, that the tendency of principles, though it be *unfavourable*, is not *prejudicial* to fociety, till it iffues in fome *overt acts* againft the public peace and order; and when it does, *then* the magiftrate's authority to punifh commences; that is, he may punifh the *overt acts*, but not the *tendency*, which is not actually hurtful; and, therefore, his penal laws fhould be directed againft *overt acts only*, which are detrimental to the peace and good order of fociety, let them fpring from what principles they will; and not againft *principles*, or the *tendency* of principles.

T H E diftinction between the tendency of principles, and the overt acts arifing from them is, and cannot but be, obferved in many cafes of a *civil* nature; in order to determine the bounds of the magiftrate's power, or at leaft to limit the exercife of it, in fuch cafes. It would not be difficult to mention cuftoms and manners, as well as principles, which have a tendency unfavourable to fociety; and which, neverthelefs, cannot be reftrained by penal laws, except with the total deftruction of civil liberty. And here, the magiftrate muft be contented with pointing his penal laws againft the evil overt acts refulting from them. In the fame manner he fhould act in regard to men's profeffing, or rejecting, religious principles or fyftems. Punifhing a man for the *tendency* of his principles, is punifhing him *before* he is guilty, for fear he *fhould be* guilty.

B E S I D E S, if the magiftrate in one country hath a right to punifh

nifh thofe who reject the religion which is there publicly profeffed, the magiftrates of all other countries muft have the fame
right ; and for the fame reafon, namely, to guard againft the
evil tendency of renouncing a religion, the maintenance of
which they think of great importance to fociety.   If thofe perfons who reject Chriftianity are to be punifhed in England, thofe
who embrace it are to be punifhed in Turkey. This is the neceffary confequence of allowing any penal laws to be enacted, and
to operate, in fupport or fuppreffion of any religious fyftem ; for
the magiftrate muft and will ufe his power according to his own
religious perfuafion.

I F it be faid, that punifhment is not to be inflicted on the mere
entertaining, but only on the zealous propagating, of the principles of infidelity ; it fhould be confidered, that the propagation of Chriftianity would, on this maxim, be obftructed, and
even precluded, where a different religion already prevails, by
making it the duty of the magiftrate to oppofe it, and punifh
thofe who attempt it.

B u t having afferted, that " all affronts to Chriftianity or en-
" deavours to depreciate its efficacy, are highly deferving of hu-
" man punifhment," or punifhment from the magiftrate, you
endeavour to prove your pofition by the following obfervation:
That " the belief of a future ftate of rewards and punifhments,
" the entertaining juft ideas of the moral attributes of the Su-
" preme Being, and a firm perfuafion that he fuperintends, and
" will finally compenfate, every action in human life, (all which
" are clearly revealed in the doctrines, and forcibly inculcated,
" by the precepts of our Saviour Chrift) thefe are the grand
" foundation of all judicial oaths, which call God to witnefs the
" truth of thofe facts which perhaps may be only known to
" him and the party attefting.   All moral evidence, therefore,
" all confidence in human veracity," you fay, " muft be weak-
" ened by irreligion, and overthrown by infidelity*."

I F

* Comment. vol. iv. p 43, 44. In the late edition it is thus altered ; " weak-
ened

IF by infidelity you mean difbelief of Chriftianity, then it will be a fair inference from this laft affertion, that there can be no human faith, no mutual confidence, no bond of fociety, and no civil government, in countries which are not Chriftian. But the fact is otherwife; and the reafon is, becaufe there are fome principles of religion and morality prevailing even in Mohammedan and heathen countries ; and thofe right principles, tho' greatly fhort of a religious fyftem, and blended with many erroneous, abfurd, fuperftitious principles ; yet, have fufficient influence in general on the minds of thofe who embrace them, to anfwer, tolerably at leaft, the purpofes of civil government, and of mutual confidence and commerce.

I ADMIT, that, provided every one who revolts from Chriftianity to Deifm renounced, together with his former profeffion, all thofe principles of natural religion on which the obligation of judicial oaths is founded, (and poffibly you underftand infidelity in this extenfive fenfe, when you fpeak of its " overthrow " ing all human confidence"): if, I fay, he were known to have renounced thefe principles, your argument would be *fo far* good, that his oath would deferve no credit, and he would be fubjected to innumerable inconveniences and incapacities, which his being deftitute of the firm confidence of other men, and being difcredited in his judicial oaths, would naturally and neceffarily bring upon him : and indeed, fuch an abfolute infidel as to all religion, natural as well as revealed, if proved to be fo, fhould not be admitted to take an oath in a court of judicature. But as for inflicting any *pofitive punifhment* upon him, merely for rejecting right *principles*, or efpoufing wrong ones, while this does not iffue in thofe *actions* which call for punifhment; *that*, I think, for the reafons already affigned, is beyond the province and jurifdiction of the magiftrate.

IN

" ened by apoftacy, and overthrown by total infidelity :" an alteration which fuperfedes the remark in the next paragraph, but leaves all that follows in its full force.

In what I have juſt now ſaid, I have ſuppoſed theſe unbelievers of Chriſtianity to reject the great principles of natural as
well as revealed religion; which, you rightly tell us, are the grand
foundation of all judicial oaths. But the truth is, many who profeſs not to believe revelation, may poſſibly believe thoſe principles as firmly as ſome nominal Chriſtians, whoſe depoſitions on
oath are not ſcrupled in courts of judicature. The belief of a
God, the moral governor of the world, the ſearcher of hearts,
the infallible judge, rewarder and puniſher of human actions, is,
as you obſerve, the only foundation of a judicial oath; and if
men *do believe* theſe articles, they ſhould not be made liable to
that puniſhment, which, on your own ſtate of the caſe, is due
only to thoſe who *do not* believe them; they ſhould not be puniſhed, I ſay, when they *do* believe them, merely becauſe they
believe them upon reaſons independent of their " being clearly
" revealed in the doctrines of Chriſt;" for their believing them
is all that your argument requires.

Indeed, we have a ceremony in adminiſtring a judicial oath,
which ſuppoſes a belief of the Chriſtian religion. But that is
by no means a neceſſary, eſſential part of a ſolemn judicial appeal to heaven; and can afford, therefore, no plea for puniſhing
thoſe who do not believe Chriſtianity, as incapable of a judicial oath, (ſuppoſing that a proper reaſon for puniſhment;) becauſe
it is obvious, the end may be anſwered by an appeal to God
in ſome other ſolemn form, without this ceremony; and our
laws have ſet an example of it in the caſe of the Quakers*.

X   I f

* I am obliged to my learned friend Mr. Dodſon for the following accurate
remark. The caſe of the Quakers, ſaith he, doth not, I think, reach the
point: for in the form of affirmation now uſed by them, there is no direct appeal to God, as there is in that preſcribed by 7 & 8 W. III. c. 34. which was
altered by 8 Geo. I. c. 6. And in criminal caſes they are not admitted as witneſſes, unleſs they will be ſworn. The caſe of the Jews is much more applicable.
They have been long admitted as witneſſes; and are ſworn upon the Penta-
teuch;

I f it be enquired, whether men fhall be fuffered with impunity to " *affront* Chriftianity and depreciate its efficacy," by reproaches and calumnies, offenfive to every Chriftian; a different cafe from fimply difbelieving, or modeftly oppofing it : I anfwer, that, provided it be unwarrantable to fupport the belief
of Chriftianity, and to confute its oppofers, by penal laws and
the fword of the magiftrate; its profeffors fhould be exceeding
tender how they animadvert, in this way, on the *manner* in which
the oppofition to it is made: a thing, comparatively of little confequence. For, though calumny and flander, when affecting
our fellow-men, are punifhable by law; for this plain reafon,
becaufe an injury is done, and a damage fuftained, and a reparation therefore due to the injured party; yet, this reafon cannot hold where God and the Redeemer are concerned; who can
fuftain no injury from low malice and fcurrilous invective; nor
can any reparation be made to them by temporal penalties; for
thefe can work no conviction or repentance in the mind of the
offender; and if he continue impenitent and incorrigible, he will
receive his condign punifhment in the day of final retribution.
Affronting Chriftianity, therefore, does not come under the magiftrate's

---

teuch; which method of fwearing them is recognized by 10 Geo. I. c. 4. f. 18.
and 13 Geo. II. c. 7. f. 3. And it is very obfervable, that the teftimony of
perfons of the Gentou religion, upon oath, taken in the manner ufed in their
country, was admitted in the court of Chancery by Lord Hardwicke in the
cafe of Omichund and Barker, Feb. 23, 1744; in which cafe he was affifted by
Lee and Willes, Chief Juftices, and Parker, Chief Baron, and the matter was
determined upon very great deliberation. See a large account of the arguments of the Lord Chancellor and Judges, in 2 Equ. Caf. abr. 397———412.
In the third book of his invaluable Commentaries, chap. 27. Mr. Juftice Blackftone cites this cafe from 1 Atkins 21. and ftates it thus : it hath been held that
the depofition of an heathen, *who believes in the Supreme Being,* taken by commiffion in the moft folemn manner, according to the cuftom of his own country,
may be read in evidence. See Lord Chief Juftice Hale's opinion as to the ad-
miffibility of witneffes not being Chriftians, in 2 Hift. Pl. Cor. 279, which was
cited and greatly relied on in the cafe of Omichund and Barker.

giſtrate's cognizance, in this particular view, as it implies an offence againſt God and Chriſt*.

* It hath been obſerved, that upon the ſame principles which are laid down in this paragraph, no profane ſwearing, blaſphemy, or breach of the Sabbath, however flagrant, ought to come under the cognizance of the magiſtrate. But this objection is grounded, I apprehend, upon a miſtake; namely, that the reaſoning in this paſſage is intended as an abſolute proof, that affronting Chriſtianity is not to be puniſhed; whereas it is ſolely deſigned to ſhew, that it is not puniſhable in *this particular view*, as an offence againſt God. Whether it be puniſhable in any other, is a point afterwards conſidered. Now it is an obſervation, and a very juſt one, of biſhop Warburton (Alliance, book I. ch. 4. p. 33, 34. edit. 4.) that the magiſtrate puniſhes no bad actions, as ſins or offences againſt God, but only as crimes injurious to, or having a malignant influence on ſociety. Accordingly the crimes mentioned in the objection do not, any more than affronting Chriſtianity, come under the magiſtrate's cognizance in this particular view: from whence, however, it by no means follows, that they may not come under his cognizance in ſome others. And I really think, it can be no invaſion of any man's right of private judgment, and of the moſt unlimited privilege of propagating his ſentiments concerning religion, in the manner in which he thinks moſt conducive to that end, if, from a regard to decency and the good order of ſociety, the magiſtrate do prohibit and puniſh profane ſwearing, blaſphemy, and breach of the ſabbath. For it is certain, that, by theſe practices, no one pretends to prove any ſuppoſed truths, or detect any ſuppoſed errors, or advance any ſentiments whatſoever: whereas, on the contrary, in oppoſing Chriſtianity, an infidel who thinks he is detecting an impoſture, may conceive it conducive to the ſtrength of his argument, and to the conviction of others, to ſet it in ſuch a light as Chriſtians will apprehend to be ſcurrilous and indecent; and in ſuch caſes it will be exceeding difficult to ſeparate the manner of oppoſition from the oppoſition itſelf, and for the magiſtrate to puniſh the former while he permits the latter. But there is no ſuch difficulty in the caſes here mentioned, common ſwearing, blaſphemy, and breach of the ſabbath. In reſpect to which I muſt however ſuggeſt this caution, that they ought to be very clearly and diſtinctly defined; and in particular, blaſphemy; ſince the idea of that, if it be extended further than to ſomething like common ſwearing, may poſſibly be extended ſo far, that laws for the puniſhment of it may be eaſily turned to the deſtruction of all religious liberty: for what is blaſphemy, in the general ſenſe of the term, but uttering ſomething diſhonourable or injurious to the Divine Being? And what controverted religious ſentiment is there, which under this general notion, by a court and jury of bigots, may not be condemned as blaſphemy? The Athanaſian ſtiles the Arian a blaſphemer,

I f you fay, that infulting and reviling religion is very offenfive to good men, and ought, on that account, to be prohibited
and punifhed: I obferve, fo are all tranfgreffions of the divine
law, very offenfive to good men; but they are not, for that reafon, all punifhable by the magiftrate. In the cafe of grofs lying,
heinous ingratitude, and many other vices which might be mentioned, though no one thinks of applying to a court of juftice on
the occafion, yet every good man will treat thefe vices, and
thofe who are guilty of them, with juft abhorrence and deteſta-
tion. And the fame, and no other, I apprehend, fhould be their
conduct, when infidels, with an offenfive indecency, vent their
impotent rancour againft the religion of Jefus.

I f you alledge, that this licentious manner of treating religion, will " depreciate its efficacy" on the minds of men, efpecially of the undifcerning and thoughtlefs, which are commonly
the major part: I anfwer, that the contempt and abufe which
infidels throw upon religion, will, in the end, entail difgrace
and infamy on themfelves. Their ribaldry and fcurrility will be
defpicable and difguftful to the more fenfible part of our fpecies;
and while there are Chriftians, efpecially Chriftian minifters, in
the world, I truft, there will always be proper perfons, who will
expofe to the moft ignorant and unreflecting, the grofs folly and
injuftice of fuch abufe; and render thofe who are guilty of it
the

mer, the Arian the Athanafian, the Calvinift the Arminian, the Arminian the
Calvinift; and thus the fame laws, differently applied as different parties prevail, will prove fatal to the religious liberty of all of them in their turn.—And
with refpect to breach of the fabbath, the penal laws againft it fhould be rather
of the negative than of the pofitive kind, and fhould only lay reftraints on civil
liberty in cafes which may be offenfive or injurious to fociety; for inftance, they
may extend to the prohibition of public diverfions, of the profecution of trade
and bufinefs, and the like. Upon thefe principles, and with thefe reftrictions,
the magiftrate, I think, may make regulations in the cafes here mentioned, with
a view to the good order of fociety, without entertaining the leaft idea of punifhing offences againft God, and without invading religious liberty, and the
moft unlimited rights of confcience.

the objects of contempt to the lowest of the people : whereas, if punished by the magiftrate, they would be the objects, probably, of their pity : a circumftance which would procure their infinuations and fuggeftions to the prejudice of religion, a much more favourable reception, than they would otherwife be like to obtain.

INDEED, difcovering a difpofition to take refuge in temporal penalties, whenever any perfons in difcourfe or writings mifreprefent and revile (or, as you ftile it, *affront*) our holy religion, and depreciate it efficacy, is acting as if we apprehended the caufe had no other and better fupport. Whereas, for three hundred years after its firft promulgation, Chriftianity maintained its full reputation and influence, though attacked in every way which wit or malice could invent) not only without the affiftance of, but in direct oppofition to the civil power. It fhone with the brighter luftre, for the attempts to eclipfe it. And the infults and calumnies of its enemies were as ineffectual to its prejudice, as either their objections, or what were more to be feared, their perfecutions. And as it was during that period, fo will it always be, if there be any ground to rely on that promife of our bleffed Saviour concerning his church, that " the gates of hell " fhall not prevail againft it*."

IN the mean time, compaffion to all ignorant, petulant, malicious adverfaries of our holy religion ; and a defire to obviate the mifchief they do, by refuting their arguments, expofing their petulance and malice, and if poffible, working conviction in their minds ; are the difpofitions which fuch contemptible attacks on the honour of the chriftian religion, and its author, fhould excite in his genuine difciples. We fhould argue with fuch men, not perfecute them ; fhould endeavour to refcue others from the danger of being infected by their principles, with cool reafoning ; but we fhould be careful how we attempt to punifh them, left we *harden* inftead of reclaiming them : left we
leave

Matth. xvi. 18.

leave room for others to imagine, that not their scoffs and insults, but their *arguments*, have *provoked us* by being unanswerable. And indeed, provided it be wrong to animadvert, by temporal penalties, on the calm reasoning of infidels against Christianity; it would, surely, be *imprudent* to punish them for what renders their arguments, if there be any, less formidable and prejudicial; I mean, their revilings and scurrillity. It is *imprudent* I say, by a prosecution, to hold up to public notice, to introduce into all conversation, and excite people's curiosity after, those scurrilous writings, which would otherwise quickly sink with their authors into perpetual oblivion. Many infidels, in modern times, have united their efforts against the Christian religion; and they have railed, at least some of them, much more than they have reasoned; but they have been heard, and confuted; and most of them are only remembered by the excellent apologies for Christianity, which they have been the occasions of producing. I hardly think they and their works would have been so soon forgotten; I am sure, our religion would not have received such honour, nor infidelity such disgrace, and such a total defeat; if instead of being answered by the learned writers, who have employed their abilities to so laudable a purpose, they had been prosecuted, fined, imprisoned, or suffered any other ignominious or cruel punishment, by the sentence of the magistrate. Those who call for the aid of the civil power, and for the infliction of pains and penalties, in support of the Christian religion, forget the character and conduct of its divine author; who when his apostles, out of zeal for his honour, would have invoked fire from heaven on the unbelieving Samaritans, because they had just *affronted* him, severely rebuked them: " Ye know " not what manner of spirit ye are of; the Son of man came not " to destroy men's lives, but to save them*.

In what I have said, let it not be supposed, that I have pleaded the cause of infidelity; No; I have pleaded that of Christianity, in
my

---

* Luke ix. 55, 56.

my own opinion at leaſt; the mild and forbearing ſpirit of which religion, I deſire more and more to imbibe, to regard all its doctrines and precepts as the rule of my faith and manners, its promiſes as the foundation of my hopes, and the ſcheme of redemption through Jeſus Chriſt as my higheſt conſolation and joy. It is indeed, from my reverence for it, and attachment to it, and zeal for its true dignity and honour, that I will ever vindicate it from the *leaſt ſuſpicion* of being a perſecuting religion†: A ſuſpicion, which, if it were juſt, would be a greater brand of ignominy, and do it more real diſcredit, than all the invidious miſrepreſentations and calumnies of its adverſaries. And this it becomes thoſe ſeriouſly to conſider, who would wipe away the diſhonour done it, by methods that would double the diſgrace, not only on themſelves, but on the noble cauſe which they profeſs to eſpouſe.—I am, Sir, *&c.*

† Several writers of the firſt rank amongſt thoſe who have appeared in defence of Chriſtianity, have declared openly, and argued ſtrongly, againſt the perſecution of infidels : particularly Dr. Lardner, in his preface to his excellent " Vindication of three miracles of our Saviour againſt Wolſton;" and in two " Letters to the Biſhop of Chicheſter," publiſhed in the late " Memoirs of his " life:" Dr. Chandler, in his preface to the " Conduct of the modern Deiſts:" and Mr. Simon Brown, in his preface to a very ſhrewd and ſenſible pamphlet againſt Wolſton, which he ſtiles " A fit rebuke to a ludicrous infidel," The performances of theſe writers ſhew, that they perfectly *underſtood* the ſtrength of their cauſe; and their averſion to the interpoſition of the civil power, that they altogether *relied* upon it, having no apprehenſions of the conſequences of a free debate, managed in any way the patrons of infidelity ſhould think proper. Indeed, no one ever made the attack in a more rude and ſcurrilous manner than Wolſton : they, however, contented themſelves with confuting his arguments and expoſing his ſcurrillity, entering their proteſt, with convincing reaſons, againſt the proſecution of him. And this conduct I cannot help thinking very much to the honour of the Chriſtian religion and its advocates.

L E T T E R

L E T T E R IV.

SIR,

WHEN you mention the ſtatute 1 Eliz. c. 2. which enacts,
that " if any perſon whatſoever ſhall, in plays, ſongs,
" or other open words, ſpeak any thing in derogation, deprav-
" ing, or deſpiſing of the common prayer, he ſhall forfeit for
" the firſt offence an hundred marks, for the ſecond offence
" four hundred, and for the third offence ſhall forfeit all his
" goods and chattels, and ſuffer impriſonment for life* :" I ſay,
when you ſpeak of this ſtatute, you not only approve of it in the
peculiar circumſtances of the time when it was firſt enacted, but
you ſay, that " the continuance of it to this time cannot be
" thought too ſevere or intolerant†." And the reaſon you aſſign
is,

---

* The expreſs words of this ſtatute called the act of Uniformity, are, That if
any perſon or perſons whatſoever——ſhall in any interludes, plays, ſongs, rhymes,
or by other *open words declare* or *ſpeak* any thing in the derogation, depraving or
deſpiſing of the ſame book (the common prayer) or of *any thing therein contained*,
or *any part thereof*——every ſuch perſon ſhall forfeit for the firſt offence an hundred marks, &c. as above.

The clauſes preceding that laſt mentioned enact, That if any parſon, vicar, or
other miniſter——ſhall preach, declare, or ſpeak, any thing in the derogation
or depraving of the ſaid book, or any thing therein contained, or any part
thereof, he ſhall for the firſt offence forfeit the next year's profit of all his bene-
fices, and ſuffer impriſonment for ſix months; for the ſecond offence ſhall ſuffer a year's impriſonment, and be deprived ipſo facto of all his ſpiritual promo-
tions; and for the third offence ſhall be in like manner deprived, and impriſoned
during life. If the perſon offending, have no benefice, nor any ſpiritual pro-
motion, he ſhall for the firſt offence ſuffer one year's impriſonment, and for the
ſecond offence impriſonment for life.

† Comment. vol. iv. p. 50, 51. In the new edition the author expreſſes himſelf thus: " The continuance of it to the preſent time, in terrorem at leaſt,
" cannot be thought too ſevere or intollerant". He alſo aſſigns ſome other
reaſons for his opinion, than thoſe which are mentioned above; and they are
all conſidered in a poſtſcript to this letter.

is, that " no one in prefent circumſtances can do this," that is,
" revile" the liturgy (the crime to which alone you ſuppoſe the
act to refer) " from any laudable motive, not even from a miſ-
" taken zeal for reformation ; it being, ſince the union, ex-
" tremely unadviſable to make any alterations in the ſervice of
" the church*.

N o w, ſuppoſing that a man cannot have any " laudable mo-
" tive for reviling and inveighing with bitterneſs againſt the
" common prayer," (for againſt this only, I ſay, you underſtand
the act to be levelled): ſuppoſing it to be a thing very culpable;
yet, what is the ſpecific nature of the crime, and wherein doth
the malignity of it conſiſt ? " It is a crime," you ſay, " of a groſ-
" ſer nature than mere nonconformity : becauſe it carries with
" it the utmoſt indecency, arrogance, and ingratitude : inde-
" cency, by ſetting up private judgment in oppoſition to pub-
" lic ; arrogance, by treating with contempt and rudeneſs what
" hath at leaſt a better chance to be right, than the ſingular no-
" tions of any particular man ; and ingratitude, by denying that
" indulgence and liberty of conſcience to the members of the na-
" tional church which the retainers to every petty conventicle †
" enjoy‡."

T h i s crime of reviling the liturgy, I perceive is a very com-
plicated one ; " it carries with it," you ſay, " the utmoſt indecency, arrogance, and ingratitude". For each of which you aſſign
a particular reaſon ; and I ſhall examine them all in their order.

Y   T h a t

---

* This argument againſt alterations, taken from the union, will be conſidered particularly in a ſubſequent letter.

† Dr. Prieſtley hath remarked a want of elegance and politeneſs in this expreſſion, unworthy of a fine writer, (Remarks p. 31.) I would obſerve an
impropriety in it, unbecoming the great lawyer. The word conventicle, if I
underſtand it right, means an unlawful aſſembly ; and is therefore improperly
applied, as it is here, to the legal aſſembly of Proteſtant Diſſenters.

‡ Comment. vol. iv. p. 50.

THAT reviling any thing, that treating with rudeneſs and contempt any man, much more a conſiderable body of men, or, the public at large, or thoſe religious forms which are uſed under the ſanction of the civil magiſtrate, and by many revered; is *indecent*, will be readily allowed. The rules of civility and good manners ought always to be obſerved; eſpecially where the public, and perſons in authority, are concerned. Never to violate them, if poſſible, is in itſelf right; and is alſo good policy; for any cauſe, inſtead of being diſſerved, will be recommended and promoted, by being defended with civility and ood temper.

BUT I cannot help ſuſpecting, Sir, that your view reaches further than this; if this be all you mean, I do not conceive why the indecency of reviling the liturgy is, particularly, ſaid to ariſe from " ſetting up private judgment in oppoſition to publick*:" I ſay, your putting the indecency of it on this footing, appears to me to be accounted for only by ſuppoſing, that you think it wrong to oppoſe private to public judgment, in any caſe; and then nonconformity and reviling the liturgy are both indecent; for the ſame reaſon, becauſe they are an oppoſition of the private to the public judgment; only one is more ſo than the other, and conſequently more indecent. And I the rather apprehend I am herein not very wide of your ſentiment, becauſe
　　　　　　　　　　　　　　　　　　　　　　　　　　you

---

* In the laſt edition the author ſtiles it " ſetting up private judgment in *vi-* " *rulent and factious* oppoſition to public *authority*." As far as reviling the liturgy implies an oppoſition which is " *virulent and factious*," I own it cannot be juſtified. But as far as it is a mere " ſetting up private judgment in oppoſiti- " on to public authority," it may; for whether it be ſtiled " public authori- " ty" or " public judgment," I think it comes to much the ſame. I ſuppoſe, the learned author would have this authority always united with, and under the influence of *judgment*: whether it be ſo or not, is another queſtion. If he is of opinion, that *mere* authority ought to be ſubmitted to in matters of religion, I beg leave to enter my diſſent from ſuch a poſition, for reaſons aſſigned in my ſecond letter, and to believe that every man is bound in ſuch caſes, to judge and act for himſelf, without regard to any human authority whatſoever.

you confider nonconformity as a crime, though not fo great as that of reviling the liturgy ; and you fo confider it, I imagine, on this particular account, as it is private judgment oppofed to the public.

A N D indeed, if it be a general maxim, that it is *indecent* to " fet up private judgment in oppofition to public ;" then it is certainly fo, to diffent from public or eftablifhed opinions and practices: then all thofe who have been the authors of any reformations or improvements, in religion, in philofophy*, in poli-

Y 2

cy,

---

* The *public judgment* of the church of Rome hath condemned for herefy the doctrine of the motion of the earth according to the fyftem of Copernicus ; notwithftanding which it hath long paffed for orthodoxy in the *private judgment* of all philofophers. The famous Galielo, having taught this point, and confirmed it by new difcoveries, was imprifoned in the inquifition on that account, obliged to recant and curfe his former opinion, and fwear that he would not teach it any more ; but that if he fhould know of any fuch heretic, or any perfon fufpected of fuch herefy, he would immediately report him to the holy office. Galilei fyftem. Cofmic. edit. Lugd. Bat. 1699. p. 483—494. Such a fatal operation had this *public judgment* formerly, in a point of *philofophy*, capable of demonftration, and now univerfally received. And the influence of it, tho' it be privately rejected by every individual, appears in the public *profeffion* of philofophers even in modern times. Two learned Romifh priefts and able mathematicians, publifhing an edition of Sir Ifaac Newton's Principia, with an excellent Commentary, in which his principles are explained and more fully demonftrated (the *monitum* or advertifement to the third book of which is dated at Rome 1742), thought it neceffary, for their fafety I fuppofe, before they entered upon the heretical doctrine De fyftemate mundi, to make, in form, the following curious declaration ; than which, however it was defigned, there never furely was a greater burlefque upon fervile fubmiffion to public judgment.

PP. Le Seur & Jacquier declaratio.

Newtonus, in hoc tertio libro, telluris motæ hypothefim affumit. Autoris propofitiones aliter explicari non poterant, nifi eâdem quoque factâ hypothefi. Hinc alienam coacti fumus gerere perfonam. Cæterum latis à fummis Pontificibus contra telluris motum decretis nos obfequi profitemur.

The declaration of the fathers Le Sieur and Jacquier.

Newton, in this third book, affumes the hypothefis of the earth's motion. The Author's propofitions could not be explained, if we did not alfo go upon

the

cy, and in the manners and conduct of life, contrary to the public standard, have been guilty of indecency.

BESIDES, it is worth observation, that the public judgment, to which it is expected such deference should be paid, amounts to no more than the vote of those who happen to be invested with power, at the time such establishments are made; which is sometimes very different from the opinion or judgment of the public at *that time*, and frequently differs widely from the judgment of the public in a *subsequent period*. But the unhappiness is, that, when the thing established, be it what it will, hath received the sanction of public authority, neither numbers, nor the respectable characters of those who disapprove it, can easily procure a reform; and even when it is in a manner grown out of all credit, so as to be espoused by very few, it still passes under the denomination of " the public judgment," against which it is " indecency to oppose the private judgment of individuals†."

                                                          BUT

the same hypothesis. Upon this account we have been obliged to appear under a feigned character. We profess, however, to follow the decrees issued by the sovereign pontiffs against the motion of the earth.

† If the Athanasian Creed, with its damnatory clauses, were now a candidate for admission into the public formulary, it would doubtless be rejected by a very large majority, both of clergy and laity; and yet it remains one of those things which are authorised by the *public judgment*.

It may not be amiss to observe, that there is not only a reluctance to making alterations in material points, but sometimes even to the appearance of making any in matters of common form : of which I think the following is a remarkable instance.

The 36th article asserts, that " the book of consecration of archbishops and " bishops, and ordering of priests and deacons, lately set forth in the time of " Edward the VIth." (in the second year of his reign, as the article afterwards saith) " and confirmed at the same time by authority of parliament, doth con- " tain all things necessary to such consecration and ordering, neither hath it " any thing that of itself is superstitious and ungodly."

The act of uniformity of Charles the II. enacts, " That all subscriptions to " the articles shall be construed and taken (for and touching the six and thir-
                                                          " tieth

BUT since a man's private judgment *may happen* to be in the right, and the public one in the wrong; whenever this be found or generally agreed, to be the case, he must make but an auk-
ward

" tieth article) to extend unto the book of Charles the IId. in such fort and
" manner as the same did heretofore extend unto the book of Edward the
" VIth."

Now this clause of the act of parliament either means to substitute the book of
Charles the IId. in the room of that of Edward the VIth. in which case, those
who subscribe the articles, are absurdly required by the words Edward the
VIth. to understand Charles the IId : or it means to add the book of Charles
the IId. (though it is not mentioned in the article) to the book of Edward the
VIth. and the subscription must be understood virtually to extend to both, as it
doth expresly to the book of Edward the VIth. And this, I take to be the
true sense of the article, from considering the last clause of it ; namely, " Who-
" soever are consecrated and ordered according to the rites of that book, since
" the second year of the aforenamed king Edward unto this time, or hereafter
" shall be consecrated or ordered, according to the same rites, we decree all
" such to be rightly, orderly, and lawfully, consecrated and ordered." Now
it can hardly be supposed, that it was the intention of the act of uniformity to
set aside this approbation of the orders of the church from the reformation, and
to substitute in the room of it only an approbation of the said orders from the
time of Charles the IId. It was rather doubtless intended to declare an approbation of both, and that the article should be hereafter extended to the book
of Edward as well as the book of Charles, in like sort and manner as it had
heretofore been extended to (an odd phrase! for it expresly mentions) the book
of Edward only. And if this be the sense of the article, all who subscribe it
must be understood according to the act of uniformity, as well as the express
words of the article, to subscribe to a book which very few have seen, and
which, though the article asserts there is nothing in it superstitious or ungodly,
contains however an oath of supremacy, in which is the following clause, " I
" will observe, kepe, mainteigne, and defende, the whole effectes and con-
" tentes of all and syngular actes and statutes made and TO BE MADE within
" this realme in derogacion, extirpacion, and extinguishment of the bishop of
" Rome and his authoritie, and all other actes and statutes made or TO BE
" MADE in reformacion and corroboracion of the kynges power, of the su-
" preme hed in yearth, of the churche of Englande." &c.—" And in cace any
" othe BE MADE" (that is shall be made) " or hath been made by me, to any
" person or persons, in maintenaunce, defence, or favoure of the bishoppe of
" Rome,

ward figure who gravely reprimands thofe that fet up the former againſt the latter. I ſhould think it, therefore, much better to come to the queſtion at once : Is the thing in deliberation right

or

" Rome, or his authoritie, jurifdicion, or power, I repute the fame, as vain
" and adnichilate, fo helpe me God, ALL SAINCTES AND THE HOLY
" EV'ANGELIST." See the forme and maner of makyng and confecrat-
yng of archbiſhoppes, biſhoppes, prieſtes, and deacons, 1549, folio ; with the
printer's name at the end: Richardus Grafton, typographus regius excudebat
menſe Martii A. M. D. XLIX. cum privilegio ad imprimendum ſolum. A copy
of this edition, through the favour of my worthy friend, the Rev. Mr. Joſiah
Thompſon, jun. is at prefent in my poſſeſſion ; and is, by the date, of the fame
impreſſion with a copy of king Edward's ordinal mentioned by biſhop Burnet,
in the preface to his third volume of the Hiſtory of the Reformation, p. iv, v.
as in the Lambeth library.

But what I would principally remark, is, that it feems very ſtrange, if the
parliament by the clauſe in the act of uniformity relative to the 36th article, intended a ſubſtitution of the book of Charles the IId. inſtead of this book of Edward the VIth. that they had not altered the words of the article to that fenfe ;
or, if they meant, as I rather think, to include the book of Charles in the fub-
fcription, as well as the book of Edward, that they did not add a clauſe to the
article, expreſsly mentioning the book of Charles the IId. This, I think, can
only be accounted for by ſuppoſing, that rather than appear to make an alteration in the article, they would ſubſtitute one book for the other, or rather add
one to the other, not by inferting a clauſe for that purpoſe in the article, but
by an arbitrary conſtruction, altering the fenfe of the article, while they retained the words.

If it be faid, that the parliament would not alter the words of an article
which had paſſed the convocation of Elizabeth, without the previous ſanction
of that body ; it amounts to a charge of the moſt abſurd fcrupuloſity in the
whole world, that they would venture to alter the fenfe of convocation, but not
the expreſſions. But this can hardly be the true reafon, the authority of parliament having been always regarded fince the reformation as ſufficient to make
laws in eccleſiaſtical matters, without the convocation ; whereas the convocation can make no laws at all, nor hath any authority without the parliament.

It is obſervable, that biſhop Hooper, who is often mentioned as refuſing to
be confecrated on account of the popiſh veſtments, objected likewife to taking
the oath of ſupremacy abovementioned, required by the book of Edward, on
account of the clauſe which concludes, So helpe me God, all fainctes, &c.
which he thought ſuperſtitious and impious ; and he argued the point before

the

or wrong? for the opinion, neither of men in power, nor of the majority, is the teſt of truth, or the rule of our faith or practice.

So that the particular reaſon on which you ground the " in-" decency of reviling the liturgy," namely, that it is " ſetting " up private judgment in oppoſition to public;" appears to me to be very inadequate and unſatisfactory.

The next article in the compoſition of this crime, namely, reviling the common prayer ; is, you ſay, " arrogance." It is " arrogant to treat with rudeneſs and contempt what hath a bet-" ter chance to be right, than the ſingular notions of any par-" ticular man."

In uſing the phraſe, " the ſingular notions of a particular " man," you put the caſe very favourably for drawing your own concluſion. To be ſure, if a man adopts ſentiments which never entered into any body's head but his own, or which no one will embrace when propoſed, the odds are againſt him. But

---

the king and council ſo much to the ſatisfaction of that pious and ſenſible young prince, that he ſtruck out the words with his own hand. Burnet's Hiſt. of Reform. vol. iii p. 202, 203. 751. Accordingly we find, that in the next edition of the ordinal, which came out by authority of parliament in the year 1552, the oath concludes thus; So helpe me God through Jeſus Chriſt. Being excuſed from ſwearing in the ſuperſtitious form to which he objected. Hooper was confecrated, the matter relating to the veſtments being compromiſed. Fox's Acts and Monuments, vol. ii. p. 120. edit. 1684 and eſpecially the Latin edition, or the quotation from it in Pierce's vindication of the Diſſenters, p. 30.

It ſhould be obſerved, that biſhop Burnet hath committed a miſtake, in printing among his records the oath of ſupremacy made by the biſhops when they did homage to Henry the VIIIth. as the oath tendered to Hooper at his confecration; that oath was different from the oath of ſupremacy required to be taken by biſhops at confecration, in king Edward's ordinal : in particular, it had not the clauſe in which they ſwear to acts that *ſhall be made* and that they hold to be void, certain oaths they *may hereafter take* ; though they both conclude with nearly the ſame form of adjuration, So helpe me God, all ſainctes, and the holy evangels.

But this is not often the case; and is not so, in particular, with regard to the debate between the church and the Diffenters; the point here in question. However, he who treats the notions of others with a rude contempt, does, I think, in most cases, appear to affect a sort of superiority, (call it arrogance, or insolence, if you please) which usually ill becomes him who assumes it, and is never very agreeable to those who are the objects of it.

But with relation to the query, Who have the fairest chance of being in the right? those who follow the lead of a public establishment? or those who are, or profess to be, impartial enquirers after truth? that, I think, is not so clear, at least on one side of the question, as you seem to imagine. Most establishments, even those which have been settled by authority of the civil power, have originated from the clergy; at least with respect to their formularies of doctrine and worship; and the magistrate hath had little more to do in the affair, than to establish what hath been already prepared to his hands. Let us, then, look into ecclesiastical history, and see what the councils, synods, convocations, and other general, national, or provincial assemblies of the clergy, have, for the most part, been, from the first famous and revered council of Nice, down to the last session of our own convocation in England. When I reflect on the policy and artifice used in the management of such assemblies; on their obfequioufnefs to the caprices of princes, and ministers of state, or of potent ecclesiastics, and even of some of their own ambitious and turbulent members; on their prejudices and passions, their private and party views, their scandalous animosities and contentions; on the small majorities by which questions of importance, intended to bind not only the men of that age but their posterity, have been determined†; on the respectable

---

† The cross in baptism, and kneeling at the communion, (which are imposed in the church of England as neceffary to the administration of these ordinances) as well as the observation of saints days, and a few other ceremonies, were carried in the convocation of Elizabeth 1562 by a single proxy. The majority

able characters which have often appeared in the minor number†; and above all, on their self-contradictions, and their mutual censures and anathemas‡: I say, when I consider these things, I own,

Z

jority of those present, *against* them, was 43 against 35; but upon adding the proxies, the majority, *for* them, was 59 against 58. Thus they obtained the honour of the *public judgment* by this *better chance of being in the right*; and the contrary opinion was degraded into *private judgment*, though hardly so as to become the *singular notion of a particular man* Strype's Annals, vol. i. p. 337—359. edit. 3. Burnet's History of the Reformation, vol. iii. No. 74 among the Records, p 662——664. edit. 1753.

† King William, in the first year of his reign, granted a commission to prepare alterations of the liturgy and canons, and proposals for the reformation of the ecclesiastical courts. In this commission, besides several others, there were such men as Tillotson, Stillingfleet, Burnet, Patrick, Tennison, Lloyd, Sharp, Kidder, Scot, Fowler. And they accordingly made very considerable alterations and improvements in the liturgy; which are highly commended by Dr. Nichols, in his *Defensio Ecclesiae Anglicanae*, p. 94——97. and which Mr. Neal, in his *History of the Puritans*, saith, would, if they had been adopted, have brought in three parts in four of the dissenters; vol. ii p. 804. edit. 4to. And this author was a good judge, since no one better understood their principles and dispositions. However, the convocation, when the matter was laid before them by a message from the crown, resolved to enter into no debates about alterations, would return no answer to that part of the king's message, and could hardly be brought to thank him for his promise of protection. Burnet's History of his own times, under the year 1689. In what a contemptible light does that majority in convocation appear, who would not so much as *hear* what was prepared for their consideration by *such celebrated divines*, the glory of the English church, acting under a royal commission! and who would not esteem it an honour to be found in such a minority! and yet their sentiments, outvoted by furious bigots, are now only *private judgment!*

‡ A few remarks upon the four first general councils, will be a sufficient illustration of what is here said. The council of Nice, held in the year of our Lord 325, consisted, we are told, of more than 300 bishops, " brought toge-" ther, some by the hope of gain, and others to see such a miracle of an em-" peror as Constantine;" who accordingly well rewarded them " by his pre-" sents as well as his entertainments." Euseb. in vit. Const. l. 3. c. 6. & 16. Sozom. l. 1. c. 25 p. 42. Theodorit. l. 1. c 11. p. 36. Sabinus saith, that " they " were weak and illiterate men." (vid. Socrat. l. 1. c. 8. p. 21. & c. 9. p. 31;) which might be true with regard to many of them. However, it is certain, all history

own they fomewhat abate my reverence for the determinations of fuch bodies, and for the eftablifhments founded by them, or

by

hiftory agreeing in it, that they were in general (polloi pleiones are the words of Socrates and Sozomen) very litigious and contentious; infomuch that the Emperor was obliged to interpofe, to take them off from their private quarrels, and from their daily cuftom of prefenting to him accufations againft one another, before he could get them to attend to the bufinefs for which they were called together, (Eufeb. de vit. Conftant. l. 3. c. 13. Socrat. l. 1. c. 8. p. 20. Sozom. l. 1. c. 17. p. 35. Theodorit. l. 1. c. 11. p. 37. Gelafius Cyzic. l. 2. c. 8); and when they did engage in it, their conduct was agreeable to their character; for the party accufed having laid before them a written confeffion of their faith, they immediately tore it in pieces; and a great tumult arifing, and thofe who prefented the paper, being cried out upon as betrayers of the faith, were fo terrified, that they all arofe, except two, and were the firft in condemning the fentiments and party they before efpoufed. Theodorit. l. 1. c. 7. p. 27. With fuch violence were matters carried in the council! And the unintelligible terms which they introduced into their creeds and definitions of faith, and impofed by dirt of authority upon others, only ferved to increafe and perpetuate the controverfies then fubfifting, and fill the world with mutual rage, and mutual perfecutions. " The confequence of which was, " that the Chriftian religion, which, for 300 years after the afcenfion of Jefus, " had been fpreading over a large part of Afia, Europe, and Africa, without " the affiftance of fecular power and church-authority, and at the convening " of the council of Nice, was almoft every where through thofe countries in a " flourifhing condition, in the fpace of another 300 years, or a little more, was " greatly corrupted in a large part of that extent, its glory debafed, and its " light almoft extinguifhed". Dr. Lardner's Credibil. vol. viii. p. 24. This council, we are informed by Socrates, l. 1. c. 11. p. 38, 39. by Sozomen, l. 1. c. 23. p. 41. and by Nicephorus Calliftus, l. 8. c. 19. tom. 1. p. 571. was on the point of decreeing the celibacy of the clergy, if they had not been diverted from it by a fpirited oration of Paphnutius, an Egyptian bifhop; and perhaps by perceiving, that it was difagreeable to the emperor; as it probably was, if we may judge by the marks of fingular refpect which he fhewed that bifhop. Socrat. l. 1. c. 11. p. 38.

    The next general council of Conftantinople, in the year of our Lord 381, was called to confirm the decifions of the council of Nice, which had not in the leaft extinguifhed the rage of controverfy. Previous to it, the emperor wrote to the inhabitants of that city, that he " would have all his fubjects to be of " the fame religion, which Peter, prince of the apoftles, had from the begin- " ning delivered to the Romans, and which was now held by Damafus, bifhop

of

by the civil power in confequence of their refolves; and I am apt to furmife, that a candid enquirer after truth would efteem

Z 2

it

of Rome, and Peter, bifhop of Alexandria," Sozom. l. 7. c. 4. Juftiniani Cod. l. 1. tit. 1. §. 1. So refpectable a father as Gregory Nazianzen, in a letter which he wrote to Procopius to excufe himfelf with the emperor for attending this council, faith, that he was " defirous of avoiding all fynods, be-" caufe he had never feen a good effect, or happy conclufion of " any one of them; that they rather increafed than leffened the evils they were " defigned to prevent. For the love of contention, and luft of power, were " there manifefted in inftances innumerable." Operum tom. 1. p. 814. epift. 55. edit. Paris 1630. And what the good father faid concerning former councils, not excepting the famous one of Nice, he found afterwards to be true of this council of Conftantinople. " Thefe conveyers of the Holy Ghoft," faith he, " thefe preachers of peace to all men, grew fo bitterly outrageous and cla-" morous againft one another, in the midft of the church, bandying into par-" ties, mutually accufing each other, leaping about as if they had been mad, " under the furious impulfe of a luft of power and dominion, as if they would " have rent the whole world in pieces." He faith afterwards, that " this was not " the effect of piety, but of a contention for thrones:" Ouk Eufebeian—Ten " d'uper Thronon Erin. And he gives a ftrange account of their indecent be-haviour, when he had juft made a fpeech to them. " Thefe furious young " men were followed by the elder," faith he, " and ruled the council." Greg. Naz. de vit. fua, operum tom. 2. p. 25, 27.

The general council of Ephefus, A. D. 431, was called on this occafion. Neftorius was of opinion, that the two natures in Chrift were not fo united af-ter the incarnation, as to occafion a mutual communication of properties. He therefore objected to calling the Virgin Mary Theotokos, the mother of God ; and would have her called Chriftotokos, the mother of Chrift. Socrat. l. 7. c. 32. Concil. tom. 1. p. 1280. edit. Harduin. The defign of the council of Ephefus was to fettle this notable difpute; or rather to condemn Neftorius. When they met, Cyril of Alexandria, the avowed enemy of Neftorius, induced the bifhops prefent, of his own party, to proceed with great precipitance and violence to the condemnation of Neftorius, before the arrival of John, bifhop of Antioch, and the bifhops who were with him; and that, in oppofition to the proteft of 60 or 70 bifhops, and of the emperor's commiffioner, whom they drove out of the affembly. Concil. tom. 1. p. 1351——1354. And then they fent an ac-count of what they had done, infcribed. " To Neftorius, a fecond Judas." Concil. tom. 1 p. 1434. When John and his party arrived, they depofed Cyril ; Concil. tom. 1. p. 1450——1455. and Cyril and his party, in return, depofed John; Concil. tom. 1. p. 1500. Evagr. l. 1. c. 5. p. 254, 255. And thus

it a much fairer chance for being in the right, to follow his own judgment; or, if any other, the judgment of a few serious, impartial,

thus there subsisted two councils, mutually condemning each other. To allay the storm, the emperor gave his sanction to the deposition of Nestorius, Cyril, and Memnon, an active partizan of Cyril's, (Concil. tom. 1. p. 1550. E. 1551. A. E. 1555. A.) and they were arrested by the Emperor's commissioner, p. 1555—1557. But he was afterwards brought (some say, by the money distributed amongst his courtiers by the deputies of Cyril, p. 1580. C.) to alter his mind; to confirm, indeed, the deposition of Nestorius, whom he banished, (p. 1670. A. B.); but to restore Cyril and Memnon. Ever since Cyril, and his party have been esteemed the legitimate council of Ephesus. Isidorus of Pelusium in a letter to Cyril, treats him very justly as well as very freely, when he represents his conduct in this council to be that of a man pursuing only his own resentments. Epistol. l. 1. epist. 310. operum edit. Paris 1638.

The fourth general council of Chalcedon, A. D. 451. was occasioned by the extraordinry transactions of a council of Ephesus in the year 449, of which Dioscorus bishop of Alexandria, was president; and in which the doctrine of the two natures in Christ after the incarnation was condemned, and the contrary doctrine of Eutyches affirmed. The menaces of the president, together with the soldiers and monks, who surrounded the council, terrified the whole assembly. Concil. tom. 2. p. 213. C. D. and Flavianus, bishop of Constantinople, who had condemned Eutyches, being accused by the president, and declared to be anathematized and deposed; and appealing therefore from him, and some bishops at the same time interposing in his behalf; the president started up, and sternly called for the emperor's commissioners, by whose command the proconsul of Asia came in with the military, and a confused mob with chains and clubs and swords. Concil. tom. 2. p. 216. and some bishops not willing to declare, and others flying away, he cried out, " If any one refuses to sign " with me he hath to contend;" (tom. 2. p. 213. B.) and then he and another bishop carried about a blank paper, (Concil. tom. 2. p. 80. F. p. 94. D. E. p. 101. E. Evagr. l. 2. c. 4. p. 288.) and obliged them all to sign it. After which it was filled up with the charge of heresy against Flavianus, and the sentence of his deposition. Flavianus still excepting against the president, he and others fell furiously upon him, beating him barbarously, throwing him down, kicking and trampling upon him, insomuch that three days after he died of the bruises he had received in the council. Liberat. Breviar. c. 12. Niceph. Callist. l. 14. c. 47. tom. 2. p. 550. edit. Paris 1630.

The general council of Chalcedon, I say, was called upon occasion of the transactions and decisions of this council of Ephesus; and after some struggle between the two contending parties, for and against Dioscorus; some crying out

partial, difinterefted enquirers, like himfelf, than to adopt the refolutions of the moft venerable fynod, in which truth and right are decided by the major vote. I would not be thought to be an advocate for an arrogant, infolent, pragmatical contempt of the opinions of others; what I mean is, that were I to be under

---

out for the condemnation and banifhment of the heretic, for Chrift had depofed him; and others, for his reftorations to the council, to the churches; (Concil. tom. 2. p. 510. B.) the party againft him prevailed, and he was depofed, (tom. 2. p. 377.) and the doctrine of the two natures, which had been condemned before, was now affirmed; the fathers crying out, "We believe as "Pope Leo doth, anathema to the dividers and confounders, we believe as "Cyril did; thus the orthodox believe, curfed be every one who doth not be- "lieve fo too". Concil. tom. 2 p. 305. E.

On this brief furvey of thefe four general councils, will the reader believe, that they are by law joined with the fcriptures, as judges of herefy, and as guides of that " *public judgment* which hath a better chance to be right than " the fingular notions, or private judgment of any particular man ?" Yet fo it is. See 1 Eliz. c. 1. fect. 36.

It may, perhaps, by fome perfons, be efteemed an act of prudence to conceal the enormities of fuch famous affemblies of Chriftian bifhops, left the honour of Chriftianity fhould fuffer by expofing them. But, I confefs, I cannot be of this opinion. Chriftianity can never fuffer, in the judgment of any impartial perfon, by the conduct of thofe turbulent and factious men, who have figured on the pub- lic theatre in fupport of *political* religion; while it hath numberlefs advocates in every age, who, by their example as well as influence, promote the intereft of *perfonal religion*; exhibiting the faireft patterns of meeknefs, humility, contempt of the world, patience, contentment, purity, and fpirituality, univerfal bene- volence and charity, as well as the moft undiffembled and fervent piety. Such men of fterling worth, fuch genuine Chriftians, who pafs through the world, like a gentle current, which fertilizes the whole adjacent country, appear with no eclat in hiftory; the good effects of their virtues being diffufed in filence; while the reftlefs and ambitious, who aim at wealth and power and pre-emi- nence, and bear down all before them, like refiftlefs torrents, which defolate whole regions, attract obfervation for the changes they produce in the world, and the materials they furnifh for the pen of the civil or ecclefiaftical hiftorians. Neverthelefs, thofe good and righteous men, who have ferved their generati- on in their particular ftations, by their private virtues, will be hereafter had in everlafting remembrance, when thofe who have ftood forth to the public as the champions of tyranny or fecular Chriftianity, will be covered with fhame and everlafting contempt.

der direction in the pursuit of truth, I had rather follow (next to the divine blessing on my own sincere enquiries) the judgment and guidance of some wise and good men, that I have known, than the public decisions of any or all the councils since the days of the apostles.

THE third article which you exhibit against reviling the liturgy, is, that it involves in it " ingratitude, by denying indul-" gence and liberty of conscience to the members of the nation-" al church". There would be little room, surely, Sir, to complain of violations of liberty of conscience; if, in contending for their respective dogmas, men never went beyond contemning and ridiculing one another: for, however censurable this may be, it certainly is not denying them liberty of conscience: that always implies restraint or compulsion, ideas very different from contempt and ridicule†.

BUT perhaps, reviling the liturgy may be censured, as ungrateful, on account of the toleration indulged to Dissenters. It is not, however, to the church the Dissenters are peculiarly indebted for this blessing‡. For though her governors promised them

---

† The author in his late edition, vol. iv. p. 50. declares reviling the liturgy to be " ingratitude, by denying that indulgence and undisturbed liberty of conscience to the members of " the national church, which the retainers to e-" very petty conventicle enjoy." So that reviling is not denying absolutely liberty of conscience, but only undisturbed liberty of conscience. But do the retainers to every petty conventicle enjoy this liberty undisturbed in his own sense of the word? I appeal to the learned gentleman himself, whether this assertion would have appeared with less grace, if that scornful expression concerning Dissenters, " retainers to every petty conventicle," had been suppressed; since it not only disturbs, according to his own idea of the word, but by implication, denies their liberty of conscience; conventicles being, as I said before, unlawful assemblies.

‡ The author of the Alliance between the Church and State, in his Postscript and answer to lord Bolingbroke, p. 2, 3. speaking both of the test-act and of the toleration, observes, that " this reform of the English constitution hap-" pened not to be the good work of the church, begun in the conviction of " truth, and carried on upon the principles of charity; but was rather owing
" to

them every mark of Christian temper and brotherly affection,
when her fears of popery ran high in the reign of James the Second ; yet, as soon as the storm subsided, these promises were
in great measure, forgotten. It is to that great prince, King
William, to whom the British constitution and liberties owe their
preservation and security ; and to those renowned patriots who
first engaged, and then supported him, in the glorious enterprize ; it is to these, and such as these, the Dissenters are, under God, alone obliged for their deliverance from unjust violence and oppression ; and for being restored, in part, to their
natural rights by the toleration. I say, to their natural rights :
for religious liberty is one of those rights to which men are entitled by nature; as much so, as to their lives and properties :
and it should be remembered, therefore, that the Dissenters
cannot be justly reckoned to be any more obliged to those who
kindly do not again deprive them of it ; than they are to those
who *as kindly*, do not seize on their estates, or take away their
lives: an obligation, which, I suppose, hath never been esteemed a reason for any *peculiar gratitude*.

AND now, Sir, notwithstanding the exceptions which I have
taken to your premises, I will leave you in full possession of your
conclusion: I will suppose, that the crime of reviling the liturgy is a complication of " indecency, arrogance, and ingratitude:"
and I will add, moreover, that it may possibly imply, (and, I
think,

" to the vigilance of the state, at one time, vainly perhaps, anxious for the
" established religion, (Char. II.) at another, wisely provident for the support
" of civil liberty." (Will. III.) The Author is certainly right with respect
to the toleration : it was entirely the work of the state. King William engaged
in it heartily; partly, no doubt, to strengthen the interest of civil liberty, of
which the Dissenters were to a man zealous friends; and partly, from a regard
to religious liberty, of which he had all his life shewn himself a firm and steady
patron. The test was not the work of Charles the IId. it was pushed on in opposition to the court by the patriots of those times, in order to secure the civil
as well as the ecclesiastical constitution from the machinations of the Papists, by
excluding them from public offices ; and the royal assent to it was procured by
the Commons stopping the bill of supply till it was passed.

think, it is the principal thing that can be implied in it, though you have not at all mentioned it,) great malignity and inveteracy against the church. But, surely, to confiscate a man's goods, and imprison him for life, for any degree of any of these evil difpositions towards the church, when discovered only by words, (though it be frequently, and they be ever so open and explicit,) and not by any injurious and dangerous overt-acts; must be considered, one would think, by persons of humanity, and doubtless therefore by you, Sir, upon further reflection, to be somewhat *too severe and intolerant.* Notwithstanding all the bitterness with which the puritans inveighed against the offices of the church, (and which they did not do, till by oppression they were provoked almost to madness,) the passing this act, in my opinion, discovered a very intolerant spirit in those who, at that time, had the conduct of public affairs.

But perhaps it may be said, that this measure was adopted only out of prudence, for the security of the national establishment. You inform us, that " the terror of these laws (for you " say, they seldom or never were fully executed) proved a prin " cipal means, under Providence, of preserving the purity as " well as decency of our national worship†." Which, give me leave to say, Sir, is passing no great compliment upon the national worship.

But however that be: what had the church to fear from the revilings of the puritans, that she must fence herself around with human terrors? We are to suppose, she had all the truth and argument, as well as the encouragement of the civil magistrate, on her side. In this case, having recourse to human terrors was bringing disgrace on a good cause, and doing credit to a bad one. For the presumption, in most men's minds, is always in favour of the cause which is oppressed and persecuted; and that this is the case, is owing, partly to a certain generosity in mankind, which inclines them to side with the weakest, and those

who

---

† Commeat. vol. iv. p. 51.

who are ill treated ; and partly to a perfuafion, which appears not wholly unreasonable, that while argument can be maintained, terror will not be employed. And for my own part, I am perfuaded, that the church, inftead of infuring its fafety by thefe methods, greatly increafed the number of its enemies, and inflamed their animofity and inveteracy. Had the governors of the church or ftate, at that time, made a few conceffions, fuch as not only the puritans, but many wife and great men in the church, defired; or, in cafe they had not thought proper to do this, if they had indulged and tolerated thofe puritans, who could not in confcience conform ; it is my opinion, the church wou'd have been in no more danger from the puritans of that age, than it is now in from the Diffenters of this. Such fevere laws occafioned the very crime they were intended to prevent: for the imbittered men's fpirits, and inflamed their paffions : and when the mind is greatly irritated, it is hardly in human nature to fpeak with temper and moderation, either of thofe by whom, or of that for which, men feel themfelves ill-treated and oppreffed.

I would further obferve, (and it is an obfervation I would fubmit to the confideration of a gentleman of your profeffion, in particular) that, on fuppofition this act was levelled only, as you feem to imagine, againft the bitter reproaches and infults of the puritans, it feems to have been drawn with too great a latitude of expreffion. I believe you will admit, and, I think, you have fomewhere faid fomething like it, that it is the excellence of any law to define offences and punifhments with the utmoft precifion, that the fubject may know diftinctly what is lawful and what is forbidden. But is this the cafe with the act before us, fuppofing it be defigned merely againft reviling and outraging the offices of the church ? For, what is the precife idea of one who declares or fpeaks any thing, in open words, in derogation of the common prayer? Surely under an expreffion of fuch latitude may be included every man, who openly declares his difapprobation of it, or as the act exprefsly faith, of any thing therein contained, or any part thereof; that is, every one who gives any of his reasons for not joining in the offices of the church; and he may, by a willing judge and jury, nay, ought, according to the literal sense of the words, to be convicted upon this statute. Now, supposing this law was intended only, as you seem to think, against insulting and reviling the liturgy; can so good a lawyer as Dr. Blackstone approve of a statute, which is so worded as to comprehend persons who are entirely innocent of the crime intended*?

BUT in truth, I cannot help thinking, that it was the actual intention of those who promoted this act, to put an effectual stop, if possible, to the puritans *arguments* as well as their revilings; and that, on this account, the act was so expressed, as to include every man who finds fault with the common prayer, though only in a way of argument. For certainly, that is, " in open " words speaking in derogation of it." The intent of the act at that time, I am afraid, was, to prevent the questioning any part of the service of the church, either in a way of reasoning or reviling.

BEFORE

---

* Having met with one or two persons who conceive what is here said not easily reconcileable with what I before advanced in p. 32. I beg leave to observe, that in p. 32. I speak of it as a *felicity*, that our laws against heresy have not precisely defined it, because in *these times of lenity and moderation*, it is not very likely that a jury will take upon them to define it, where the law hath left it *doubtful and undefined*, and them at *liberty* to put a favourable construction. But the sentiment I here suggest is, that if the judgment of the learned Commentator concerning the crime against which 1 Eliz. c. 2. §. 14. is levelled, be right, then there is a want of precision of *another* kind, not arising from the *uncertainty* of the expression, but from the *latitude* of it, which *comprehends*, and thereby *binds down* the jury (without leaving any room for the interposition of their lenity) to convict, persons who, in his opinion, are innocent; and therefore he ought to have condemned this law for the *impropriety* as well as severity of it; whereas in the former case, the impropriety might have been *excused* for the sake of the good consequence arising from it through the lenity of the times. What I have said in these two passages being thus brought into one point of view, I apprehend there will not appear to be the least inconsistency between them.

BEFORE Dr. Blackstone, therefore, had declared his approbation of this statute, and much more of the continuance of it to the present time, he should have considered, what persons and what cases, according to its literal and just construction, and perhaps according to its original intention, may be affected by it; and whether he would chuse to vindicate it in its full extent. In every view it appears to me very surprising, that you, Sir, who have expressed yourself, on various occasions, with so much liberality of sentiment, should think " the continuance of this " act not too severe and intolerant."

AFTER such a declaration, I cannot be much surprised at your passing this encomium on the reign of Elizabeth, notwithstanding it produced such severe laws against nonconformity, that " the reformation was then finally established with tem- " per and decency, unsullied with party-rancour, or personal " caprice and resentment*." An impartial review of the ecclesiastical history of those times, as it is exhibited by Fuller, Strype, and other credible historians of the church of England; is, I think, sufficient to convince us, that there was, in that reign, a great deal of ill-temper, party-rancour, and personal pique and resentment in the governors of the church, which entered much more than it should have done into their deliberations and conduct concerning ecclesiastical affairs. The queen, it is true, at the entrance of her reign, discovered great policy and caution, in the measures she employed to take down the fabrick of Popery, which her sister queen Mary had re-edified. Nevertheless, through the whole course of it, there were few demonstrations of temper and moderation in her, or in those governors of the church whom she principally esteemed and preferred; whereas there were many proofs and examples of unjust and cruel severity, towards those Protestants who disliked the least article in her ecclesiastical settlement, or who expressed,

A a 2 though

---

* Comment. vol. iv. p. 48.

though in ever fo humble and modeft a manner, their defire of a further reformation. The truth is, fhe had entertained fuch lofty conceptions of her fpiritual as well as temporal prerogative, and was difpofed to maintain it, upon all occafions, with fuch rigour; as cannot be eafily reconciled with any juft notions of religious liberty, or with any regard to the facred and inviolable rights of confcience.

I am,

Sir, &c.

P O S T-

P O S T S C R I P T

T O

L E T T E R IV.

SIR,

I SHALL not be thought deficient, I hope, in that amiable virtue, candour, of which you have fet a laudable example; if I obferve, that fome of the alterations in the late edition of your Commentaries, are not perfectly fatisfactory. In particular, the account in this edition, as well as that in the former, of the claufe in the act of uniformity, 1 Eliz. c. 2. §. 9. againft declaring or fpeaking any thing in open words, in derogation or depraving of the liturgy, appears to me to be liable to feveral objections, "The continuance of this claufe," you fay, "to this "time, in terrorem at leaft," (thus you now chufe to exprefs yourfelf) "cannot be thought too fevere or intolerant; when "we confider, that it is levelled at the offence, not of thinking "differently from the national church, but of railing at that "church and its ordinances, for not fubmitting its public judg-"ment to the private opinion of others. For though it is clear," you add, "that no reftraint fhould be laid upon rational and "difpaffionate enquiries into the rectitude and propriety of the "eftablifhed mode of worfhip, yet contumely and contempt are "what no eftablifhment can tolerate." And then you remark, that "a rigid attachment to trifles, and an intemperate zeal for "reforming them, are equally ridiculous and abfurd. But the "latter is at prefent the lefs excufable, becaufe from political "reafons fufficiently hinted at in a former volume, it would "now be extremely unadvifable to make any alterations in the "fervice of the church." And in fupport of this obfervation, that "contumely and contempt are what no eftablifhment can "tolerate,"

" tolerate," you infert this marginal note : " By an ordinance*,
" 23 Aug. 1645, which continued till the reftoration, to preach,
" write, or print any thing in derogation or depraving of the
" directory for the then eftablifhed prefbyterian worfhip, fub-
" jected the offender, upon indictment, to a difcretionary fine,
" not exceeding fifty pounds.   (Scobel, 98.)"

THE firft remark, which I think proper to make, relates to
the approbation here given to acts in terrorem : to acts which
are attended (like that in particular now under confideration)
with penalties too fevere to be executed, confiftently with any
principles of humanity, or even equity ; which requires a due
proportion between the punifhment and the crime.   And fuch
laws cannot, I think, be confidered as the offspring of political
wifdom, fo much as of an arbitrary and tyrannical difpofition:
for the laws of a wife ftate fhould only be fuch, if I am not miftaken, as may be carried into effect, with reafon and juftice.
The common law of England, in particular, is the voice of reafon ; and its ftatutes fhould always fpeak the fame language.

IT is not fufficient to allege, that thefe laws are made only in
terrorem: an allegation, I fay, which can never vindicate them ;
for this obvious reafon, becaufe they never contain in them a
declaration, that they are made only in terrorem ; indeed if they
did, they would abfolutely defeat their own intention.   That
fuch laws are not executed therefore, and that acts of feverity
and cruelty are not in confequence of them, and under their
fanction, committed, is not at all owing to the laws themfelves,

                                                                but

* The words of the ordinance are, That what perfon foever fhall with intent
to bring the faid directory into contempt and neglect, or to raife oppofition
againft it, preach, write, print, or caufe to be written or printed, any thing
in the derogation or depraving of the faid book, or any thing therein contained,
or any part thereof, fhall lofe and forfeit for every fuch offence, fuch a fum
of money as fhall at the time of his conviction be thought fit to be impofed
upon him by thofe before whom he fhall have his tryal, provided that it be not
lefs than five pounds, nor exceeding the fum of fifty pounds.

but folely to the fpirit of the times. And the laws themfelves are neither better nor worfe, becaufe they do not happen to be executed. To form therefore a right judgment concerning them, we fhould examine them as to what they are in their own nature, and on fuppofition they will be executed ; and approve or condemn them, as they appear in this view, to be either reafonable or otherwife. Suppofe a profecution is commenced, that the law hath its courfe, and that the penalty is inflicted, the proper queftion is, What fhall we think of the law in thefe circumftances? And in the cafe before us, where the penalty is one hundred marks for the firft offence, four hundred for the fecond, and forfeiture of goods and chattels and imprifonment for life for the third offence, of fpeaking in open words in derogation of the common prayer ; I believe, on fuppofition of the actual infliction of this penalty, efpecially in the laft inftance, I may fafely appeal to the moft zealous partizan of the eftablifhed liturgy, whether there is any proportion between the punifhment and the crime.

Besides, the fubject fhould always be able to learn his condition under any law, from the law itfelf ; and not be obliged to recur, for this purpofe, to confiderations wholly foreign to it ; fuch as the fpirit of the times, and the chance that it will not be executed. This is not being under the government of law, under a known and equitable rule ; it is being at mercy ; it is being fubject to fortuitous events, of which no eftimate can be taken. Now every law is unreafonable, which leaves the fubject in a condition fo infecure : Every law deferves to be condemned, which brings the infliction of an unreafonable and difproportionate punifhment, within the power of every one who takes upon him to be an informer or profecutor ; and which affords, therefore, no fecurity from injuftice and oppreffion (for every penalty more fevere than the offence deferves, is, in proportion, unjuft, and oppreffive) ; I fay, every fuch law fhould be exploded, as leaves no ground of exemption from injuftice and oppreffion, but the bare prefumption

that

th at there will be no profecutor, and confequently that the law will not be executed: which really amounts to this very bad compliment upon the law, that the people will difcern the iniquity of it, and have more wifdom and moderation than thofe who enacted it.   However, it muft be confeffed, this is not always to be expected; and therefore (to ufe your own fervent expreffions concerning the laws in terrorem againft the PAPISTS) " it ought not to be left in the breaft of every mercilefs bigot to " drag down the vengeance of thofe occafional laws upon inof" fenfive, though miftaken, fubjects; in oppofition to the le" nient inclinations of the civil magiftrate, and to the deftructi" on of every principle of toleration and religious liberty*."

I F

* Comment. vol. iv. book 4. chap. 4. page 57. Penal laws are never warrantable againft any mere fyftem of religion: and yet they may be juftified againft the fyftem of the church of Rome, becaufe it is not merely a corrupt and erroneous fyftem of religion, but a wicked confpiracy for the extirpation of all who oppofe her enormous fuperftitions and ufurpations: and hath uniformly appeared to be fo, wherever her power hath been predominant.   Upon this conviction, very fevere ftatutes have been enacted againft the papifts, in thefe kingdoms, at thofe particular periods fince the reformation, when peculiar danger was apprehended from their machinations.   Thefe laws are neverthelefs every day violated with impunity.   And the reafon is, that they have feldom or never been executed; becaufe they are of fo fevere and fanguinary a nature, that the idea of executing them, fhocks the humane and liberal fentiments of the age.   It is, notwithftanding, always requifite to be on our guard againft the prevalence of Popery, that implacable enemy to the general liberties of mankind, as well as in particular to our own happy conftitution.   But the danger, I apprehend, would be more effectually prevented by laws which might be properly executed, than by laws which the genius and fpirit of the times have rendered as dormant as if they were obfolete.   The fyftem of laws eftablifhed in Holland would perhaps deferve confideration.   That wife people, I am informed, permit no Jefuits at all in their country, and no priefts but natives; no money to be carried out of their dominions upon a religious account, no attempts to make profyltes, and the like.   And in cafe of a breach of any one of thefe regulations, the place of worfhip belonging to the Roman Catholics, (for under the preceding reftrictions, they are tolerated in Holland) in the diftrict where the offence is committed, is immediately fhut up.   This makes it to
be

I F any one plead the danger arising from impunity, as an
excuse for the severity of that law in particular, which we have
now in contemplation ; I profess, I cannot perceive, as I observed in my fourth letter, any such mighty danger arising from
mere words spoken in derogation of the common prayer, separate from any violent and outrageous overt acts, as will be a
tolerable excuse for penalties so enormously severe*.

B b   You

be the interest of their religion, for every individual to observe the laws of his
country ; and the consequence is, that there is hardly ever a convert attempted
to be made to Popery ; and the Catholics. the descendants of popish ancestors,
or those who come to settle in the provinces, are preserved, or weaned, from
any attachment to a foreign interest ; and at the same time, having no share in
the magistracy, and their numbers and persons being well known, the danger
which might be apprehended from their principles, is in great measure precluded : perhaps in a greater degree, than where the laws are so severe, that,
except in case of overt acts of treason or rebellion, they can never be executed.

I have made these observations, because I apprehend, laws in terrorem will in
any case answer very little purpose. I am however persuaded, that to guard
against the prevalence of Popery, by every method which appears to be calculated for that end ; in Protestants, whom Papists stile heretics, and as such
esteem fit for nothing but extirpation in this world, and damnation in the next,
is mere self-defence. And, thanks to the Catholics, whilst they have among
them such writers as the author of the life of Cardinal Pole, who in this protestant kingdom has the audacity to write a cool apology for the flames which
were kindled in Smithfield by queen Mary, they will not let us overlook the necessity of taking every measure requisite for our security, against their pernicious and persecuting principles and practices.

* It is very extraordinary, that this act inflicts the same penalty upon open
words spoken in derogation of the common prayer. as upon the overt act of obstructing the reading of it. It enacts, " That if any person whatsoever shall in
" any open words, declare or speak any thing in the derogation of the common
" prayer: or by open fact, deed, or by open threatnings, shall unlawfully
" interrupt or let any parson, vicar, &c. to sing or say common and open pray-
" er, or to minister the sacraments, in such manner and form as is mentioned
" in the said book ; he shall for the first offence forfeit one hundred marks, for
" the second four hundred, for the third all his goods and chattels, and suffer
" imprisonment for life." 1 Eliz. c. 2. §. 9, 10, 11. Is the offence of speaking
against the common prayer, of the same magnitude with obstructing the reading of it, perhaps by violence ? If not, where is the wisdom and justice of making the penalty, in these two very different cases, the same?

You endeavour, however, to fupport your opinion, that " the
" continuance of this act to the prefent time, in terrorem at
" leaft, is not too fevere and intolerant," by fuggefting, that
" it is levelled at the offence, not of thinking differently from
" the national church, but of railing at that church and its or-
" dinances for not fubmitting its public judgment to the private
" opinion of others." I readily admit, that the act is not levelled againft thinking differently from the national church:
it would be a grofs abfurdity, if it were; inafmuch as mere
thought can never come under the cognizance of any human
law whatfoever. But there is furely a medium, in all cafes, between thinking and railing; I mean afferting and arguing: and
therefore fuppofing (but not granting) this act to be intended
merely againft railing, I think, with fubmiffion, you fhould have
attempted, at leaft, to define the crime more accurately than you
have done; that under the notion of railing, a man's merely declaring his fentiments, and arguing in fupport of them, may
not be conftrued to be within the intent of this act. Any one
who confiders the ufual courfe of religious controverfy may obferve, that what preffes clofe upon an adverfary, what cannot be
eafily anfwered, is very apt to be exclaimed againft as mifrepre-
fentation and abufe; and the difputant, who only reafons, if he
fets his argument in a light calculated to convince or confound
his adverfary, is prefently charged with railing. Nothing is
beftowed more indifcriminately, than fuch language; for bigots
of all parties, who fee no difficulty on their own fide, take it for
granted, when they cannot get rid of an untoward confequence
charged upon them and their principles, that the fault is neither
in the caufe which they efpoufe, nor in their management of it;
and therefore they cry out upon foul play in their antagonifts,
upon their mifreprefenting and reviling what perhaps they only
exhibit in a right point of view. To draw the line between reafoning and reviling, in every cafe, is indeed no eafy matter; and
I muft beg your excufe, Sir, if I prefume to fay, that I believe
you found it fo, by the lax and uncertain ftate in which you

have

have left this queſtion; oppoſing only the two extremes of thinking and railing to each other, and leaving it in doubt in what claſs, whether of things allowed, or of things prohibited, is to be ranked reaſoning in ſupport of direct poſitions and plain declarations. But was it right to leave a point of this conſequence wholly doubtful and undetermined? Becauſe, in particular caſes, it may be difficult to mark the difference between aſſerting and reaſoning on the one hand, and railing or reviling on the other, was it right, that no exception ſhould be made in favour of a man's declaring his ſentiments, and ſupporting them in the beſt manner he is able in the way of reaſoning and argument?

You admit it, I own, to be clear, " that no reſtraint ſhould " be laid upon rational and diſpaſſionate enquiries into the rec- " titude and propriety of the eſtabliſhed mode of worſhip." In what degree *enquiries* concerning the propriety of the eſtabliſhed mode of worſhip may come within the intendment of the act, or whether they do at all, I will not pretend to determine. Enquiring, in the proper import of the term, may not perhaps amount to *declaring* or ſpeaking any thing in open words in derogation of, that is, advancing a plain poſition againſt, the liturgy, or any part of it. But then, I apprehend, the queſtion is not ſo much concerning mere enquiries, as concerning direct poſitions and arguing in ſupport of them*; the act, as I before obſerved,

B b 2

* A learned biſhop obſerves, that " it is ſomething odd, to have two creeds" (the Nicene and Athanaſian) " eſtabliſhed in the ſame church, in one of which " thoſe are declared accurſed, who deny the ſon to be of the ſame uſia, or hy- " poſtaſis, with the father;" ex eteras upoſtaſeos e ouſias phaſkontas einai — " toutous anathematizei e katholike kai apoſtolike Ekkleſia. Symb. Nicen. vid. Socrat. Hiſt. Eccl. l. i. c. 8.) " and in the other it is declared, they cannot " be ſaved, but periſh everlaſtingly, who do not aſſert, that there is one hypoſ- " taſis of the Father, and another of the Son." See the late biſhop of Clogher's Eſſay on Spirit, p. 146. edit. 2. I ſhould be glad to know under what head this *direct charge* is to be arranged; whether it amounts to *declaring* any thing in derogation of the liturgy? and conſequently, whether it comes within the intendment of the act?

ferved, being plainly levelled againſt allowing thoſe who diſlike the liturgy, or ſcruple the uſe of it, to aſſign and defend the grounds of their opinion and practice ; and that even when attacked by others. So that whatſoever be the caſe concerning mere rational and diſpaſſionate enquiries into the propriety of the eſtabliſhed mode of worſhip, I preſume it is very plain, from the expreſs words of the ſtatute, that every poſitive aſſertion or *declaration* of a perſon's ſentiments concerning the impropriety of that mode in any one reſpect (the act referring not only to the book in general, but to " every part of it, and eve- " ry thing therein contained") comes within the meaning of " ſpeaking in open words in derogation of the common prayer." And this obſervation, if it be juſt, as I think it is, ſuperſedes all occaſion of diſtinguiſhing between aſſerting and reaſoning on the one hand, and railing or reviling on the other ; becauſe it ſhews, that the act alike comprehends and condemns both of them. And therefore, Sir, unleſs you intend to prohibit every ſuch aſſertion or declaration of opinion concerning the impropriety of any part of the eſtabliſhed mode of worſhip, though ſupported by the moſt ſubſtantial reaſons, I hope you will, as with ſubmiſſion I think you ſhould, retract your approbation of theſe ſevere clauſes in the act of uniformity.

I f any rail at the church and its ordinances, I am not the advocate of ſuch perſons. Railing is always unwarrantable, and never ſerviceable. And yet I ſuppoſe, if it hath ever been employed againſt the common prayer, it hath ſeldom been for the reaſon you aſſign, that the church " will not ſubmit her public " judgment to the private opinion of others." I rather think, in ſuch caſes, it is generally owing to an imagination at leaſt, that the object of ridicule is really contemptible; and that the public judgment is not ſo very ſacred, as to ſanctify every thing which hath the ſanction of public authority. Whether this apprehenſion be ſufficient to juſtify ſuch conduct, is a different conſideration.

Y o u

You endeavour, I perceive, to support your approbation of this act, by remarking, that " contumely and contempt are " what no establishment can tolerate:" and in confirmation of this, you have inferted this note in the margin, that, " by an " ordinance 23 Aug. 1645, preaching, writing, or printing any " thing in derogation or depraving of the directory for the then " established prefbyterian worfhip, fubjected the offender upon " indictment to a difcretionary fine, not lefs than five, and not " exceeding fifty pounds." I am forry, Sir, you fhould pay fo great a compliment to this ordinance (fo much beyond what I think it deferves) as to produce it in defence of this favourite act of Elizabeth. It is fo far from being, in my humble opinion, an authority fufficient to give countenance to a thing difputable or exceptionable; that the framers of it were very culpable in following the bad example fet them by that act. And yet it fhould in juftice be obferved, that even in this inftance of retaliation (which, I admit, cannot be juftified) they affigned a far more moderate penalty than was before done ; a fine not lefs than five, yet never exceeding fifty pounds, being much below one hundred marks for the firft offence, four hundred for the fecond, and forfeiture of goods and chattels and imprifonment for life for the third. And this they laid, not as in the cafe before them, upon " declaring or fpeaking any thing in open " words," but only upon " preaching, writing, or printing, " in derogation or depraving of the directory, with intent to " bring it into contempt or neglect, or to raife oppofition againft " it."

But notwithftanding, Sir, the favourable light in which you have placed this ordinance, I cannot prevail upon myfelf to approve it. For fure I am, whatever religious inftitutions cannot be fupported, without the aid of fuch penal ftatutes or ordinances to fecure them from contempt and ridicule, had better not be fupported at all. If reafon and argument are on their fide, contempt and ridicule in the end, will do them no real

pre-

prejudice; and provided reason and argument are not on their side, it is no matter how soon they are discarded. By this, Sir, you may perceive, that I have no better opinion of penal laws in support of a Presbyterian, than of an Episcopal establishment, The Presbyterians, I confess, formerly copied too nearly the example of the Episcopalians. The genuine principles of universal and impartial liberty were very little understood by any; and all parties were too much involved in the guilt of intolerance and persecution. The Dissenters in our times freely acknowledge this, and condemn the narrow principles of many of their predecessors; having no objection to transmitting down to posterity, in their true colours, the acts of oppression and intolerance of which all sects have been guilty; not indeed, as is sometimes done, with a view of encouraging such conduct in one party by the example of others; but of exposing it alike in all, and preventing it wholly, if possible, in time to come.

THE observation, which you make at the close: namely, that " a rigid attachment to trifles, and an intemperate zeal for " reforming them, are equally ridiculous and absurb;" would, I admit, be very just, and quite applicable to the present case, provided only the things in question were merely trifles. But that is gratis dictum; and, I believe, you will allow, that in matters of this nature, the most venerable ipse dixit deserves no regard: and that even your authority, Sir, respectable as it is, cannot claim the privilege of being substituted in the room of reason and evidence.

WITH submission, Sir, the power of decreeing rites and ceremonies, and authority in controversies of faith, claimed by the church; the authoritative absolution of sin, in the visitation of the sick*; the expressions of strong hopes of the happiness of some

---

* The rubrick orders, " that the sick person shall be moved to make a special " confession of his sins, if he feel his conscience troubled with any weighty " matter. After which confession the priest shall absolve him, (if he humbly and heartily desire it) after this sort :

" Our

some perhaps of the worst of men, in the burial of the dead; and the pronouncing damnation, in the creed ascribed to Athanasius; certain, inevitable and everlasting damnation, upon every one that doth not believe the whole of it* ; and in general

ral

" Our Lord Jesus Christ who hath left *power to his church* to absolve all sin-
" ners who truly repent and believe in him, of his great mercy forgive thee
" thine offences : And by his authority *committed to me*, I absolve thee from all
" thy sins, in the name of the Father, and of the Son, and of the Holy Ghost,
" Amen."

And how this authority *is committed* to the priest, may be seen in the office of ordination, where the bishop, putting his hand on the head of the person to be ordained, faith, " Receive the Holy Ghost——Whose sins THOU dost forgive
" they are forgiven; and whose sins THOU dost retain, they are retained; in the
" name of the Father, of the Son, and of the Holy Ghost. Amen."

There is something similar in the office of confirmation, where the bishop lays his hand on each individual, " *to certify him by this sign*" (as the collect expresses it) " of God's favour and gracious goodness towards him." Though the twenty-fifth article, by the way, affirms, that " confirmation hath not any " visible *sign* or ceremony ordained of God".

If those expressions and actions are understood according to their obvious import, and as I fear they are often understood, as in the one case conveying, and in the other exercising extraordinary powers; they mean *too much*. If they are understood, as they are sometimes explained, or explained away rather; they are in danger of being considered as nothing better than *solemn trifling*, as " grasping at the shadow of an authority" (to use the words of the late Dr. Stebbing in his instructions of a parish minister to his parishioners on the subject of popery, part 2. p. 37, 38) " which we must all renounce. What else do " we, when we pretend to absolve conscience ? We may use an hundred dif-
" tinctions, if we please : we may say, that the absolution is not authoritative,
" but declaratory ; or, that it is not judicial, but ministerial : but if you would
" speak to be understood, you must say, that with respect to any real internal
" effect it is NOTHING ; and you will speak *truth* too : for all the rest, if you
" will preserve to God his *prerogative* to forgive sin, are words without mean-
" ing." I only add, that it would be more manly, rational, christian, to alter such passages, than to attempt to explain them : which, I apprehend, it is impossible to do, in a way consistent with reason and scripture.

* It is observable, that with respect to those concerning whom the Athanasian creed declares, that they shall WITHOUT DOUBT *perish everlastingly* ; the burial

ral, the impoſing ſuch unſcriptural forms to be uſed in the public ſervice, and ſuch doctrinal articles to be ſubſcribed, as many
wiſe and good men in the church can with difficulty, if at all
reconcile to their real ſentiments : theſe and ſeveral other particulars which might be mentioned, with all due deference to
your judgment, Sir, are no trifles. And though I am not diſpoſed to caſt unjuſt or ſevere reflections upon any of the public
forms, I really cannot help hinting upon a proper occaſion (with
all due reſpect to the ſtatute) how things appear to me; how indeed they have appeared to others, not to Diſſenters only, but
to many who have been the glory of the Eſtabliſhed Church ;
and have, nevertheleſs, wiſhed for alterations in theſe and many other particulars; ſuch alterations, as you, Sir, eſteem very improper to be attempted ; becauſe, you ſay by the act of u-
nion between England and Scotland, the conſtitution and worſhip of the two churches reſpectively are rendered immutable : a
point, which deſerves to be diſtinctly examined. I am, Sir, &c.

LET-

burial office, appointed to be read over the ſame perſons, if they are not ex-
communicated, thanks God that he hath in GREAT MERCY *taken them to him-*
ſelf, and HOPES *that they reſt in* Chriſt.

It is not my deſign to enter upon the particulars of the controverſy between
the Church and the Diſſenters. They may be ſeen on the Diſſenting ſide, in
all their ſtrength, in the|Diſſenting Gentleman's (I think, unanſwerable) Letters
to Mr. White. I only obſerve, that if the power and authority, claimed in
the twentieth article, of decreeing rites and ceremonies and deciding controverſies of faith, be once proved, the debate will be brought to a ſhort iſſue : but
till then, the ground of diſſent will remain firm ; ſince there can be no obligation upon us, in point of conſcience, to comply with any rite or ceremony, or
any deciſion of faith, which we do not ourſelves perceive to be divinely appointed ; and that, whether it be of greater or leſs importance : nay, it is rather our duty to oppoſe the *impoſition* of all ſuch rites or ſuch articles, out of regard to the ſovereign authority of Chriſt ; which, in ſuch caſes, is the ſole
ground of obligation upon Chriſtians.

LETTER V.

SIR,

THE attempts to procure a further reformation in the church have been many and various. But while I enjoy my liberty as a Chriſtian, and a Proteſtant Diſſenter, I am not ſolicitous, on my own account, whether any alterations are made in the conſtitution or liturgy of the church of England. I deſpair of ever ſeeing the terms of conformity ſo enlarged and liberal, as to invite me into the eſtabliſhment. But when I conſider, that there are perſons already in the communion, and even in the orders of the church, who deſire, and endeavour to obtain, a reformation of various particulars which they, as well as Proteſtant Diſſenters, think ought to be reformed; I am ſorry, on their account, and for the intereſt of religion in general, whenever I ſee difficulties thrown in the way of a deſign ſo laudable, and ſo deſireable. In this view, it is with no ſmall concern, that I obſerved you laying ſo much ſtreſs on the following ſentiment: That " an alteration in the conſtitution or " liturgy of the church of England, would be an infringement " of the fundamental and eſſential conditions of the union be- " tween England and Scotland, and would greatly endanger " that union*."

I WILL firſt make ſome remarks upon this queſtion, according to your ſtate of it ; and then explain the particular view in which, I think, it ought to be conſidered.

I OBSERVE that you allow, that, notwithſtanding the act of union, and the conditions therein enacted, there is a competent authority in the Britiſh parliament for making ſuch alterations

C c

in

* Comment. vol. i. p. 98.

in the church*. And if so, whether the parliament should venture to exercise that power, is merely a question of prudence
and expedience. You declare your opinion that, " it will en-
" danger the union." With submission, I cannot conceive,
there could be any great danger in a parliamentary review and
alteration of such things, as it would be agreeable to the members of the church of England themselves should be altered ;
and especially if it be apparent to the whole world, that the design takes its rise in the church of England itself. The Scots
would then have no reason to be alarmed; and I hardly think
they would be so ; because the case here supposed, is no precedent for any alterations in their church, except what they themselves shall desire. Could we suppose, indeed, an attempt made
of alterations in the church of England, at a time when the Scots
had reason to apprehend a design, formed in England, to make
alterations in the church of Scotland ; and that alterations here
were only made to furnish a kind of precedent for carrying that
design into execution ; they might, and probably would, be a-
larmed. But I cannot see, for my part, any dangerous consequences in the parliament's making what are generally considered to be real improvements (even tho' it should not be thought
absolutely necessary to make them†) in either church, provided
it

---

* " It may be justly doubted," saith the learned Commentator, " whether
" such an infringement of the act of union (though a manifest breach of good
" faith, unless done upon the most pressing necessity) would consequently dif-
" solve the union : for the bare idea of a state without a power somewhere
" vested to alter every part of its laws, is the height of political absurdity."
Comment. vol. i. p. 97. 98. note. And in the Reply to Dr. Priestley, p. 44.
speaking of the *power* of alteration, he saith " it must necessarily reside in the
" supreme legislature of the united kingdoms." Again, p. 46. " Indeed I
" have allowed, that the *power* of new modelling the churches both of Eng-
" land and Scotland (however dangerous its exertion might be) still resides in
" the parliament of Great-Britain."

† See Comment. vol. iv. p. 51. where the author saith, " it would now"
(since the union) " be extremely unadvisable to make any alterations in the ser-
" vice of the church ; unless it could be shewn, that some manifest impiety or
" shocking absurdity would follow from continuing it in its present form."

it be done only in conformity with the general sentiments and desire of the respective churches themselves. We see, in fact, that the passing the patronage-act, in respect to the church of Scotland, was attended with no such formidable consequences as you seem to apprehend; though it was an infringement of the union, the more dangerous, because that act was passed under the influence of Queen Ann's last ministry, in opposition to the general sentiments of the Scottish nation.

In what I have said, I have left all consideration of the intention of the act of security of the church of England, included in the act of union between the two nations, entirely out of the question. But after all, permit me to ask, Whether it was not the spirit and design of these acts of security in both churches to prevent the incroachments of one upon the other, after the union took effect? It must certainly be admitted, that an apprehension of such incroachments upon each other, was the *occasion* of those acts; for if it had not been for the dangers apprehended by each church from the other, those acts of security of the two churches had never been passed at all: and from the *occasion* we may infer the *design*.

Besides, if no alteration must be made in either of the two churches, because the act of union hath settled things immutably in each: then the act of union amounts to a declaration of the legislature, that they would, and their posterity should, always think and act exactly as they did at that time: which, as Dr. Priestley observes, in his letter to you, published in the St. James's Chronicle of October 10, 1769, is so absurd, that one would not willingly impute it to two such august assemblies as the parliaments of both kingdoms.

But there is another view in which this point may be considered, independently of any enquiry, what was the design of the two parliaments, or the two nations, at the time when the act of union was enacted; and which, I think is the true one: and it is this:

I BELIEVE

I BELIEVE it will be admitted, that in all *pacta conventa*, or union treaties, those conditions which are previously insisted upon by either of the contracting parties in its own favour, and in which the interest of the others is not involved; though they are ratified in ever so solemn a manner, are nevertheless alterable, with the free consent of that party who is alone interested therein. This is perfectly consonant to reason, and to the nature of such solemn pactions. Indeed, no conditions can be made so unalterable, that they cannot be reversed in the case which is here supposed; that is, where the only party interested in the condition, and who insisted upon it for his own behoof, releases the obligation, and consents to have it altered. And if this principle be allowed, the propriety of the application of it to the present case will appear, if we consider, that the union between England and Scotland, though an incorporating union in many, was not so in all respects; and particularly that in their ecclesiastical capacities, or with regard to their respective churches, the two nations, who were the original contracting parties; still continue separate bodies: I say, the two nations were the original contracting parties; for this should be carefully observed, that, strictly speaking, the two parliaments were not the contracting parties, but the two nations; for whom, and on whose behoof, the parliaments were only agents, or plenipotentiaries, executing an express or implied trust. And if so, either of the two churches, or nations, may authorize an alteration of any condition stipulated merely in its own favour, and in which the other hath no interest; that is, the English or the Scottish nation or church, may recede from the condition demanded and enacted in its own favour, even though most solemnly declared to be immutable. And on this footing, I mean on the free consent of the party interested therein, the parliament of Great-Britain may make the alterations in question.

INDEED, you tell us, that " without dissolving the union,
" you do not see how the sense of either nation could now be
" se-

" separately taken;" (that is) " how the Scots Peers or Com-
" moners could be prevented from voting either for or againſt
" the repeal of the acts of uniformity, in caſe it were moved in
" either houſe†." And I admit, that as the two parliaments are
now ſunk into the one parliament of Great Britain, the ſenſe of
the two nations cannot be ſeparately taken in parliament. But
if the ſenſe of the two churches, or nations, in their ſeparate eccleſiaſtical capacity, may be known, that will be a ſufficient
foundation for the parliament to proceed upon. For inſtance,
if any alterations were requeſted of the parliament by the generality of either of the two churches or nations; or, if, upon a
motion in parliament for ſuch alterations, and ſuch motion being ſufficiently known, they were not in a reaſonable time petitioned againſt by any conſiderable number, the parliament
might preſume a general conſent, and muſt form their judgment of this from the notoriety of the fact.

And this is the footing upon which, I think, the caſe ſhould
be put; and not merely upon a competent authority in the
Britiſh parliament to make alterations in the two churches.
And I am of this opinion, becauſe the parliament of Great-Britain is to be conſidered as *guardian*, or in *truſt*, for both churches;
and therefore cannot have any *authority*, that is, *right*, inherent
in itſelf (for *nemo poteſt, quod non jure poteſt*) to diſpenſe with the
conditions of the union, which were previouſly declared to be
unalterable, *in thoſe particular reſpects in which the two nations
ſtill continue ſeparate bodies;* here, I think, nothing but the conſent, expreſſed or implied, of each of theſe bodies, as to the condition ſtipulated in its own favour, can be ſufficient warrant for
an alteration‡.

L ET

† Reply to Dr. Prieſtley, p. 43.

‡ The learned Commentator obſerves (Comment. vol. i. p. 98. note) that
" ſuch an incorporate union" as that between England and Scotland, " is well
" diſtinguiſhed by a very learned prelate from a *fœderate alliance*, where ſuch
" an infringement" of it, as making alterations in either of the churches,
" would certainly reſcind the compact." Now it happens, that England and
Scotland,

LET this be illuftrated by the cafe of the Diffidents in Poland: Can it be thought, that there was an authority in the Polifh diet to vacate the folemn *pacta conventa*, and the rights and privileges of the Diffidents grounded upon them? I apprehend, the Diffidents difallow, and proteft againft, fuch right or authority in the diet; and, I think, with reafon; but they would have no fuch reafon to complain of any infraction of the original fettlement, if no alterations had been made but at their own requeft, or with their own free confent.

ON the whole, this ftate of the queftion appears to me to be the only one that is confiftent with the general nature of government as a truft*, with the facred regard due to fuch *pacta conventa*,

Scotland, in their ecclefiaftical capacities, are not *incorporated*, but only in a *fœderate alliance*; and therefore, by his own argument, the parliament can have no right to make alterations in either of the two churches, *without its confent*; fince the compact would be thereby refcinded: but with fuch confent, it certainly may; volenti non fit injuria.

* The learned author obferves, that " the bare idea of a ftate without a " power fomewhere vefted to alter every part of its laws, is the height of political abfurdity." (Comment. vol. i. p. 97, 98. note. A pofition, which I apprehend, ought to be, in fome meafure, explained and limited. For, if it refers to thofe particular regulations, which take place in confequence of immemorial cuftom, or are enacted by pofitive ftatute, and at the fame time are fubordinate to the fundamental conftitution, from which the legiflature itfelf derives its authority; it is admitted to be within the power or truft vefted in the legiflature to alter thefe pro re nata, as the good of the fociety may require. But this power, or authority of the legiflature to make alterations cannot be fuppofed to extend to the infringement of thofe effential rights and privileges, which are referved to the members of a free ftate at large, as their undoubted birthright and unalienable property. I fay, in every free ftate there are fome liberties and privileges, which the fociety have not given out of their own hands to their governors, not even to the legiflature: and to fuppofe the contrary (if I may be allowed the expreffion) would be the height of political abfurdity; for it is faying, that a ftate is free and not free at the fame time; or, which is the fame thing, that its members are poffeffed of liberties, of all which they

may

conventa, as the act of union, and with the rights thereby referved to each of the two churches; and, on thofe accounts, to
be much preferable to acknowledging on the one hand, a power
in the parliament to difpenfe with fuch folemn conditions, when,
and as far as, *they* fhall think theie is fufficient ground for it;
or to holding, on the other hand, fuch conditions to be unalterable, whatever change of circumftances may render an alteration, in the general opinion, expedient and neceffary.

I N fhort, this argument, drawn from the immutability of the
church in confequence of the act of union, between the two
nations, feems to me to be an ufeful engine to be played off by
thofe who are averfe to any alterations; but I believe, (I fpeak
only

may be divefted at the will of the legiflature; that is, they enjoy them during
pleafure, but can claim no property in them.

In a word, nothing is more certain than that government, in the general nature of it, is a truft in behalf of the people. And there cannot be a
maxim, in my opinion, more ill grounded, than that there muft be an *arbitrary* power lodged fomewhere in every government. If this were true, the
different kinds of government in the world would be more alike, and on a level, than they are generally fuppofed to be. In our own government in particular, though no one thinks with more refpect of the powers which the conftitution hath vefted in every branch of the legiflature; yet I muft be excufed
in faying, what is ftrictly true, that the whole legiflature is fo far from having
an *abfolute power,* that it'hath not *any power* in feveral cafes that might be mentioned. For inftance, their authority does not extend to making the Houfe of
Commons perpetual, or giving that Houfe a power to fill up their own vacancies; the Houfe of Commons being the reprefentatives of all the Commons of
England, and in that capacity only a branch of the legiflature; and if they
concur in deftroying the foundation on which they themfelves ftand; if they
annihilate the rights of their conftituents, and claim a fhare in the legiflature
upon any other footing, than that upon which the conftitution hath given it to
them; they fubvert the very truft under which alone they act, and thereby forfeit all their authority. In fhort, they cannot difpenfe with any of thofe effential rights of the people, refpecting their liberties, properties, or lives, the prefervation of which ought to be the great object of government in general, as it
is of our conftitution in particular. See an excellent paffage to this purpofe in
Dr. Hutchefon's Syftem of Moral Philofophy, book 3. chap. 7. vol. 2. p. 267.
at the beginning.

only in general,) would not have much ftrefs laid upon it by thofe who are inclined to them.

HOWEVER, if it be fo, that the act of union renders every tittle and iota of the church conftitution and liturgy immutable; this confideration furnifhes the ftrongeft argument for *their* feparating entirely from the church, who are diffatisfied with the prefent ftate of things in it; inafmuch as this invariable fettlement precludes all hope of future amendment.

IN your anfwer to Dr. Prieftley you fay, you " have neither " leifure, inclination, nor ability to dip yourfelf in theological " controverfy*." Will you fuffer me to remind you, Sir, that, if this be the cafe, you fhould not have *decided* a theological controverfy, on which volumes have been written, in fo fummary a manner as you have done, when you fay, " that many " Diffenters divide from the church upon matters of indiffer- " ence, or in other words, upon no reafon at all†."

To judge of the propriety and truth of this affertion; I firft obferve, that it is not agreed on both fides, that the things in queftion are indifferent. And, I think, whoever reads the Diffenting Gentleman's excellent letters to Mr. White, and confiders his objections to the prefent terms of conformity, muft at leaft admit, that a great deal may be advanced to prove, that the things in debate are not indifferent, but fuch as every judicious, as well as confcientious perfons, may reafonably fcruple to comply with. However, even fuppofing them to be indifferent, I obferve,

THAT the authority by which they are injoined, and made neceffary to the inftitutions of Chrift, and to a participation of Chriftian ordinances, may be reafonably called in queftion. The twentieth article of the church of England afferts, indeed,
" that

---

* Reply to Dr. Prieftley, p. 37, 38.

† Comment. vol. iv. p. 52.

" that the church hath power to decree rites and ceremonies,
" and hath authority in matters of faith." But this the Diffenters muſt be allowed to controvert. They aſſert, that Chriſt
alone hath this authority ; that no power can make that necef-
ſary, which he hath not made neceſſary; and that what is indifferent in its own *nature*, ought to be left indifferent in *practice*,
and ſhould not be bound upon Chriſt's ſubjects either by civil or
eccleſiaſtical laws; neither of which can, in this caſe, be of any
validity, as being both alike of human origin.

That " all things ſhould be done decently and in order*,"
they admit ; and in the ſenſe of the apoſtle Paul, they aſſert
with as much zeal as any other perſons. But they think, there
is a manifeſt difference between circumſtances of natural decency and order, which are neceſſary to be agreed upon and obſerved, in order to the performance of any divine worſhip at all;
and ſuch rites and ceremonies, ſuch additions to divine inſtitu-
tions, as are not at all neceſſary, in the reaſon of the thing, or
by any law of Chriſt; but only injoined by a human, that is, in
this caſe, incompetent authority. " A power in the church to
" decree rites and ceremonies, and authority in matters of faith",
is a principle ſo extenſive in its influence, that under the ſhadow
of it, have grown up all the enormous innovations and ſuperſti-
tions of the church of Rome† : And if Diſſenters ſhould diſco-

D d ver

* 1 Cor. xiv. 40.

† The following obſervations of Dr. Prieſtley, upon this head, in his View
of the principles and conduct of the Proteſtant Diſſenters, p. 59, are very ſen-
fible. " It ſhould be conſidered," ſaith he, " that a *power of decreeing rites and*
" *ceremonies*, is a power abſolutely indefinite, and of the very ſame kind with
" thoſe claims, which, in things of a civil nature, always give the greateſt a-
" larm. A tax of a penny is a trifle ; but a power of impoſing that tax is never
" conſidered as a trifle, becauſe it may imply abſolute ſervitude in all who ſubmit
" to it. In like manner the enjoining of the poſture of kneeling at the Lord's
" Supper is not a thing worth diſputing about in itſelf, but the authority of
" enjoining it *is*; becauſe it is, in fact, a power of making the Chriſtian reli-
" gion as burdenſome as the Jewiſh, and a power that hath actually been car-
" ried to that length in the church of Rome. Nor do we ſee any conſiſtence
" in

ver any averfion to giving countenance to fuch a principle, and
its genuine confequences, excufe me, Sir, if I think, they are
more than pardonable in fo doing, and fhould not have been reprefented as acting upon no reafon at all.   I am, Sir, &c.

" in the church of England rejecting the authority of Rome in thefe things,
" and impofing her own upon us."———

Again, p. 66. " Our anceftors, the old puritans, had the fame merit in op-
" pofing the impofition of the furplice, that Hampden had in oppofing the
" levying of fhip-money.   In neither cafe was it the thing itfelf they objected
" to, fo much as the authority that enjoined it, and the danger of the prece-
" dent.   And it appears to us, that the man who is as tenacious of his *religious*
" as he is of his *civil liberty*, will oppofe them both with equal firmnefs.

" All the difference then, in the conduct of men who equally value their li-
" berty, will be in the *time* and *manner* of oppofing thefe incroachments upon
" it.   The man of a ftrong and enlarged mind will always oppofe thefe things
" in the beginning, when only the refiftance can have any effect ; but the weak,
" the timid, and fhort fighted, will attempt nothing till the chains are rivet-
" ted, and refiftance is too late.   In civil matters, the former will make his
" ftand at the levying of the firft penny by *improper authority* ; and in matters of
" religion, at the firft, tho' the moft trifling ceremony, that is, without reafon,
" made neceffary ; whereas the latter will wait till the load, in both cafes, is
" become too heavy to be either fupported or thrown off."   And by thefe reafons he fupports his remark, p. 58. that " the oppofition made by the firft
" nonconformifts to the injunction of a few ceremonies, was an argument of
" great *ftrength of mind*; and that they acted upon more juft and enlarged views
" of things, than thofe who fuperciliouffy affect to ftigmatize them as men of
" *weak minds*."   Whether the puritans underftood the principles of liberty fo
thoroughly, and acted upon fuch enlarged views of things, as they are here
reprefented to have done, I will not pretend to fay.   Of this, however, I am
very certain, that all thefe obfervations are true and juft as applied to the modern Diffenters.

LETTER VI.

SIR,

I OBSERVE in your Commentaries a very remarkable paſſage, which aſſerts the abſolute neceſſity of excluding all Diſſenters from civil offices, as a thing *eſſential* to the *very idea* of a national eſtabliſhment.—You ſay, " He," (that is the ma-
" giſtrate) is bound to protect the eſtabliſhed church, by admit-
" ting none but its genuine members to offices of truſt and emo-
" lument: for if every ſect was to be indulged in a free com-
" munion of civil employments, the idea of a national eſtabliſh-
" ment would at once be deſtroyed, and the Epiſcopal church
" would be no longer the church of England*." That is ex-
traordinary indeed! Some have talked of the ſecurity which may ariſe to the church from this excluſive privilege; and you intimate it yourſelf, when you ſay, it is the magiſtrate's duty to *protect* the church by this method. Others have inſiſted up-
on I know not what kind of alliance or contract, in which this excluſive privilege was ſtipulated for the church. But that the church would loſe her *exiſtence* and *eſſence* without it, ſeems to be very ſtrange. What! cannot the church be eſtabliſhed in the poſſeſſion and enjoyment of her own peculiar temporalities, her tythes, prebends, canonries, archdeaconries, deanries, and biſhopricks by law, unleſs ſhe engroſs all civil as well as eccleſiaſtical offices to herſelf? Can there be no legal eſtabliſhment of, and no legal and national proviſion made for, a *church*, unleſs all the offices and emoluments of the *ſtate* are annexed to it? Was there no national church properly eſtabliſhed by the law in England till the teſt-act was enacted, which appropriated all civil offices to perſons of her communion, in the reign of Charles the

D d 2

Second?

* Comment. vol. iv. p. 53.

Second ? And is there none now in Scotland, where civil offices are not confined to the Prefbyterians, who have been hitherto fuppofed to be the ecclefiaftical eftablifhment in that country? Is there, I fay, no fuch eftablifhment in Scotland? is the very idea of it deftroyed, and the Prefbyterian church no longer the eftablifhed church of that part of the united kingdom? I apprehend this will hardly be affirmed ; and if fo, an exclufive right to civil offices cannot be effential to the very idea of a church-eftablifhment*.

INDEED, I would not willingly fuppofe any thing fo unjuft can be effential to an ecclefiaftical eftablifhment. For certainly good fubjects, if they are by law deprived of the capacity of ferving their king and country, in thofe offices for which they are qualified, and which poffibly they might otherwife obtain, are injured by fuch exclufion. I do not fay, that the actual poffeffion of civil offices is the right of any fubject ; but a capacity of being elected or appointed to them, is the right of every good fubject ; and being deprived of that capacity is plainly an injury ; and every injury done a man merely for his religion, and not on a civil account, is, in my opinion, a degree of perfecution: I know no other definition of perfecution, than that it is an injury

* The paragraph, which gave occafion to the preceding remarks, is greatly altered in the new edition: it now runs thus: " He," that is the magiftrate, " is bound to protect the eftablifhed church: and, if this *can be better effected* by " admitting none but its genuine members to offices of truft and emolument, " he is certainly *at liberty fo to do* ; the difpofal of offices being matter of favour " and difcretion." He is bound to protect the eftablifhed church, faith the learned Commentator : the truth is, he is bound to protect all good fubjects, of every religious perfuafion ; but none of any perfuafion, at the expence of all the reft, and by encroaching on their undoubted rights, amongft which we are to reckon, though not the *actual poffeffion* of offices, yet certainly a *capacity* of being appointed to them; which is not a " matter of favour and difcretion ;" for every good fubject hath a natural right, not to be profcribed as unworthy of the public confidence. Whether fufficient reafon can be affigned, for infringing this right in regard to Proteftant Diffenters, is confidered in the fubfequent part of this letter.

jury inflicted on a perfon for his religious princip'es or profeffion only.

A TEST-LAW, appropriating all civil offices to the members
of the church, hath been vindicated, even on fuppofition of its
being contrary to the law of nature, by inftances of municipal
laws, made, in direct oppofition to the law of nature, for the
public good*. But in fuch cafes, the advantage to the public
ought

---

* See the Bifhop of Glouceficr's Alliance between Church and State, p. 320.
edit. 4.

In Mr. Fofter's late vifitation fermon (preached at Chelmsford May 22,
1770) entitled, " The eftablifhment of the church of England defended upon
" the principles of religious liberty." I find the ftrefs of the argument for an
eftablifhment, together with an exclufion of all but its own members from civil
offices, laid upon the following fentiments : " What fecurity," faith the author, " doth the eftablifhment require for its prefervation and defence ?" To
which he anfwers, " It only doth not put arms into the hands of its enemies.
" It requires only, that thofe who profefs to diffent from its doctrines fhould be
" excluded from offices of power and influence in the government, that is, they
" are kept out of fituations which would render their opinions dangerous to
" that mode of religion which the conftitution hath adopted and made its
" own." p. 13. " For every ftate, as well as every individual," he faith,
" hath a right to judge for itfelf in matters of religion, or to choofe its own
" religion." p. 14. With refpect to what is here advanced, as the foundation of the whole fuperftructure, that " every ftate hath a right to chufe its own
" religion as well as every individual ;" I obferve, that the ground of this inference in thefe two cafes, is very different. The reafon, upon which every
individual hath a right to choofe his own religion, is, becaufe religion is the
refult of perfonal conviction, and the rewards of it fought and obtained, not
by collective bodies, but by individuals, as the fruit of their own perfonal character and conduct. In the cafe of a ftate, or civil fociety, choofing a particular
religion, thofe grounds of election which I have mentioned can have no place :
the fole intereft which a civil fociety can have in this matter, is its promoting the
good order of the community; and this is effectually provided for by the magiftrates encouraging the general principles of religion and morality which prevail amongft all parties, and which are by no means peculiar to any peculiar
fyftem or mode of worfhip.

Again, I obferve, that by " the ftate's choofing its own religion," the author

ought to be very apparent, and of confiderable moment; and even then, is rather to be confidered as an *excufe* for fuch deviations

thor means, choofing a religion in order to its being eftablifhed, with exclufion of all but its own members from civil offices and emoluments. A very different cafe from that perfonal choice, which every individual makes of a religion for himfelf. Had he meant no more than that the feveral members of the ftate, or the magiftrates and perfons in office, have a right, as individuals, to judge for themfelves as much as any other members of the community; the obfervation would have been true, but nothing to the purpofe. But the right of an individual to choofe the religion which he is to profefs and practife, and the right of a ftate to choofe the religion which it is to eftablifh, and on the profeffors of which it is to beftow an exclufive title to its civil offices, are things widely different; particularly in this refpect, that the former, the right of an individual to choofe his own religion, interferes in no refpect with the rights of any other perfon; whereas the latter, the right claimed by a ftate firft to choofe, and then to eftablifh with an exclufive teft, a particular religion, does incroach upon the rights of others, by laying upon them an incapacity of enjoying thofe privileges and advantages to which, in common with their fellow fubjects, they have a natural claim.

However, " fuch an eftablifhment, with exclufion of all but its own mem-
" bers from civil offices," the author faith, " is a meafure neceffary to be a-
" dopted, in order to prevent the ill effects of the peculiar opinions of others,
" firft upon their own paffions, and in confequence upon the peace and order
" of that fociety, which having chofen and eftablifhed a different mode of
" religion, muft have the fame right to preferve what it hath thus eftablifhed,
" that it hath to preferve itfelf." Upon this I would obferve, that the defence and prefervation of fociety in general, and all its members, from the ill effects of the peculiar opinions of the different fects of which it confifts; that is, from violence (for the weapons of reafon and argument, he immediately adds, are left untouched in their hands) I fay, the defence and prefervation of all the members of fociety are abundantly provided for, if the magiftrate, as confervator of the public peace, interpofe to prevent their perfecuting, or any way molefting each other. To confider, as the author does, perfons of different religious perfuafions as " enemies" when he reprefents the fecurity of a religious eftablifhment to be that " it only doth not put arms into the hands of its enemies," is, I think, no very liberal notion. But if they are fo, I do not fee but the influence and authority of the magiftrate over the whole community may controul that enmity, and keep it within proper bounds; nor can I think, that partiality to any one fect, taking it into his peculiar good graces to the exclufion of all the reft, will be likely to affuage that enmity; it rather feems

calculated

tions from the law of nature, or general principles of equity, in the prefent imperfect ftate of fociety, than as a full and abfo-lute

calculated to enflame it, to create no fmall jealoufy in thofe who have the mono-poly of civil offices and emoluments, and no lefs envy in thofe who are deprived of them. It is very obfervable, that a fpirit of domination and contention a-rofe in the Chriftian church in proportion to the increafe of the emoluments and power of its ecclefiaftics; and that till Chriftianity was incorporated with the ftate or civil conftitution, in the time of Conftantine, there were no ex-amples of the debates and divifions among Chriftians, iffuing in actual perfecu-tion of each other, on account of difference in religious fentiment; but no foon-ner were wordly emoluments connected with the profeffion of it, and either be-ftowed by the court, or obtained by the fuffrages of the people, than the great ftruggle was, who fhould poffefs them exclufively; and the feveral parties, as the moft effectual means of annihilating each others pretenfions, fell to hereti-cating, anathematizing, and perfecuting one another. But if the Emperor had favoured all alike, had either diftributed temporal emoluments among them equally, or rather had conferred them upon none, I apprehend the peace of the church and the world would not have been fo fcandaloufly violated, as it hath been, by contentions for riches and power among the feveral Chriftian fects, and efpecially their refpective ecclefiaftics, and by their mutual perfecuti-ons and violence. The large temporalities with which the church was foon endowed, and the principality which was at length beftowed on the pope raif-ed the church of Rome, and the whole fabrick of popery, to the enormous height to which they afterwards arrived. And from popery the Proteftants brought with them, and retained among them after the reformation, an un-happy attachment to the fhackles of human authority, and of human inventi-ons and definitions; and as the natural confequence, a rigid, intolerant fpirit. In a word, if we examine the matter clofely, we fhall find, that human inven-tions in divine worfhip, human definitions of faith, and the exclufive enjoyment of wordly emoluments, as the reward of adhering to a particular fyftem which happens to be eftablifhed; thefe are the things, which have produced whate-ver there is of an hoftile fpirit amongft the various fects of religionifts, and cre-ated all that neceffity (if there be any) of mutual felf-defence on which the au-thor fo much enlarges. Abolifh human inventions, and human definitions, which human pride for the credit of the refpective parties is always concerned to fupport, and remove that monopoly of worldly emoluments for which this author pleads fo ftrenuoufly; and, religion being no longer a matter of fecular intereft, the fpeculative differences concerning it will hardly excite more con-tention than different fchemes of philofophy; and its different modes, than different manners and cuftoms in civil life. Men will eafily apprehend, as foon

lute *juftification* of them. However, fhould an excluſion of good ſubjects from civil offices on a religious account appear, upon examination,

ſoon as their ambitious and intereſted views ceaſe to miſlead their judgments, that the eſſence of religion, which lies in a few general principles, and in good affections and habits, may very well conſiſt with an almoſt infinite variety of ſpeculative opinions, and external modes and forms; and unity of affection will eſtabliſh that peace and tranquillity in the chriſtian church, which by fruitleſs endeavours after uniformity of ſentiment and practice, hath been in great meaſure, I had almoſt ſaid, wholly baniſhed from it. Nor can I think, that where men live together in peace and harmony, a diverſity of religious ſentimen ts and practices is in itſelf an evil, or any way prejudicial to ſociety. I am ſure, if it be, ſome more effectual meaſures ſhould be taken than have yet been taken, to put an end to that variety of ſentiment which ſtill ſubſiſts amongſt the members of the national church, notwithſtanding they ſubſcribe and uſe the ſame creeds and formularies; nor ſhould that remarkable diverſity between the mode of worſhip in pariſh churches and cathedrals, be any longer permitted. Indeed, for the ſame reaſon no toleration ſhould be allowed ; becauſe, under a toleration, there will perhaps be as great a variety of religious ſentiments and modes, as if there were no eſtabliſhment at all: and perhaps a greater ; for as Biſhop Stillingfleet ſomewhere obſerves, "whatever limits, divides;" excluſive eſtabliſhments, founded upon human creeds and human canons, prevent the ſcripture from being regarded as the only rule of faith and order, and the only center of union. It is the advancing of theſe into the room of the ſcriptures, which hath been the grand ſource of all the ſects, and all the ſharp contentions among them, which have ever diſgraced and divided the Chriſtian church. And can we then reaſonably aſſert the neceſſity of excluſive eſtabliſhments, as a cure for the evils which they themſelves have cauſed ?—Whatever uniformity hath been produced by them in reſpect to human creeds and forms, (in which for my part I can ſee no advantage) they have often produced likewiſe, either a great degree of bigotry where the compliance hath been ſincere, or of hypocriſy, where, as hath been frequently the caſe, men have been induced to profeſs and practiſe what they diſapprove and condemn.

To the objection, that upon the principles of this ſermon, " a ſtate hath a " right to eſtabliſh and defend a falſe religion as well as the true one,—the " Koran, the Viedam, and every other the moſt abſurd, and even impious ſyſ" tem of doctrine and worſhip ;" the author replies, that he " acknowledges " the conſequence," p. 15. " But then doth not the ſame objection," ſaith he, " lie equally againſt the right of an individual to chooſe his religion, and " defend his choice ? This right," he adds, " cannot be completely exerciſed " in either caſe, but at the hazard of chooſing a falſe religion." But there is
this

examination, not to be at all for the public good, then the very foundation of this defence (such as it is) of an exclusive test is entirely destroyed. The question therefore is, What is that public good arising from a test law, and the exclusion of good subjects from civil offices, which overbalances the right that every such subject hath, on principles of reason and equity, to a capacity of being appointed to such offices?

E e

Upon

this essential difference in the two cases, that the individual who chooses a false religion, seldom doth any prejudice by that wrong choice to any but himself : whereas a state choosing, and establishing a false religion, with an exclusive right of civil employments (which amounts not only to defence, but to encouragement) lays such inducements thereby in the way of all its subjects to embrace a false religion, as few comparatively are able to withstand; and entails likewise this false religion on posterity, by laws, which, while there are great worldly emoluments annexed to the observance of them, will not easily be repealed or altered. And thus such motives as are with the generality irresistible, to the embracing of a false religion, are established and perpetuated, to the entire and perpetual exclusion perhaps of the true religion. And this consequence is the more likely to follow, if, as the author asserts, " every state must have " a right to require, that those who are appointed to the duty of public in- " struction by the state—shall instruct the people in those doctrines which it " hath established, and no other." p. 17. But none of these bad consequences follow from that personal choice, which an individual makes of a false religion. And it is surprising, that these two cases should ever be considered as parallel, or that any sensible man, as the author certainly is, should argue from the one to the other. In a word, true religion, as well as true philosophy, is, I think, more likely to prevail and flourish upon the foot of its own intrinsic evidence, than by the interposition of human authority ; which we see, in fact, over the largest part of the world, by far, establishes a false religion, and excludes the true; and indeed nothing else can be expected, when religion depends for its reception and establishment upon princes and politicians, who are too often under the dominion of such maxims and views as are diametrically opposite to its genuine principles and spirit. Whereas if the obstacles, every where raised by human authority to the entrance and prevalence of true religion, were removed ; and this heavenly guest suffered to recommend herself to all by the lustre of her native charms, and the evidence of her divine original ; I believe, the event would be a wonderful demonstration of the truth of that old adage : Magna est veritas, et prævalebit.

Upon the moſt general view of this point, it cannot appear to be for the good of the *magiſtrate*, or the *ſtate*, to be deprived of the power of availing itſelf of *the ſervices of any good ſubjeƐts*. It is, ſurely, for the advantage of the ſtate, that none ſhould be rendered incapable of civil employments but thoſe whoſe affections or principles render them ſuſpected to the civil government; that is, who do not give proper teſtimony of their being good ſubjects: for the more numerous the perſons are who are capable of ſuch appointments, the greater is the probability of a proper choice, provided thoſe who make it diſcharge their duty to the public with fidelity and judgment.

It may be alledged, perhaps, that the magiſtrate hath wiſely conſented to grant the church this excluſive privilege in order to obtain the *greater good* of the ſpecial ſervices of the church, in inforcing the duties of imperfect obligation, ſuch as gratitude, hoſpitality, generoſity, &c. which human laws cannot effectually inforce; and of an alliance with her, and a right by grant from the church to a ſupremacy over her, and to the power of appointing her miniſters and officers.

With regard to the ſervice which the church does the ſtate, by inforcing the duties of imperfect obligation, and by which ſhe is ſuppoſed to merit, in part, her excluſive privilege to civil offices; I obſerve, that if this be a reaſon for allowing capacity of civil employments to good ſubjects of any one religious perſuaſion, it is a valid reaſon for extending it to good ſubjects of all religious perſuaſion, and in particular, to the Proteſtant Diſſenters. For, in their religious aſſemblies, theſe virtues are inculcated, perhaps with as good effect, and with as much utility to ſociety, as amongſt Chriſtians of any other denomination. Upon this ſtate of the caſe, therefore, no ſufficient cauſe can be aſſigned, why they ſhould be excluded from a reaſonable and proportionable ſhare of the favour of the ſtate.

As

A s for the church's giving up her independence and fupre-macy, and the appointment of her officers or minifters, to the ftate; it may be proper to enquire, to what this condefcenfion, on the part of the church, may be fuppofed to amount. And here it fhould be remarked, that the ftate hath a right to a fupre-macy over all perfons, whether clergy or laity, of every religi-ous perfuafion, within her dominions; a right, founded in the nature of civil government, independent of any grant from the church; and in this fenfe, the church could confer upon the ftate no fupremacy which it had not before; fhe could not give it any new fubjects, or increafe its civil power.

The meaning, therefore, of this grant of fupremacy muft be, that the church admitted the ftate to a fupremacy in caufes ecclefiaftical, and to the appointment of her church officers; in lieu of which fhe claims an exclufive right to the poffeffion of civil offices. And thefe, it is faid, are the terms of the grand alliance between the church and ftate, upon which is grounded the equity of a teft-law, excluding all from the poffeffion of ci-vil offices, except the members of the eftablifhed church. But it doth not appear, that any fuch terms were ever concerted and agreed between the church and the ftate; it appears, on the contrary, that no fuch *can be* fuppofed or *implied*, on any fair and equitable principles. For, all the peculiar temporalities of the church being folely the grant of the ftate, and her particu-lar form and conftitution being eftablifhed by its laws, the go-vernment of the church of courfe belonged to that authority which formed and endowed it; and when the ftate appoints the minifters and officers of the church, fhe doth it upon this foot-ing, that the provifion made for their fupport is her donation and eftablifhment. Now, on this ground, the ftate was in undif-puted poffeffion of all the power of church-government, and of the appointment of church-officers, which fhe at prefent en-joys, before any teft was appointed, or nonconformifts were by law excluded from civil offices. This exclufive right, therefore, now claimed by the church, to the offices of the state, could be no part, no term, no condition, of the supposed *original* treaty of alliance between the church and state. The claim is entirely *novel*; it is an usurpation upon the state, an attempt to introduce a new term or condition into the original contract, which ought therefore to be rejected as inadmissible.

If it be said, that the church hath purchased this exclusion of Protestant Dissenters from civil offices, by consenting to a toleration of their religious profession and worship; I observe, that this free enjoyment of their religious liberty was a natural right, of which they were never deprived but with manifest injustice; and the granting of their religious liberty, therefore, or the repairing of one act of injustice, can never be considered as a sufficient reason, or tolerable excuse, for a violation of their civil rights; that is, committing another act of injustice.

If it be further alledged, that the church's exclusive enjoyment of civil offices comes in as a balance to the toleration, as an accession of strength to the church; in order to counterpoise the danger which might accrue to her, were Dissenters admitted to a free enjoyment of civil offices*: (whereas her security before

---

* Thus argues the author of The Alliance, &c. p. 296, 297. and gives himself the credit of being of the same sentiments with King William, whom he stiles, perhaps justly, the best and greatest of our monarchs; applauding his equal conduct in his different stations of Prince of Orange and King of England: which conduct he thus represents. "When King James, a *Papist*, de-
" manded of his son-in-law, with whom he was then on good terms, his ap-
" probation of a *toleration* and *abolition of the test*, the Stadtholder readily con-
" curred with the scheme of a *toleration*, but utterly condemned an *abolition of*
" *the test* When afterwards he became King of a free people, the *Protestant* Dif-
" senters, likewise, in their turn, demanded both. His conduct was uniformly the same. He gave them a *toleration*, but would not consent to *abolish*
" *the test*." The only fault I find with this account is, that it is not *history*,
but *fable*. The fact is, that when King James asked the Prince's approbation
of the abolition of the test, he meant, and the Prince understood him to mean,
a repeal of it as to the *Papists*, as well as the Protestant Dissenters; and it was
with

before the toleration confifted in this, that every man, whether in or out of office, was by law confidered as a member of the church,

with refpect to the former, the Prince refufed his approbation. When afterwards he became King of England, he was fo far from refufing the *Proteftant Diffenters* the repeal of the teft as to *them*, that he had the defign very much at heart ; he fignified it in council, and in a fpeech on the occafion, earneftly recommended it to his parliament, that while he " doubted not they would fuf- " ficiently provide againft Papifts, they would leave room for the admiffion of " all Proteftants that were willing and able to ferve :" adding, " This con- " junction in my fervice will tend to the better uniting you amongft yourfelves, " and the ftrengthening you againft your common adverfaries." And accordingly, when a claufe for repealing the teft as to Proteftant Diffenters, which was inferted in the bill for fettling the oaths, was rejected ; the King, being refolved to purfue his defign, procured another claufe to be propofed to be inferted in the fame bill, in order to qualify all perfons for places, who, within a year before or after their admiffion into them, had received the facrament, either according to the ufage of the church of England, or *in any other Proteftant congregation :* which claufe was alfo rejected, notwithftanding the influence of the court in its favour. See Tindal's continuation of Rapin, vol. i. p. 120, —123. edit. 8vo. 1758. The conduct of the Prince and the King was equal and confiftent; but, as we have feen, totally different from the ideas of this author.

It fhould be obferved, that the original defign of the teft was, not to exclude the Proteftant Diffenters, but the Papifts. See Burnet's Hiftory of his own Times, vol. i. p. 347——352. firft edit. It was brought in by the patriots in the reign of Charles the Second, under their apprehenfions of Popery and a popifh fucceffor ; and is ftiled, an " Act for preventing dangers which " may happen from Popifh Recufants ;" and the fame is faid to be its defign in the preamble. And when, during the debate in the Houfe of Commons, it was obferved, that it was drawn in fuch a manner as to comprehend the Proteftant Diffenters, the court-party endeavoured to avail themfelves of that circumftance in order to defeat the bill. But the diffenting members difappointed them, by declaring, that they had rather confide in the juftice and generofity of parliament to pafs fome future bill in their favour, than be the occafion of retarding or defeating the fecurity, which the prefent bill was calculated to afford to the liberties of their country. And this genuine patriotifm facilitated the paffing of a bill then depending in the Commons, for their relief from the penal laws; (See Grey's Parliamentary Debates, vol. ii. p. 36. 38, 85.) which being fent up to the Lords, and coming down with fome amendments; whilft the

church, and indifpenfably obliged to conformity): I fay, fhould be this alledged, it will come under confideration, when we examine

the Commons were debating thofe amendments, the parliament was fuddenly prorogued through the refentment of the court, and the intended favour to the Diffenters prevented. See Grey's Parliamentary Debates, vol. ii. p. 180. And when afterwards, in the year 1680, a bill in favour of the Diffenters, repealing the 35 Eliz. c. 1. paffed both Houfes, and lay ready for the royal affent, the court ventured upon a very extraordinary expedient; the clerk of the crown was ordered to convey away the bill; and, accordingly it was never afterwards to be found. Burnet, ubi fupra, p. 494, 495.

In the fame feffion, on the 16th of December, a bill was brought into the Commons, " for uniting his majefty's Proteftant fubjects to the church of Eng-" land," (See the Journal) which repealed the declaration of affent and confent, and fome other particulars ufually objected to by the Diffenters. See Grey's Parliamentary Debates, vol. viii. p. 201. And whereas, it was apprehended this bill might not comprehend all the Diffenters within the pale of the church, there was another bill brought in at the fame time " for exempting his majefty's Proteftant fubjects diffenting from " the church of England, from the penalties of certain laws;" which is the title of the prefent toleration act. Both thefe bills were read a fecond time; the former the 21ft, and the latter the 24th of December; and referred to the fame committee. But though the difpofition of the parliament was thus favourable to the Diffenters, it hath been afferted by fome writers in favour of the Teft, and I believe, generally taken for granted, that the defign was to exempt Diffenters only from the penal laws, and not from thofe laws which excluded them from offices. But whoever confults the Journals will find, that on the 24th of December in the fame feffion, a bill was ordered into the Commons to repeal the Act 13 Car. 2. ftat 2. c 1. entitled, " An act for the well go-" verning and regulating of Corporations;" which had been made on purpofe to exclude Diffenters from Corporation offices. On the 6th of January this bill was read a fecond time, and referred to a felect Committee. And in the mean time, on the 3d of January, a bill came down from the Lords, entitled, " An " Act for diftinguifhing Proteftant Diffenters from Popifh Recufants." I have no doubt, that this bill was defigned to exempt Proteftant Diffenters from the Teft-act; which was profeffedly made to prevent dangers which may happen from Popifh Recufants, and there are no other perfons exprefsly mentioned in the act to whom it can refer. The order of the Houfe of Lords (as I find by the Journal) to the Committee concerning Proteftant Diffenters, on the 29th of November, is, " that they prepare a bill for explaining fuch laws, as were in-
" tended

mine the nature of the *security* which the *church* derives from an exclufive teſt. For if this plea of public good, as the bafis of

" tended only againſt Popiſh Recufants, and are put in execution againſt Pro-" teſtant Diſſenters, to their great grievance;" without any direction, either then or afterwards, as far as I can find, for inferting a claufe to except the Teſt-act; a ſtep which feems to have been very requifite, if the Teſt-act was not to be affected by this bill; for that act was exactly in the fame predican e it with the other laws againſt Popiſh Recufants; it mentioned them only, and yet by conſtruction was capable of being extended, and accordingly was extended, to Proteſtant Diſſenters. Befides, if the bill had been intended to have no further influence and operation than merely upon the old penal laws againſt Popiſh Re-cufants, and not upon the Teſt-act, it would have been entirely needlefs ; the fecurity of the Diſſenters from thofe laws being effectually provided for by the bill at that time depending in the Commons for exempting his majeſty's Pro-teſtant fubjects, diſſenting from the church of England, from the penalties of certain laws ; which, as appears from Grey's Parliamentary Debates, was de-figned to procure the Diſſenters the full liberty of their religious profeſſion, free from the moleſtation of penal laws. The bill, therefore, for diſtinguiſhing Pro-teſtant Diſſenters from Popiſh Recufants, I am perfuaded, was defigned to com-prehend a virtual repeal of the Teſt as to Proteſtant Diſſenters ; and the rather, fince, underſtood in this latitude, it feems a proper counterpart to the bill for the exprefs repeal of the Corporation-act, at that time depending in the Com-mons: and indeed the Teſt-act could no way be repealed, with refpect to Pro-teſtant Diſſenters, fo properly, as by diſtinguiſhing between them and Popiſh Recufants; the act being defigned to remain in force, with refpect to the latter, againſt whom it was originally intended. It is, I think, remarkable, that, as far as appears, there was no divifion upon any one of the bills which I have mentioned. Neverthelefs they were all defeated by the fudden prorogation of the parliament on the 10th of January, but four days after the laſt bill was fent down from the Lords; the Commons being apprized of the king's intention on-ly time enough to pafs in hafte a few votes on the ſtate of the nation ; the laſt of which is in thefe words : " That it is the opinion of this Houfe, That the " profecution of Proteſtant Diſſenters upon the penal laws, is at this time grie-" vous to the fubject, a weakening of the Proteſtant intereſt, an encourage-" ment to Popery, and dangerous to the peace of the kingdom." The par-liament was foon after diſſolved by proclamation. Thus the continuance of the Teſt-act, to the prefent time, and the exclufion of the Diſſenters from all public offices, is the reward they enjoy for their generous and difintereſted patriotifm.

It

of an exclusive test, does not relate to the good of the state, perhaps it may be the good of the church.

A N D, doubtless, it is for *her good*, in one sense; namely, for her *emolument*, that her members only should enjoy civil offices. But, provided this claim does not appear to be *just* as well as profitable, it would be an ill compliment to the church to suppose her capable of continuing and maintaining it. And where, indeed, *is the equity* of her demanding, besides that ample provision which is made for her support by law, and to which the whole nation contributes, an exclusion of all who are not in her communion from the opportunity of serving their king and country, and enjoying the honours or emoluments of such services? Where is the equity, I say, that instead of being satisfied, not merely with her own peculiar revenues, but with that share of civil offices and emoluments which would fall to the members of

It may be further observed, that this particular test, receiving the sacrament according to the rites of the church of England, as it was designed, so it was calculated, to exclude the Papists, rather than the Protestant Dissenters; for the former, it was apprehended, would not comply with the established church in this office above all others; and to increase the difficulty on their part, they were expressly required, besides the oaths of allegiance and supremacy, to renounce transubstantiation; whereas it was, at that very time, no uncommon thing for Protestant Dissenters, to receive the sacrament occasionally in the church of England, in order to express their charity towards it as a part of the church of Christ. This was the case with Mr. Baxter, Dr. Bates, and others of their leading clergymen, as well as many of their laity. Indeed, after the test was enacted, many of these altogether abstained from this practice; because they would not act upon a suspicious motive, and because they totally disapproved the use of a religious ordinance as a civil test. But this consequence of appointing the sacrament as a test, was not likely to be foreseen at the time the act was enacted. And therefore, I think, we may on the whole infer with reason, that it was not particularly levelled against the Protestant Dissenters. If it had been the design of the legislature, to exclude all from civil offices but those who have a real affection for the constitution and worship of the church, they would doubtless have appointed the test to be, not merely once taking the sacrament at church, but a stated and constant conformity to all its religious services.

of her communion, and which undoubtedly would be by far the largeſt and moſt conſiderable, ſhe muſt poſſeſs an excluſive right to the whole? and where, in reaſon and juſtice, is her title to ſuch a monopoly ? The kingdom of Chriſt is not of this " world;" and religion, much leſs any peculiar form of it, can be no foundation for a claim to all civil offices and emoluments in any country ; becauſe *dominion is not founded upon grace*, nor are the *ſaints of any communion*, as ſuch, entitled to all thoſe good things, which thoſe who are poſſeſſed of dominion have to be‑ ſtow.

Theſe are principles ſo juſt and indiſputable, that ſome of the warmeſt friends of eſtabliſhments and excluſive teſts have been forced to confeſs, that they are neither of them, founded in *truth*, but in *utility;* that when a particular religion is eſta‑ bliſhed by law, and fenced with the ſole and excluſive privilege of enjoying civil offices and emoluments; this is not done on account of its being the *true religion*, but the *religion of the majo‑ rity*; which, as ſuch, is taken into alliance by the ſtate, and ſo eſtabliſhed and privileged for the public good. Provided there‑ fore, it can be ſhewn, that this goodly fabrick no way contri‑ butes to public utility, it cannot any longer be ſupported, but muſt fall to the ground.

As for the ſuppoſition, that it conduces to the utility of the *ſtate*, that I have already conſidered. As for the utility of the *church*, if by that be meant her profit or emolument, ſhe ſhould, as I before obſerved, inſiſt upon no gain but that which is fair and honourable, none to the prejudice of other good ſubjects, where they have a juſt and equitable claim.

But if this public utility is underſtood to refer to the *ſecuri‑ ty* and *protection*, which is apprehended to be afforded to the church, by the excluſion of all others, except the members of her own communion, from civil offices; that is a point which remains now to be conſidered: For you tell us, " that the ma‑ " giſtrate is bound to *protect* the eſtabliſhed church, by admitting " none but is genuine members to offices of truſt and emolument."

The

THE danger of the church, and the ſtrength of that ſecurity which is afforded by a teſt-law, in caſe ſhe be in danger, hath, I think, been greatly magnified. Indeed, her danger ſeems to be a mere chimera. I am perſuaded, the church would be in no danger from the Proteſtant Diſſenters, who have very little diſpoſition to moleſt her; and would have leſs ſtill, if ſhe left them in full poſſeſſion of their civil rights. The removal of any odious mark of diſtinction, and ground of jealouſy and envy as it leaves men more at eaſe, ſo in greater good humour with themſelves and others, and very little diſpoſed to quarrel about modes of faith and modes of worſhip. That is not, indeed, at all the temper of the preſent age; nor is it likely to be ſo of their poſterity, unleſs the ſpirit of perſecution ſhould ariſe in the church or ſtate. That would ſet in motion a certain ſpring and elaſticity there is in human nature, which riſes againſt oppreſſion. But in quiet and peaceable times when principles of moderation and liberty univerſally prevail, this elaſtic ſpring is wholly relaxed. And the more liberal and equitable, therefore, the temper and conduct of the church and ſtate are, towards men of different religious perſuaſions, who are good ſubjects, the leſs danger is there of moleſtation to either. An equitable diſpoſition in the church, to permit all without exception to enjoy in their full extent, their natural rights, would be a much greater ſecurity to her, than any excluſive or even penal laws. For the principles of impartial liberty form the prevailing character of the preſent age, and are, in a manner, univerſal amongſt the Proteſtant Diſſenters. Liberty, religious liberty eſpecially, is their idol; in their attachment to which, for the moſt part, they are more tenacious, than they are in their affection to any peculiar diſtinguiſhing tenets, which divide them from the church, or from one another. And this liberty they would no more violate in others, than be eaſy to ſee it violated in themſelves.*

BUT

* Dr. Burton, (in his Commentariolus Thomæ Secker, Archiep. Cantuar. memoriæ ſacer.) ſpeaking of the oppoſition which hath been made to the ſcheme

of

BUT if any could be found, who were difposed to give the church moleftation, while fhe hath fo vaft a majority in the kingdom,

F f 2

of eftablifhing bifhops in America, exclaims, " Iniqui homines & maligni ! qui " libertatis, quam ipfi fibi arrogant effrænatam, jus aliis a fe diffidentibus " concedi nolunt !" I am not certain whether thefe words refer to the American Prefbyterians and Independents, or to the Englifh Diffenters. Perhaps the Doctor would have no great objection to our underftanding them both of the Americans and Diffenters; for he does not feem to have much complaifance for either. However that be, I may venture to fay of both, that fo far from fhowing themfelves, by their oppofition to this fcheme, to be the enemies, I apprehend, they have fhewn themfelves to be the friends of liberty. When they are convinced, that the fcheme of fending bifhops to America hath not the advancement of ecclefiaftical power in view, and will not be prejudicial to the liberty of chriftians of other perfuafions; when the plan fhall appear to be folely this, not only that the bifhops fhall be invefted with the mere powers of confirmation and ordination, and of regulating their own clergy, but fhall be excluded, by exprefs act of parliament, or by provincial acts previoufly paffed, and folemnly ratified by act of parliament, in fome fuch manner as the acts of fecurity of the two churches, in the union between England and Scotland) from enjoying the leaft degree of temporal power; (always fuppofing, that the fallaries for their fupport fhall be drawn only from thofe who profefs to be of the Epifcopal perfuafion;) then, I apprehend, if I may judge of the Americans by what I have heard of them, and of the Diffenters by thofe with whom I am acquainted, they will be fo far from oppofing, that they will be advocates for fuch a fcheme. And in fo doing they will allow others the very fame liberty which they claim themfelves. For, though they are friends to liberty, they are enemies to temporal power in the hands of ecclefiaftics, prefbyters as well as bifhops. Some things have dropped from the archbifhop, in his letter to Mr. Walpole, which give ground to furmife, that the whole of what is intended, is not fo mild and moderate as his panegyrift fuppofes. " The " propofal is, faith the archbifhop, that the bifhop fhall exercife fuch jurifdic- " tion over the clergy of the church of England in thofe parts, as the late " bifhop of London's commiffaries did, or *fuch as it might be thought proper that* " *any future commiffaries fhould,*" (and who knows what that may be?) " if " this defign were not to take place," p. 2. And to the queftion, " How a- " ny perfons can undertake to promife, that no additional powers fhall hereaf- " ter be propofed and preffed on the colonies, when bifhops have once been " fettled ? he anfwers, that ftrictly fpeaking, nothing of that nature can ever " be promifed in any cafe," p. 6. 7. And he faith, " that there feems no necef-

fity

kingdom, and especially in both Houses of Parliament, (and I cannot see, that the repeal of the test would make any altera-

tion

" fity, that the affair ever should come into parliament; for, as the law now
" stands, suffrag in bishops may be ordained with the king's approbation; and the
" bishop of London may send these, instead of presbyters, for his commissaries,"
p. 21. If the American Presbyterians and Independents, and their friends the
Dissenters in England, are more jealous than they need be of the scheme of
sending bishops to America, it is owing to the evident reluctance there is in the
most moderate patrons of this scheme, to the Episcopal power being laid under
any positive restraint or limitation, and to their expressing a desire of having
that matter left entirely open; as well as to the conduct of the society for propagating the gospel, who expend a great disproportion of their revenues in countries where Christianity is already in a flourishing condition: with what other
view than to proselyte the inhabitants to Episcopacy, it is difficult to say; they
employ a great number of missionaries in the northern colonies, and very few
comparatively in the southern: I say the southern episcopal provinces have been
comparatively neglected, from the time that a few presbyterian or independent
ministers in New-England conformed to the church, and came to England for
orders; to defray the expence of whose settlement, as missionaries in the colonies from whence they came, the society came to a RESOLUTION " to suspend
" complying with any other of the many requests made them for the supply of
" several vacant churches upon the continent of America." Abstract for 1722.
p. 46. And from that period these colonies have been objects of peculiar attention. It is natural for this conduct to create a jealousy in the Presbyterians and
Independents in those parts, of an undue spirit of incroachment in these episcopalian brethren: especially, as their missionaries are, many of them of the old
jure divino stamp, who think Episcopacy and the uninterrupted succession, essential to the validity of religious ordinances, and to the Christian as well as
the ministerial character: who declare, in the words of Bishop Beveridge,
that " the apostolical line hath through all ages been preserved entire, there
" having been a constant succession of such bishops—as were truly and proper
" ly successors to the apostles by virtue of that apostolical imposition of hands,
" which being begun by the apostles, hath been continued from one another e-
" ver since their time down to us; by which means, the same spirit which was
" breathed by our Lord into his apostles, is together with their office transmit-
" ted to their lawful successors, the pastors and governors of our church at this
" time:" (Beach's Calm and Dispassionate Vindication of the Professors of the
Church of England. p. 5.) Who assert, that without this uninterrupted succession, " there can be no ministers of Christ," p. 4. that the people's acceptance with God depends upon it, p. 8. and that " if the power was once lost,
" none

tion in this respect) the apprehension of danger from the Dissenters being admitted to such offices as a few amongst them may
be

" none could renew it or begin a new succession, till Christ was pleased to send
" new apostles," p. 6. and that " could this point once be made clear, that
" this succession hath been interrupted, it would also prove further, that Christ
" hath neglected to provide for his church in a case so essential to the very
" Being of it, notwithstanding his having expressly promised to be ever with it
" to the end of the world : that if the succession be once broken, and the power
" of ordination once lost, not all the men on earth—not all the angels in hea-
" ven, without an immediate commission from Christ, can restore it." Dr.
T. B. Chandler's Appeal to the Public in behalf of the Church of England in
America; published at New-York 1767. A pamphlet now before me, wrote at
the *appointment* and according to the *directions* of a CONVENTION of missionaries,
to promote the design of sending bishops to America.

Upon these principles it is not at all surprising to find missionaries asserting,
that " not only without any authority from God or Man, from Church or
" State, but in defiance of both, were the New-England Churches first set up."
Beach. p. 27. For they imagine that the Church of England is, in virtue of
the act of uniformity, established in the colonies; laying it down as a maxim,
that " colonies transplanting themselves, carry the laws of their mother coun-
" try with them." Wetmore's Appendix to Beach's Vindication, p. 63. A
very different opinion from that of Bishop Gibson expressed in a letter to Dr.
Coleman, May 24, 1735, that " the religious state of New-England is found-
" ed in an equal liberty to all Protestants, none of which can claim the name
" of a national establishment, or any kind of superiority over the rest." Agreeably to a declaration of the *Lords Justices*, in a letter to Governor Dunbar in
the year 1725, that " there is no regular establishment of any national or pro-
" vincial church in these plantations." Now it is but natural that missionaries
of the principles before-mentioned should declare it to be " the business they
" are employed in to endeavour to proselyte men from every sect to the com-
" munion of the established church." Wetmore's Vindication, p. 6. In which
they do but obey a standing instruction of the society, that " they frequently
" visit their respective parishioners, those of their own communion, to keep
" them steady in the profession and practice of religion, as taught in the church
" of England, and those that oppose them or dissent from them, to convince
" and reclaim them*."

I may

* For the quotations from Mr. Beach and Mr. Wetmore, and from Dr. Coleman's Life, I
am indebted to Mr. Hobart's Second Address to the Members of the Episcopal Separation in
New-England ; a pamphlet published at Boston. 1751.

be qualified for, and likely to obtain, muſt be entirely groundleſs. It is my firm opinion, that the repeal of the teſt would be
a greater

I may now appeal to any man of common underſtanding, what impreſſions
ſuch enormous claims advanced by the miſſionaries in the colonies, are likely
to make upon their non epiſcopalian inhabitants; and whether they are not
calculated to raiſe in them incureable jealouſies of the growth of epiſcopal or eccleſiaſtical power. It is very unhappy, if the ſociety, as the Archbiſhop intimates, p. 4. can procure " few to go from hence, in the character of miſſion-
" aries, but perſons of deſperate fortunes, low qualifications, and bad or doubt-
" ful characters ;—a great part of whom," faith he, are " Scotch; and I need
" not ſay," he adds. " what chance there is, that epiſcopal clergymen of that
" country may be diſaffected to the government."

In what I have ſaid, I have no more deſign than the Archbiſhop had, to fix
an odium on the ſociety; I wiſh both its conduct and its miſſionaries may in e-
very reſpect be unexceptionable and honourable; and to that end, that thoſe
members of it who are men of wiſdom and moderation, may be always diſpoſed
to take that lead in its councils and determinations, which their numbers and
influence muſt naturally give them. However, I could not, upon occaſion of
this rhetorical attack of Dr. Burton, but think it very expedient juſt to point
out ſome of the grounds of thoſe apprehenſions, which the ſcheme of ſending
biſhops to America hath raiſed in the colonies. And I really think, in this
ſtate of things, the Americans, thoſe eſpecially who are not of the Epiſcopal
perſuaſion, may reaſonably expect ſome ſtrong barrier ſome effectual ſecurity,
ſuppoſing biſhops ſent to America with ſpiritual characters only, againſt their
aſſuming, or poſſeſſing afterwards, any degree of temporal authority. And unleſs this be done, the oppoſition of them and their friends here, to ſuch a deſign, is no proof that they are enemies to the liberties of others, but only that
they are willing to preſerve their own.

What I have ſaid is on ſuppoſition, that the ſtate interpoſes in ſending biſhops
to America. But the Preſbyterians and Independents in thoſe parts apprehend,
that if biſhops are ſettled among them *by the ſtate*, it will deſtroy that *equality*
which ſubſiſts, and which, (notwithſtanding what Dr. Burton aſſerts to the
contrary) they are willing ſhould ſubſiſt, between themſelves and Epiſcopalians;
and will give the latter a *ſuperiority* to all other denominations. They have no
objection to the Epiſcopalians procuring themſelves biſhops, or perſons inveſted
with a *ſpiritual power* of ordaining confirming and ſuperintending (as Dr. Chaun-
cy of Boſton in his controverſy with Dr. T. B. Chandler expreſsly aſſerts) provided they will be contented to ſtand upon the foot, upon which *they them-
ſelves* ſtand, of *permiſſion* and *protection*, not of *authority*; of *toleration*, not of a *ſtate-
eſtabliſhment.*

a greater difadvantage to the Body of Diffenters, than to the eftablifhed church; that it would rather diminifh than increafe their numbers. For, in general, men are not much inclined to fhock all the princip'es on which they have acted; and defert a party with which they are connected, at once on a lucrative motive; but they may be gradually foft n d and relaxed in their principles, by the new connections into which the poffeffion of public offices would introduce them, by the influence of general cuftom, and of what is efteemed polite and fafhionable, and by the example of their fuperiors, or of the majority; provided they are not difgufted and revolted by any ungenerous compulfion or reftraint. In fuch circumftances, no confiderable numbers, if any, would be found mad enough to embark in the dangerous enterprize of overturning an eftablifhment, fo well guarded and fenced by law, as that of the church of England, and to which the nation hath been fo long accuftomed. And provided, in any future time, fhe fhould be improved in her conftitution, in her public forms, and in the terms of conformity to her lay and minifterial communion, there would be no human profpect, fcarcely a poffibility, of fhaking her foundations, fhould any be inclined to attempt it. For, the broader the bafis on which fhe ftands, fhe ftands the firmer. And therefore, comprehenfive, not exclufive meafures fhould, in all prudence be adopted and purfued by thofe who would approve themfelves her trueft and beft, as well as warmeft friends.

I F, to all thefe confiderations, you fhould oppofe the deftruction of the ecclefiaftical conftitution, in the laft century, by the fectaries: I beg leave to obferve, that the true caufe, and at bottom the only caufe, of the overthrow of the church at that time, was, that her leading men and governors had been, in fome cafes,

eftablifhment. And indeed, if the ftate do interpofe in fettling bifhops in America, then, as I faid before, all circumftances confidered, fome effectual fecurity againft their affuming, or being permitted to affume, improper powers may in all reafon be expected.

cafes the authors, and in others the inſtruments, of civil as well as eccleſiaſtical tyranny. Their oppreſſions and perſecutions had been deeply felt by the puritans, who had ſome zeal for religion ; and their ſlaviſh doctrines, and arbitrary meaſures, pernicious and fatal as they were to civil liberty, had given ſuch a turn to men's minds in general, as enabled ſome religious zealots, in conjunction with the Scots, who inſiſted upon the deſtruction of Epiſcopacy before they would move to the aſſiſtance of the Parliament when their affairs were at a low ebb, to overturn the eccleſiaſtical conſtitution. But what is the inference from hence? that the permitting of the Diſſenters to enjoy the common rights of good ſubjects, would endanger the church a ſecond time? I think the reverſe : that, as the tyranny of the church and ſtate proved, by a ſtrange concurrence of circumſtances, the ruin of both; lenity and ſome degree of the ſame magnanimity in this caſe, which you ſay, was diſcovered in the toleration, would, in this inſtance as well as in the former, tend to her eſtabliſhment and preſervation. For, as we ſee in fact, that every inſtance of it, which hath been hitherto exerciſed, hath had that effect ; we have reaſon to conclude, that every further inſtance of it would undoubtedly have the ſame.

BESIDES, what ſecurity can be derived to the church from a man's now and then receiving the ſacrament in it, for the ſake of a good place ? That is, I own, a mark of *his affection for the place*; but very little, I am ſure, of his affection for the church; to which he may, notwithſtanding a compliance obtained by a bait ſo alluring, be ſtill a falſe friend, or a determined enemy.

AND, as there are theſe objections to a teſt in general, affecting Proteſtant Diſſenters; ſo there are ſome, I think, no inconſiderable ones, to the particular nature of the teſt by law appointed ; namely, that leading perſons to take the ſacrament with wrong views, who would not otherwiſe do it

at

at all, and who have no proper notions of, and right difpofitions for it, it gives ground to confider it as an abufe of
a facred ordinance, which was appointed for the ends of religion only, to temporal and worldly views and purpofes ; and
as a ftrong temptation to hypocrify : and though they are
criminal who do not refift it ; yet, neither are they innocent,
who lay the fnare in their way.

I am,

Sir, &c.

G g　　　　　　　　　　　　L E T-

L E T T E R VII.

SIR,

IT will be found, I believe, that the obfervations which I have occafionally made upon the character of the Proteftant Dif-fenters are ftrictly juft: that their principles are calculated to render them the firm and invariable friends of the civil conftitu-tion of their country. You obferve, that " in all ages and " countries *civil and ecclefiaftical tyranny* are mutually productive " of each other*." I think it muft be equally true, that *religi-ous* and *civil liberty* have a reciprocal influence in producing and fupporting one another; and accordingly the Proteftant Diffen-ters are at leaft as likely as any, to be warmly and fteadily at-tached to both. I cannot forbear, therefore, taking notice, with furprize, of a paffage in your chapter of *Præmunire*, which, notwithftanding I have endeavoured to put the moft favourable conftruction upon it, I cannot reconcile to the fuppofition of your having any tolerable idea, what the principles are which generally prevail amongft the Proteftant Diffenters. After a ve-ry extraordinary panegyrick upon the church of England, and the clergy of her perfuafion†, of which I am not inclined in

the

---

* Comment. vol. iv. p. 103.

† " It is the glory of the church of England, you fay, as well as a ftrong " prefumptive argument in favour of the purity of her faith, that fhe hath " been (as her prelates on a trying occafion once expreffed it : Addrefs to Jam. " II. 1687.) in her principles and practice ever moft unqueftionably loyal. The " clergy of her perfuafion, holy in their doctrines, and unblemifhed in their " lives and converfation, are alfo moderate in their ambition, and entertain " juft notions of the ties of fociety and the rights of civil government. As in " matters of faith and morality they acknowledge *no guide but the fcriptures*, " fo, in matters of external polity and of private right, they derive all their " title from the civil magiftrate; they look up to the king as their head, to

" the

the leaſt, to diſpute the propriety, you give us a ſtriking con-
traſt in theſe remarkakable words: " Whereas the principles of
" thoſe who differ from them, as well in one extreme as the o-
" ther, are equally and totally deſtructive of thoſe ties and ob-
" ligations by which all ſociety is kept together ; equally en-
" croaching on thoſe rights, which reaſon, and the original
" contract of every free ſtate in the univerſe, have veſted in the
" ſovereign power ; and equally aiming at a diſtinct indepen-
" dent ſupremacy of their own, where ſpiritual men and ſpiri-
" tual cauſes are concerned*."

G g 2

POPISH

" the parliament as their lawgiver, and pride themſelves in nothing ſo juſtly,
" as in being true members of the church emphatically *by law* eſtabliſhed.
" Whereas the principles of thoſe who differ," &c. It cannot be doubted,
that a clergy ſo holy and moderate and unambitious, and ſo warmly attached
to the SCRIPTURES *as their* ONLY *guide in matters of faith and morality*, and to
the civil magiſtrate in reſpect to matters of external polity, will do their utmoſt
to procure a reform of various particulars in their eccleſiaſtical conſtitution, diſcipline and worſhip ; and eſpecially a repeal of the twentieth article, by which
the CHURCH is ſaid to have *power to decree rites and ceremonies*, and *authority in
matters of faith* ; and likewiſe of the law, by which the *four firſt general councils,
conjunction* with the ſcriptures, are made judges of hereſy.

* Comment. vol. iv. p. 103. This paſſage being altered in the new edition,
runs thus: " Whereas the *notions of eccleſiaſtical liberty* in thoſe who differ from
" them, as well in one extreme as the other *(for I here only ſpeak of extremes)* are
" equally and totally deſtructive, &c." What notions of eccleſiaſtical liberty
the learned gentleman aſcribes to the church of Rome, I know not; unleſs by
this phraſe he means that independence upon the ſtate, and that ſuperiority o-
ver it, which ſhe does indeed arrogate to her governors. But though this claim
as I have ſaid above, is inconſiſtent with the rights of civil government and the
foundations of ſociety ; yet the notions of eccleſiaſtical, or rather religious liberty, amongſt the Proteſtant Diſſenters are eſſentially different. Liberty in
their ſenſe is not a claim of power, much leſs of ſupremacy, as in the church
of Rome : it is on the contrary a proteſt againſt all power in matters of religion, either in themſelves or others; for they allow of no power but that of the
civil magiſtrate. An obſervation, which is ſufficient to ſhew, that their notions of liberty do not interfere with any rights of ſociety or of civil government.

By

Popish principles, undoubtedly, are one extreme to which you here allude ; and, I think, diffenting principles, at leaft, when they are carried to their utmoft length, muft be the other. It is true, the examples, which you immediately produce in fupport of this branch of your affertion, are of fome enthufiafts both at home and abroad in the laft century. " The dreadful effects," you fay, " of fuch a religious bigotry, when actuated " by erroneous principles, even of the Proteftant kind, are fuf- " ficiently evident from the hiftory of the Anabaptifts in Ger- " many, the Covenanters in Scotland, and that deluge of fec- " taries in England, who murdered their fovereign, overturned " the church and monarchy, fhook every pillar of law, juftice, " and private property, and moft devoutly eftablifhed a king- " dom of the faints in their ftead."

The only objection I think proper to make to the fentiment fuggefted in this round and warm paragraph, is, that it cannot vindicate the univerfality of your cenfure on the principles of thofe who, among Proteftants, differ from the church ; unlefs upon fuppofition, that the principles of all Proteftant Diffenters are of the fame nature and tendency with thofe, which being carried to an extreme by the Anabaptifts in Germany, and the Fifth-monarchy-men in England, in the laft century, produced very extravagant confequences. This conftruction offers itfelf

fo

By the parenthefis, which the author hath inferted, " (for I here only " fpeak of extremes)" I fuppofe he means to fuggeft, that in this paffage he had not the Diffenters directly in view, but the Anabaptifts in Germany, and the Fifth-monarchy-men in England, and the like enthufiafts in the laft centu- ry. Neverthelefs this very parenthefis confirms the apprehenfion, that he ef- teems the principles of thefe enthufiafts to be only the extremes of diffenting principles; that they are the fame in kind, though not in degree, thefe enthufi- afts having carried them to the utmoft length. What follows therefore in this letter, to fhew the effential difference and abfolute contrariety between the prin- ciples of the Diffenters on the one hand, and the principles of thefe Enthufiafts and of the Papifts on the other, holds equally good againft the paffage as it is now amended, as it did in its former ftate.

fo readily, that, if it was not your intention to ftigmatize the Diffenters of the prefent age in any degree, but only fome particular enthufiafts of the laft age both at home and abroad, it might furely have been expected, that fome exceptive or qualifying expreffions fhould have been inferted in their favour. And after what you have faid of the modern Diffenters, in your Reply to Dr. Prieftly, I hope this will be done in future editions.

In the mean time, as I apprehend this paragraph will be underftood to intimate, that the Diffenters hold principles unfriendly to fociety, and to civil government; principles which, in the extreme, have produced the moft fatal effects, both at home and abroad; in juftice to them, (though not in oppofition to you, if you really do not intend this cenfure for them,) I fhall offer a few remarks, in order to fhow, that the principles of the Diffenters are entirely the reverfe, both of popifh principles, and of thofe enthufiaftic principles which you mention, and can never produce the dreadful confequences to civil government which flow from either.

The church of Rome, indeed, afferts her own fupremacy over the civil power, in every country*. And accordingly fhe demands

---

* This claim the church of Rome hath always advanced, and wherever fhe hath had opportunity, exercifed; without ever in a fingle inftance giving it up. Since the Reformation, the times have been daily growing more unfavourable to the exercife of that enormous power, which formerly held the civil authority all over Europe in abfolute fubjection and dependence. But the church, ever attentive to her favourite fupremacy, ftill takes every method to prevent its further depreffion, and even to reftore it, if poffible, to its former glorious exaltation. With this worthy defign, a large folio volume, in Latin, in a fmall type, was printed in England (without any name of place or printer) in the year 1753, (of which I have a copy now in my hands,) under the care of the Jefuits, and the impreffion fent to Portugal, for the ufe of the ecclefiafticks in that kingdom. It is intitled, Opufculum-Theologico-Juridicum, de utroque Recurfu: in Judicem, fcilicet, competentem et incompetentem: quinque libris diftinctum: in quibus agitur, in lib. 1. De Recurfu ad Judicem competentem, puta ab Ecclefiaftico ad Ecclefiafticum, de fæculari ad fæcularem, vel ad Ecclefiafticum

demands an abfolute fubmiffion in all her members, fubverfive not only of the rights of a free people, but of all the obligations of fociety, and the very foundations of civil polity. She claims an utter exemption of all ecclefiaftical perfons, and of all their rights and poffeffions, from the jurifdiction and authority of the magiftrate. But is there the leaft fimilarity to this, in the fentiments of the Proteftant Diffenters? No, certainly. It is their opinion, I own, that the magiftrate fhould not expect, much lefs exact, obedience or fubmiffion in matters purely religious; and that, in things pertaining to confcience, it is the duty of the fubject to act upon the principle of the apoftles and primitive Chriftians; that is, to " obey God rather than " men[x]." But then there is nothing in this fentiment, in the fmalleft degree, inconfiftent with *civil obedience*: " rendering " unto

---

fiafticam Superiorem: in 2do vero, De eodem ad Judicem INCOMPETENTEM; puta, ab ECCLESIASTICO ad SAECULARIA TRIBUNALIA, &c. So that, according to the doctrine which this book is intended to eftablifh, by an infinite number of reafons and authorities (fuch as they are) from the decrees of Popes, of councils, of the holy office of Inquifition, and of numberlefs Romifh canonifts, and cafuifts, the *civil* power hath NEVER any controul over the *ecclefiaftical*, but the *ecclefiaftical* ALWAYS over the *civil*. And even the power, affumed and exercifed by the Popes in the darked ages, of depofing emperors, kings, and all other princes and magiftrates, is explicitly afferted and maintained. This work, fo much adapted to promote the glory of holy church, is publifhed under the patronage of the King of Kings: Sub *Regis Regum* patrocinio, omnibus Regibus Principibus, ad Judicibus, tum Ecclefiafticis, tum Saecularibus, dicatum. The author the bifhop of *Algarve*: Autore Excellentiffimo ac Reverendiffimo D. Ignatio a S. Terefia Portucalenfi, Excanonico Regulari S. Auguftini Congregationis S. Crucis Colimbrienfi, Archiepifco Goano Primate Orientis, Indiani Status femel. et iterato. Saeculari Ex gubernatore: Poftea vero Ecclefia Algarlienfis Epifcopo, et ejufdem Regni Armorum Gubernatore. It is a performance calculated to free the votaries of Rome not only from the obligations of civil but of *moral* authority; furnifhing fuch diftinctions, evafions, and decifions, with regard to the moft FLAGITIOUS and even UNNATURAL crimes, as amply inftruct men how to commit them *falva confcientia*. Is not this aftonifhing, in modern times, in a man of letters, and, as I have been informed, polite and convertible?

Tantum RELLIGIO potuit fuadere malorum!

[x] Acts v. 29.

" unto God the things which are God's," is no objection to
" rendering unto Cæfar the things which are Cæfar's†." The
Diffenters are fo far from fetting up the fuppofed interefts of religion, or, as you exprefs it, " fpiritual men," or " fpiritual
" caufes," againft lawful magiftracy, or the peace and good
order of fociety, that they allow of the exemption of none from
the authority of the civil magiftrate; holding all to be equally
under his jurifdiction; and that no plea of facred character, or
of religion and confcience, is to be admitted in bar to his pro-
cedure, in matters of a criminal, or merely civil nature. And
as, in their opinion, it is his duty to *protect* all *good fubjects*
in the profeffion of their religious principles; fo, without any
regard to their religious principles or profeffions, he is to *punifh*
all *offenders* againft the *peace* of fociety. Now, how is this " fet-
" ting up an independent fupremacy of their own, where fpiri-
" tual men and fpiritual caufes are concerned?" If, as they fay,
all men are to judge for themfelves, and act accordingly, in matters of faith and worfhip, and the falvation of their fouls; if, in
thefe refpects, they are not to controul, ufurp upon, and do-
mineer over one another, and are at the fame time to be *fubject
to the civil magiftrate*; this appears to me to be fo far from fetting up an *imperium in imperio*, that it leaves no *imperium*, no fupremacy, indeed, *no power at all*, in fociety, *but that* of the civil
magiftrate. Thefe principles, therefore, can never iffue in a
diftinct independent' fupremacy of thofe who profefs them,
whether *fpiritual men* or others. The principles of the Papifts,
indeed, directly lead to and fupport this fupremacy: the principles of the Diffenters are diametrically oppofed to it.

AND as their principles are quite of another nature, another
genius and complexion, than thofe of the Papifts; fo are they,
than thofe of the enthufiafts whom you have mentioned. I
know no Diffenter on earth who holds, that *dominion is founded
in grace*, and that *the faints muft rule the world*; or any principles which have the leaft tendency and afpect towards fuch a
conclufion.

† Matth. xxii. 21.

conclufion. On the contrary, they all to a man affert, that religion is fo far from vefting in its profeffors a title to *dominion*, that it is no exemption from *civil fubjection*. It is in matters of confcience only, they apprehend, they are alone accountable to God; and that not fo as to excufe thereby any criminal overt acts, inconfiftent with the peace of fociety: *thefe*, the magiftrate muft punifh, from whatever principle they proceed, from any or none, and whatever plea of that fort is offered in their favour. Some enthufiafts formerly, particularly thofe you have cenfured, made one compofition of religion and politics; the Diffenters, on the contrary, keep them wholly diftinct, as being of a different nature, and relating to different purpofes, and different interefts; the one to the foul, the other to the body; the one to the prefent world, the other to the future. Thefe enthufiafts were ftrenuous affertors of the monarchy of King Jefus, that his kingdom was of this world: the Diffenters zealoufly maintain, in conformity with reafon and fcripture, that " Chrift's kingdom is not of this world*," and doth not at all interfere with the office of the magiftrate; who, in their opinion, is fupreme over all perfons within his dominions, of whatever religion, of any or none. I will venture to affirm, that it is impoffible to erect the fyftem of thefe enthufiafts, as a fuperftructure, on the principles of the Diffenters, as a foundation. The principles of the latter are totally incompatible with the whole fcheme of the former, and of all others, moft effectually overturn and deftroy it. In a word, their principles, with refpect both to church authority and to civil government, are precifely the fame which the late Bifhop Hoadly advanced and fupported in an unanfwerable manner; doing thereby fuch fervice to the caufe of true Proteftantifm, and of the royal fucceffion in the Houfe of Hanover, as will always be remembered with gratitude by the true friends of that auguft family, and of the liberty of their country.

I SHALL

---

* John xviii. 36.

I s HALL only add, in juftice to Dr. Prieftley, whom you call a willing critic, (I fuppofe, you mean one inclined to put not the moft favourable conftruction upon your expreffions) that, I believe, every Diffenter, I am fure, every one with whom I have converfed, who had read that page in your Commentaries, which contains a comparifon between the principles and the conduct of the Papifts and the Sectaries, underftood you, in the moft obnoxious paffage of all, in the fame fenfe in which he did; namely, as referring to the modern Diffenters; and were perhaps as much offended with it as he was: I refer to that claufe, wherein you fay, " As to the Papifts, their tenets are undoubtedly cal-
" culated for the introduction of all flavery, both civil and religi-
" ous; but it may with juftice be queftioned, whether the fpi-
" rit, the doctrines, and the practice of the Sectaries ARE better
" calculated to make men good fubjects*."

I s HALL not fcruple to affirm, that there are no better fubjects, and no better friends to the conftitution of their country as a limited monarchy, defined and improved by the glorious Revolution, than the Proteftant Diffenters†: they pray for the con-

H h   tinuance

---

* Comment. vol. iv. p. 52.

† " The Diffenters are fincere well wifhers to the civil part of our prefent happy eftablifhment; and they are to be efteemed and loved for it," faith the late Abp. Secker, in his letter to Mr. Walpole concerning bifhops in America, p. 24, 25. Dr. Burton, the Archbifhop's panegyrift (in his Commentariolus Thomæ Secker, &c. p. 27.) hath given a different character of certain perfons, whom he ftiles, " Diffentientium greges quidam:" After mentioning the Archbifhop's fcheme of fending bifhops to America, he adds: fremunt tamen illico et tumultuantur Diffentientium greges quidam irritabiles et pervicaces; iidem in Republicâ Cives feditiofi in Ecclefiâ Principatum adepti, Tyranni intolerabiles. Whether the author levels this invective againft the Prefbyterians and Independents in the colonies, or the Diffenters at home, I will not be pofitive. If he means the Americans, they perhaps would tell him, that he hath grofsly mifreprefented both their civil and their religious principles, and would excufe him on the fcore only of that nobe privilege, which Atticus allows all rhetoricians:
Conceffum

tinuance of the Proteftant fucceffion in the prefent illuftrious royal family, and for the *falus regis et populi*, in the words, and with
the fervour, with which father Paul prayed for the Republic
of Venice in his dying moments : Esto Perpetua !

But I have done: you have promifed to correct thofe paffages in your next edition; and I have no doubt, you will
make that correction in fuch a manner as will be entirely fatif-
factory*,

In thus addreffing you, Sir, I would not be thought to entertain a fondnefs for controverfy. I know full well, how feldom it is, that controverfies anfwer any valuable end. They
often four and imbitter men's minds, and give a keenefs and a-
crimony to their tempers; befides engroffing a great deal of
time

Conceffum eft rhetoribus ementiri in hiftoriis, ut aliquid dicere poffint argutius.
Cicero de claris oratoribus, c. 11.   But if he means the Diffenters, I am con-
tent to afcribe it folely to his total ignorance of their character ; otherwife he
would know, that ecclefiaftical authority, and much more ecclefiaftical tyranny, in the hands of either prefbyters or bifhops, is their entire averfion. As for
fedition, that charge, I think, is unjuft even againft their anceftors the puritans;
who in general, were not a whit more feditious, or more enemies to limited
monarchy, and lawful authority, than thofe great patriots of the church of
England who at that time oppofed the defigns of an arbitrary court, and the
dangerous incroachments of prerogative upon civil liberty. And as to their de-
fcendants, the modern Diffenters, let his oracle the Archbifhop be their com-
purgator; who had reafon to know them better than his panegyrift, as he was
not only born of diffenting parents, but received his education, together with
the late excellent Bifhop Butler, in one of their academies, under a tutor (one
Mr. Jones, as he is called in the late review of his Grace's life and character, p.
2.) whofe great learning and abilities would have been no little honour to either of our univerfities : Circumftances, by the way, which this gentleman, in
his great ingenuity and liberality of fentiment, hath thought proper to pafs over
in filence; whether, becaufe he imagined they would be a difgrace to the
Archbifhop, or an honour to the Diffenters, or both, I pretend not to determine.

    * The author hath left them out in the laft edition of the Commentaries. A
degree of candor, worthy not only of applaufe, but of imitation !

time and attention, which moſt men may employ to much better purpoſes. I am ſo convinced of this, that nothing ſhould
have engaged me to appear in the character of a polemical writer, even ſo far as I have now done, in laying before you, and the
public, the preceding remarks, if I had not been fully-perſuad-
ed, that ſome poſitions and ſentiments which you have advanced, have an unfavourable aſpect (and the more ſo as coming
from an author of your diſtinguiſhed reputation) on the glorious cauſe of religious liberty : a cauſe nearly connected with,
and of great importance to, the intereſts of truth, and the preſent and future happineſs of mankind.

Thus, Sir, have I freely, and I hope, inoffenſively, pointed
out ſome of the *ſuppoſed* blemiſhes in your otherwiſe excellent
and elaborate work; which many, who have a great opinion
both of the author and of his performance, wiſh to ſee corrected.
And, I am perſuaded, they will be ſo, as far as you ſhall be convinced they are *real* blemiſhes: Whether they are or not, muſt
be left, Sir, to your conſideration, and to the judgment of the
impartial public.

I am,

with great reſpect, &c.

PHILIP FURNEAUX.

APPENDIX:

CONTAINING

AUTHENTIC COPIES

OF

The ARGUMENT of the late Honourable Mr. Juſtice
FOSTER in the Court of the Judges Delegates,

AND OF

The SPEECH of the Right Honourable Lord MANSFIELD
in the Houſe of Lords, in the Cauſe between the City
of London and the Diſſenters.

ADVERTISEMENT.

IT is proper the reader should be apprized, previous to the perusal of the following argument and speech, that in the year 1748, the Corporation of London made a by-law, with a view, as they alledged, of procuring fit and able persons to serve the office of sheriff of the said Corporation ; imposing for that end a fine of four hundred pounds and twenty marks upon every person who, being nominated by the Lord Mayor, declined standing the election of the Common-hall ; and six hundred pounds upon every one who, being elected by the Common-hall, refused to serve the office. Which fines they appropriated to defraying the expence of building the Mansion-house.

Many Dissenters were nominated and elected to the said office, who were incapable of serving ; it having been enacted by the Corporation-act (13 Car. II. stat. 2. c. 1.) that no person should be elected into any Corporation-offices, who had not taken the sacrament in the church of England within a year preceding the time of such election ; and several of them, accordingly, paid their fines, to the amount of above fifteen thousand pounds. Some at length refused to pay their fines, apprehending they could not be obliged, by law, to fine for not serving an office to which they were, by law, uneligible. The city, therefore, brought actions of debt against them in a court of their own, called the Sheriff's Court, for the recovery of those fines. After many delays the cause came to a hearing in the case of Allen Evans, Esq; and judgment was given for the Plaintiff in September 1757. The defendant Evans brought the cause before the Court of Hustings, another city-court, to which an appeal lay ; and the judgment was there affirmed by the Recorder in the year 1759. The Defendant then, by writ of error, brought
the

the caufe before the Court of Judges Delegates, called the Court of St. Martin's : the Delegates were Lord Chief Juftice Willes, Lord Chief Baron Parker, Mr. Juftice Fofter, Mr. Juftice Bathurft, and Mr. Juftice Wilmot. Lord Chief Juftice Willes dying before judgment given, the reft of the delegates delivered their opinions feriatim, July 5, 1762, and unanimoufly reverfed the judgment of the Sheriff's Court and Court of Huftings. On this occafion the following excellent argument of Mr. Juftice Fofter was delivered. The Corporation then by writ of error brought the caufe before the Houfe of Lords, when all the Judges, who had not fat as delegates, except Mr. Juftice Yates who was ill, gave their opinions feriatim, Feb. 3d and 4th, 1767, upon a queftion put to them by the Houfe. After which Lord Mansfield in his place as a peer, made the juftly-admired fpeech which is here publifhed ; concluding it with moving, that the judgment be affirmed ; which was done .immediately without any debate, or a diffentient voice.

Th is was a caufe of great expectation; it was interefting to the Diffenters not only in London, but in every Corporation in the kingdom ; fince they might, any of them, follow the fteps of the city of London; make a by-law to fine thofe who refufed to ferve Corporation-offices, under pretence of procuring fit and able perfons; and then choofe Diffenters who had not taken the facrament at church within a year preceding the time of fuch e-lection, to any number they thought proper ; who, provided the city of London had fucceeded in this leading caufe, would have had the alternative, of fubjecting themfelves to a profecution and to heavy penalties, if they ferved the office under the inca-pacity incurred by the Corporation-act ; or of paying their fines, to any amount the Corporation fhould think fit to impofe.

I n the argument upon this caufe, the extent and influence of the Act of Toleration, and whether it abolifhed the crime as well as the penalties of nonconformity, came under confideration : which is directly in point to the fubject of my firft letter.

I HAVE

I HAVE had an opportunity of perufing copies, taken in court, of the arguments of Mr. Juftice (now Lord Chief Juftice) Wilmot, Mr. Juftice Bathurft, and Lord Chief Baron Parker; who, together with Mr. Juftice Fofter, compofed the Court of Judges Delegates. Their refpective arguments contain very judicious and pertinent obfervations and cogent reafonings, in fupport of the unanimous judgment given for the Defendant; and they all affert the influence and operation of the Toleration-act in the extent in which I have pleaded for it, as removing the crime as well as penalties of nonconformity. Mr. Juftice Wilmot fays, " It hath taken away both the reatum et pœnam:" and " that it is no greater offence in the Defendant not to have " received the facrament according to the rites of the church of " England, than it is not to be worth fifteen thoufand pounds:" the qualification for the office of fheriff. Mr. Juftice Bathurft fays, " The Defendant's difability was occafioned by a volunta- " ry omiffion, but not default, unlefs it was his duty to receive " the facrament." And " if the Defendant is not by any law " obliged to receive the facrament annually, he is guilty of no " default in omiting to do it. Here the Defendant, by bring- " ing himfelf within the toleration-act, fhews it was not his du- " ty to receive the facrament." And whereas it was objected, " That this averment of Mr. Evans, that he could not take the " facrament according to the rites of the church of England, " could not avail him: that it could only be known to the " Searcher of all hearts, and the contrary could not be prov- " ed;" Lord Chief Baron Parker replies, that " Lord Chief " Juftice Holt in Larwood's cafe was of a different opinion; " the plea was difallowed for want of that averment. The con- " trary may be proved, by his having accepted a profitable of- " fice requiring that qualification, or by other circumftances, " fhewing that he really had no fuch fcruples. But if no evi- " dence can be given of that infincerity, he *ought to be, and is* " *excufed by law.*" But though thefe learned judges all agreed in the opinion concerning the toleration-act, that it abolifhed

the

the crime of nonconformity, as well as the penalty ; yet none of them gave their reafons for it fo fully as Mr. Juftice Fofter : on which account his argument is more appofite to my particular purpofe than that of any other of the Judges Delegates. And befides arguing this point in a very convincing manner, he hath likewife given a mafterly expofition of the 12th fection of the Corporation-act, in which Lord Chief Baron Parker declared his concurrence with him : and on thefe two points the merits of the caufe principally depended.

W H E N the Judges delivered their opinions in the Houfe of Lords, they were naturally led, by the wording of the queftion which the Houfe put to them on the motion of Lord Mansfield, into a particular confideration of the meaning of the Toleration-act ; and the fubftance of what was then faid (together with fome excellent obfervations and reafonings which were peculiar to himfelf) may be feen to very great advantage in the fpeech of that Noble Lord which is here prefented to the world.

T H E R E is one remark which it may be proper to make, that whereas in Larwood's cafe, the Court of King's Bench would not admit his allegation that he was a Diffenter, becaufe it was made in his rejoinder, and not in his plea ; fo that his rejoinder was a departure from his plea ; and the Court could not take notice of the Toleration-act unlefs it was pleaded, becaufe it was a *private* ftatute: one of the learned Judges in the Houfe of Lords, obferving upon this, declared his opinion, that the Court determined wrong in Larwood's cafe, the Toleration-act not being a private, but a *public* ftatute. And for this he affigned the the following reafons : that there is no diftinction between a public and a private ftatute in point of authority, but only of notoriety and univerfality. Now the Diffenters were a body of people well known in the kingdom, and even mentioned in feveral acts of parliament, and had public ftatutes enacted againft them before the Toleration-act, which were repealed by that act ; and therefore it fhould in all reafon be confidered as a pub-

lic

lic act: Especially, as in reality it virtually affects all persons in the kingdom, setting them at liberty, and giving them a legal right to become Nonconformists, if they are so disposed. And the preamble to the act mentions another consideration as the design of the legislature in passing it, which is of the most public nature, and of universal influence: It saith, " Forasmuch as " some ease to scrupulous consciences in the exercise of religion, " may be an effectual means to unite their majesties protestant " subjects in interest and affection : Be it enacted," &c. Now is it possible to conceive, that an act, which related to a body of people at that time so well known as the Dissenters, which repealed several public statutes, which gives liberty of dissent to every one who chooses to avail himself of it ; and which was designed to unite all protestant subjects in interest and affection ; is it possible to conceive, that this can be a private act? If so, by what criterion can we distinguish between private acts and public ones? But to return :

THE authenticity of the copy, here published, of the argument of that upright and able lawyer, the late Mr. Justice Foster, will appear from the following letter of his worthy Nephew : and whatever be the defects of my own performance, to which that gentleman is very partial ; and of how little advantage soever the publication of it may be to the world, I reckon it no inconsiderable one to myself, that it hath procured me the acquaintance and friendship of Mr. Dodson.

APPENDIX. No. 1.

A Letter from MICHAEL DODSON, Esq; to the AUTHOR.

REVEREND SIR,

I ADMIRE the letters which you have addressed to the Honourable Gentleman to whom the world is indebted for the celebrated Commentaries on the laws of England, and think that you have very clearly proved in the first letter, that such of the Dissenters as comply with the terms of the toleration-act, are not in the eye of the law guilty of any crime by reason of their nonconformity. But though the observations which you have made for this purpose seem to be abundantly sufficient, yet I presume that it will be agreeable to you to see the argument of the late Mr. Justice Foster, in the cause between the city of London and the Dissenters, as delivered by him at Guildhall in July 1762, when the judges delegates gave judgment for Mr. Evans the plaintiff in error; and I now send it you exactly copied from his own notes, at the same time giving my consent to the publication of it in an appendix to your letters.

I am, with great respect,

Reverend Sir,

Your most obedient humble servant,

Clifford's Inn,
Aug. 25, 1770.

MICHAEL DODSON.

I i 2

Mr.

Mr. JUSTICE FOSTER's *Argument in the Case of* ALLEN EVANS, *Esq; against Sir* THOMAS HARRISON, *Chamberlain of London.*

THE merits of the cafe will turn on the Corporation and To-leration-acts taken together. One works a difability on the part of the plaintiff in error; the other fhews that this dif-ability doth not arife from any criminal neglect in him. The Corporation-act * prohibits the election of Nonconformifts; the Toleration-act † renders nonconformity no longer a crime.

THE intention of the legiflature in framing the Corporation-act was to exclude all Nonconformifts from corporation offices. The preamble after a fhort mention of the late troubles goes on and faith, " To the end that the fucceffion in fuch corporati-" ons may be moft probably perpetuated in the hands of per-" fons well-affected to his majefty and the eftablifhed govern-" ment—and for the prefervation of the public peace both in " church and ftate, Be it enacted," &c.

THIS exclufion was to be effected two ways. The firft was by removing all Nonconformifts who were then in office or fhould come into office before the 25th of March 1663. The fecond, by providing againft the admiffion of them for the fu-ture.

WITH regard to thofe then in office commiffioners are ap-pointed with extraordinary powers, powers new and unknown to the conftitution, which nothing but the moft urgent neceffity, real or imaginary, could have juftified. For they were im-powered among other things, at their will and pleafure to remove all corporation officers *if they fhould deem it expedient for the pub-lic*

* 13 Car. II. ftat. 2. c. I. † 1 W. & M. feff. 1. c. 18.

lic safety, and at their will and pleasure to fill up all vacancies occasioned by such removals or otherwise.

THIS commission expired on the 25th of March 1663. And it is observable, that during this commission no mention is made of the Sacramental Qualification. The well-known zeal of the commissioners, men picked and chosen for the purpose, with regard to the exclusion of Nonconformists who had been rendered very odious, made an express provision for that purpose needless as to them.

BUT when elections were to return into their old channel, subject only to charter and custom, it was thought necessary to put electors, whose zeal in the cause might by time and a change of circumstances be abated—it was thought necessary to put them under a new restraint ; and to make this restraint perpetual. This is done by the 12th section of the act : " Provided also and " be it enacted, that from and after the expiration of the said " commission, no person or persons shall for ever hereafter be " placed, elected or chosen in or to any the offices or places a- " foresaid, that shall not have within one year next before such " election or choice taken the sacrament of the Lord's Supper " according to the rites of the church of England ; and that e- " very such person and persons so placed, elected or chosen, shall " likewise take the aforesaid three oaths, and subscribe the said " declaration at the same time when the oath for the due exe- " cution of the said places and offices respectively shall be admi- " nistred ; and in default hereof, every such placing, election " and choice is hereby enacted and declared to be void."

THIS clause consists of two Branches independent and un- connected with each other. The first regards the persons hav- ing the right and power of election and nomination to corpora- tion-offices : The second, the candidates alone.

THE first is, in my opinion, prohibitory on the electors ; it lays a restraint upon them in the exercise of their antient right

and diſcretionary power in the matter of the election, and con-
fines them to perſons conforming to the eſtabliſhment in the
manner preſcribed by the act. No perſon not previouſly qualified as the act directs, ſhall for ever hereafter be elected. What
is this but ſaying, That no corporation having the right of e-
lection ſhall for ever hereafter elect any perſon not ſo previouſly qualified?

THE ſecond Branch of the clauſe regards only the candidate,
and upon a ſuppoſition that he may have been eligible and actually elected, requires ſomething further to be done by him,
the taking and ſubſcribing the three oaths and declaration ; and
in default hereof declares the election void.

I THEREFORE do not found my opinion on this branch of
the ſtatute, but on that which prohibits the election of perſons
not previouſly qualified. For in true Grammar and plain conſtruction, what is the meaning of the words, *in default hereof
the election ſhall be void?* In default of what ? Plainly in default of
ſomething required by the act to be done by the candidate after
his election ; not in default of what this act doth not require of
him.

I SAY what *this* act doth not require; for though it ſhould
be admitted that the Rubrick did injoin conformity in the inſtances therein mentioned, yet ſtill in the conſtruction of the words,
in default hereof, as they ſtand in this clauſe, we muſt confine
ourſelves to thoſe duties which *this* act alone doth require.

I RETURN now to the firſt Branch of the clauſe. If it be prohibitory on the electors, as I think it is, the conſequence will be
that if they having due notice of the incapacity of the candidate,
will proceed to elect a perſon declared by the ſtatute not eligible,
this ſhadow of an election will be a mere nullity; as being made
in contravention to the ſtatute, a contravention on the part of
the electors wilful, open and undiſguiſed.

IN

In the prefent cafe it muft be admitted, that the electors had due notice of the incapacity of the Defendant in the action, fince he in his plea avers it, and the Plaintiff hath not put it in iffue.

This being fo, it will, I think, be impoffible to maintain that a right of action can accrue to the Corporation from a proceeding prohibited by the ftatute, and confequently null and void from the beginning.

In the cafe of the Mayor of Guildford againft Clarke * the Court held, " That to make a default in the Defendant there " muft have been an election antecedent; and that the election " of fuch an one as the Defendant *is abfolutely prohibited by the* " *ftatute.*"

Thus the cafe ftands with regard to the Corporation.

On the other hand, what is the cafe of the Defendant? he is now called upon under a penalty to ufurp an office upon the Crown, which ufurpation will fubject him to a criminal profecution and to a heavy punifhment. Strange dilemma this! You fhall, faith the Plaintiff in the action, ufurp upon the crown, or forfeit the penalties of the By-law. Can the By-law purge the ufurpation? It cannot. And can it at the fame time oblige the Defendant, confcious of his own incapacity, and apprized of the danger of the ufurpation, to venture on it? I think not.

It hath been faid, that all corporations have a right to the fervice of their members. They certainly have this right under proper limitations, but ftill it is a right fubject to the controul of the legiflature, and in the matter of the election they muft fubmit to fuch regulations and reftraints as the ftatute hath laid on them.

It hath been faid, Shall perfons who live in open contempt of all Gofpel inftitutions fhelter themfelves under this act? It is
sufficient

* 2 Vent. 247, 248.

ſufficient at preſent to ſay, that their caſe was not in the contemplation of the legiſlature at the time this act was made, and conſequently the Act cannot be extended to them. The Act was plainly levelled at perſons of a quite different character; I mean the Proteſtant Nonconformiſts.

BESIDES, the Defendant doth not take ſhelter under the idle excuſe which the objection puts into the mouths of Debauchees and Unbelievers; but having pleaded the Toleration-act, which will be conſidered in its proper place, he avers, that he doth not live in the neglect of Goſpel Ordinances, though he entertains ſome ſcruples touching the mode of adminiſtration in the Eſtabliſhed Church; and he hopes the Act of Toleration hath diſpenſed with conformity in that reſpect.

A GREAT deal hath been ſaid touching the diſtinction between Acts and Proceedings, void in themſelves and only voidable; and touching the conſtruction of Statutes declaring certain proceedings void.

THE anſwer I ſhall at preſent give to what hath been ſaid on that head is, that the point now in queſtion will not turn on that branch of the ſtatute which declares the election void, but upon that which abſolutely prohibits it, and conſequently renders it a mere nullity. If I am right in this, nothing that hath been urged upon the head of *void* and *voidable* will be applicable to the preſent caſe.

IT hath been ſaid, that the conſtruction now contended for is over-partial to Diſſenters, it excuſeth them from offices of Burden. But doth it not at the ſame time exclude them from all offices attended with Honour and profit? And it would ſound extremely harſh to ſay, that the ſame law which, for the reaſons given in the preamble, excludes them from the one, *as perſons unworthy of public truſt*, hath ſtill left them liable to the other, be the truſt that attends the office what it may. The
Shrievalty

Shrievalty is indeed an office of burden, but we all know that it is likewise an office of great importance and signal trust.

IT was said in Larwood's case*, and I believe it had great weight with those Judges who thought him liable to serve the office, that no man can by his own plea disable himself, or excuse one fault by another.

IT is sufficient on the present occasion to say, that Larwood's case totally and substantially differs from the present. Larwood had not properly pleaded the Toleration-act, and therefore could not take advantage of it. The present Defendant hath properly pleaded it, and shewn himself entitled to the benefit of it.

AND he doth not plead it in order to excuse one fault by another, but in order to shew that the Rubrick, which requires all persons to communicate with the Established Church three times at least in the year, is not now obligatory on him. The Toleration-Act, he saith, hath taken away the force and effect of the Rubrick, with regard to him. Whether it hath or hath not done this remains to be considered. And I am clearly of opinion with my Brothers who have spoken before me, that it hath.

THIS opinion I ground not barely on some particular branches of the Act, but likewise on the Spirit and general Frame and Tenour of it.

IT is not to be considered merely as an act of connivance and exemption from the penalties of former laws ; it doth, in my opinion, declare the public worship among Protestant Dissenters to be warranted by law, and intitled to the public Protection.

IT no less than four times, upon different occasions, speaks of

K k

the

---

* Reported in 4 Mod. 269. 12 Mod. 67. 1 Ld. Raym. 29. Salk. 167. and other books.

the religious worship practised among them as a mode of worship *permitted and allowed* by that act. What is this but saying, that it was warranted by Law? The magistrate may sometimes connive where he cannot punish or reform? but what the legislature permits, allows and takes under its protection, ceaseth from that moment to be an offence.

WHEN it enforceth former laws made for obliging all persons to resort to divine service on the Lord's Day, the attendance upon divine worship among the Dissenters is made equivalent to their attendance at the Churches established by Law.

WITH regard to the special penalties inflicted by the Act upon persons maliciously and contemptuously disturbing public worship, the places for religious worship among Protestant Dissenters are expressly put upon a level with Cathedrals, Parish-churches, and Chapels. I say, with regard to the special penalties of this Act, they are put upon a level. For though persons disturbing the public worship in the Established Church may be liable to prosecutions of another kind, yet with regard to the penalties inflicted by this act, dissenting meeting-houses and parish churches stand upon the same foot.

And persons officiating as Teachers or Preachers in their congregations are exempted from serving on juries and executing public offices in as full a manner, and I presume upon the same principles, as the established Clergy are exempted by the common law.

BESIDES, let the Toleration-act be considered barely as exempting Protestant Dissenters from the penalties of all former laws inflicted *singly* on account of their nonconformity. In this light at least it must be considered. And considered in this light it will be very difficult to conceive that the Legislature intended to leave them still open to ecclesiastical censures for not complying with this Rubrick.

THUS

THUS much I thought proper to fay touching the general frame and apparent intention of the Toleration-act. But the point will not ftand upon inferences and conclufions drawn from the fpirit and frame of the act. It exprefsly provides that they fhall not be profecuted in any Ecclefiaftical Court for or by reafon of their nonconformity to the Church of England.

IT may be eafily fhewn that all profecutions founded on the Rubrick were carried on in the ecclefiaftical courts, and not elfewhere : confequently a perfon intitled to the benefit of this Act, is not now obliged to conform to the Rubrick.

I CONCLUDE therefore that the Corporation-Act being prohibitory on the Electors, every election made in contravention to it with notice of the incapacity of the Candidate, and of his legal excufe founded on the Toleration-act, is a mere nullity. And that the Act having difpenfed with the Defendant's conformity to the Rubrick, the judgment againft him muft be reverfed.

K k 2   A P P E N-

APPENDIX. No. 2.

THE

SPEECH

OF THE RIGHT HONOURABLE

LORD MANSFIELD,

IN THE

House of Lords, Feb. 4, 1767.

IN THE

CAUSE between the City of LONDON and the DISSENTERS.

It is proper, as an Introduction to the following Speech, to prefix the Question which the House of Lords put to the Judges; as also their Opinions upon it: A Question, which the Noble Lord who moved it hath worded with such precision, that it is hardly possible the point on which the Cause turns, should be mistaken on any future occasion.

EXTRACT from the JOURNALS of the HOUSE OF LORDS.

Die Jovis 22 Januarii 1767.

Chamberlain of London.
against
E V A N S.

} C OUNCIL (according to order) were called in to be further heard in the cause upon a writ of error brought into this House, wherein the Chamberlain of the City of London is Plaintiff, and Allen Evans, Esq; Defendant; and the council for the Defendant having been heard; as also one council for the Plaintiff by way of reply; the council were directed to withdraw.

A N D it being proposed, that the Judges be directed to deliver their opinions upon the following Question:

Q. W H E T H E R upon the facts admitted by the pleadings in this Cause, the Defendant is at liberty, or should be allowed to object to the validity of his election on account of his not having taken the sacrament according to the rites of the church of England within a year before, in bar of this action?

T H E same was agreed to, and the said Question was accordingly put to the Judges.

W H E R E U P O N the Judges desiring some time might be allowed them for that purpose;

ORDERED,

ORDERED,

THAT the further hearing of the said Cause be adjourned to Tuesday next; and that the Judges do then attend to deliver their opinions upon the said Question.

Die Martis 27 *Januarii* 1767.

THE order of the day being read for the further hearing of the Cause wherein the Chamberlain of the city of London is Plaintiff, and Allen Evans, Esq; is Defendant, and for the Judges to deliver their opinions upon the Question proposed to them on Thursday last; the Lord Chancellor acquainted the House, That the Judges differed in their opinions, and that they desired, that further time might be allowed them for giving their opinions upon the said Question.

ORDERED,

THAT the further hearing of the said Cause be adjourned to this day sevennight; and that the Judges do then attend to deliver their opinions upon the said Question.

Die Martis 3 *Februarii* 1767.

THE order of the day being read for the further hearing of the Cause upon the writ of error, wherein the Chamberlain of the city of London is Plaintiff, and Allen Evans, Esq; is Defendant, and for the Judges to deliver their opinions upon the Question proposed to them on Thursday the 22d day of January last; the Lord Chancellor acquainted the House, That the Judges differed in their opinions; and thereupon they were directed to deliver their opinions seriatim, with their reasons.

ACCORDINGLY,

MR. Justice Hewitt was heard, and gave his reasons, and concluded with his opinion, that the Defendant is at liberty, and should be allowed to object to the validity of his election, on

account

account of his not having taken the facrament according to the rites of the church of England within a year before, in bar of this action.

Mr. Juftice Afton heard, and was of the fame opinion, and gave his reafons.

Mr. Baron Perrott heard, and gave his reafons, and concluded with his opinion, That the Defendant is not at liberty, nor ought to be allowed to object to the validity of his election on account of his not having taken the facrament according to the rites of the church of England within a year before, in bar of this action.

Mr. Juftice Gould heard, and was of the fame opinion as Mr. Juftice Afton, and gave his reafons.

O R D E R E D,

T h a t the further confideration of the faid Caufe be adjourned till to-morrow; and that the Judges do then attend.

Die Mercurii 4 *Februarii* 1767.

T h e order of the Day being read for the further hearing of the Caufe upon the writ of error wherein the Chamberlain of the city of London is Plaintiff, and Allen Evans, Efq; is Defendant ; and for the Judges to attend.

Mr. Baron Adams was heard, and gave his reafons, and concluded with his opinion, That the Defendant is at liberty, &c.

Mr. Baron Smythe heard, and was of the fame opinion, -and gave his reafons.

Mr. Juftice Clive heard, and was of the fame opinion, and gave his reafons.—Thus far the journals.

As foon as the Judges had given their opinions, Lord Manffield made the following fpeech.

L l

Lord

Lord MANSFIELD's *Speech in the House of Lords, in the Case of the Chamberlain of London against* ALLEN EVANS, *Esq;*

MY LORDS,

AS I made the motion for taking the opinion of the learned Judges, and proposed the question your Lordships have been pleased to put to them ; it may be expected, that I should make some further motion, in consequence of the opinions they have delivered.

IN moving for the opinion of the Judges, I had two views : The first was, that the House might have the benefit of their assistance, in forming a right judgment in this cause now before us, upon this writ of error : The next was, that, the question being fully discussed, the grounds of our judgment, together with their exceptions, limitations, and restrictions, might be clearly and certainly known ; as a rule to be followed hereafter, in all future cases of the like nature : And this determined me as to the manner of wording the question, " How far the De-" fendant might, in the present case, be allowed to plead his " disability in bar of the action brought against him ?"

THE question, thus worded, shews the point upon which your Lordships thought this cause turned ; and the answer necessarily fixes a criterion, under what circumstances and by what persons such a disability may be pleaded, as an exemption from the penalty inflicted by this by-law, upon those who decline taking upon them the office of Sheriff.

IN every view in which I have been able to consider this matter, I think this action cannot be supported.

IF they rely on the Corporation-act ; by the literal and express provision of that act no person can be elected, who hath
not

not within a year taken the facrament in the Church of England : the Defendant hath not taken the facrament within a year : he is not therefore elected. Here they fail.

I f they ground it on the general defign of the legiflature in paffing the Corporation-act ; the defign was to exclude the Diffenters from office, and difable them from ferving. For in thofe times, when a fpirit of intolerance prevailed, and fevere meafures were purfued, the Diffenters were reputed and treated as perfons ill-affected and dangerous to the Government : The Defendant therefore, a Diffenter, and in the eye of this law a perfon dangerous and ill-affected, is excluded from office, and difabled from ferving. Here they fail.

I f they ground the action on their own by-law ; fince that by-law was profeffedly made to procure fit and able perfons to ferve the office, and the Defendant is not fit and able ; being exprefsly difabled by Statute-law; here too they fail.

I f they ground it on his difability being owing to a neglect of taking the facrament at church, when he ought to have done it ; the Toleration-act having freed the Diffenters from all obligation to take the facrament at church, the Defendant is guilty of no neglect, no criminal neglect. Here therefore they fail.

T h e s e points, my Lords, will appear clear and plain.

T h e Corporation-act, pleaded by the Defendant as rendering him uneligible to this office, and incapable of taking it upon him, was moft certainly intended by the legiflature to prohibit the perfons therein defcribed being elected to any corporation-offices, and to difable them from taking fuch offices upon them. The act had two parts : Firft it appointed a commiffion for turning out all that were at that time in office, who would not comply with what was required as the condition of their continuance therein, and even gave a power to turn them out though they fhould comply: and then it further enacted,

L l 2

that

that from the termination of that commiffion no perfon hereafter who had not taken the facrament according to the rites of
the Church of England within one year preceding the time of
fuch election, fhould be placed, chofen, or elected, into any office of or belonging to the government of any corporation :
and this was done, as it was exprefsly declared in the preamble
to the act, in order to perpetuate. the fucceffion in corporations
in the hands of perfons well-affected to the government in
church and ftate.

I т was not their defign, as hath been faid*, " to bring fuch
" perfons into corporations by inducing them to take the facra-
" ment in the church of England ;" the legiflature did not
mean to tempt perfons who were ill-affected to the government,
occafionally to conform : It was not, I fay, their defign to bring
them in ; they could not truft them, left they fhould ufe the
power of their offices to diftrefs and annoy the ftate.   And the
reafon is alledged in the act itfelf : it was becaufe there were
" evil fpirits" amongft them ; and they were afraid of evil fpirits
and determined to keep them out : And therefore they put it out
of the power of electors to choofe fuch perfons, and out of
their power to ferve ; and accordingly prefcribed a mark or character, laid down a defcription whereby they fhould be known
and diftinguifhed by their conduct previous to fuch election ;
inftead of appointing a condition of their ferving the office, refulting from their future conduct, or fome confequent action to
be performed by them : they declared fuch perfons incapable of
being chofen, as had not taken the facrament in the church within a year before fuch election ; and without this mark of their
affection to the church, they could not be in office, and there
could be no election.

But as the law then ftood, no man could have pleaded this
difability, refulting from the corporation-act, in bar of fuch an
action as is now brought againft the Defendant ; becaufe this
                                                        difability

* By Mr. Baron Perrott.

difability was owing to what was then in the eye of the law a crime; every man being required by the canon-law, received and confirmed by ftatute-law, to take the facrament in the church at leaft once a year: The law would not permit a man to fay, that he had not taken the facrament in the Church of England; and he could not be allowed to plead it in bar of any action brought againft him.

But the cafe is quite altered fince the act of Toleration: It is now no crime for a man, who is within the defcription of that Act, to fay he is a Diffenter; nor is it any crime for him not to take the facrament according to the rites of the church of England: Nay, the crime is, if he does it contrary to the dictates of his own confcience.

If it is a crime not to take the facrament at church, it muft be a crime by fome Law; which muft be either Common or Statute-law, the Canon-law inforcing it depending wholly upon the Statute-law.   Now the Statute-law is repealed as to perfons capable of pleading that they are fo and fo qualified; and therefore the Canon-law is repealed with regard to thofe perfons.   If it is a crime by Common-law, it muft be fo, either by Ufage or Principle.   There is no ufage or cuftom independent of pofitive law, which makes Nonconformity a crime.   The eternal principles of Natural Religion are part of the Common-law: The effential principles of Revealed Religion are part of the Common-law; fo that any perfon reviling, fubverting or ridiculing them, may be profecuted at Common-law.   But it cannot be fhewn from the principles of Natural or Revealed Religion, that, independent of pofitive law, temporal punifhments ought to be inflicted for mere opinions with refpect to particular modes of worfhip.

Persecution for a fincere, though erroneous confcience, is not to be deduced from reafon or the fitnefs of things; it can only ftand upon pofitive law.

It

I T hath been faid*, that " the Toleration-act only amounts
" to an exemption of Proteftant Diffenters from the penalties of
" certain laws therein particularly mentioned, and to nothing
" more ; that if it had been intended to bear, and to have any
" operation upon the Corporation-act, the Corporation-act
" ought to have been mentioned therein ; and there ought to
" have been fome enacting claufe, exempting Diffenters from
" profecution in confequence of this act, and enabling them to
" plead their not having received the facrament according to
" the rites of the Church of England, in bar of fuch action."
But this is much too limited and narrow a conception of the
Toleration-act : which amounts confequentially to a great deal
more than this ; and it hath confequentially an influence and o-
peration upon the Corporation-act in particular. The Toleration-act renders that which was illegal before, now legal ; the
Diffenters way of worfhip is permitted and allowed by this act ;
it is not only exempted from punifhment, but rendered innocent and lawful ; it is eftablifhed : it is put under the protection,
and is not merely under the connivance, of the law. In cafe
thofe who are appointed by law to regifter Diffenting places of
worfhip, refufe on any pretence to do it, we muft, upon application, fend a Mandamus to compel them.

N o w there cannot be a plainer pofition, than that the law
protects nothing, in that very refpect in which it is in the eye
of the law, at the fame time, a crime. Diffenters within the
defcription of the Toleration-act, are reftored to a legal confideration and capacity ; and an hundred confequences will from
thence follow, which are not mentioned in the Act. For inftance, previous to the Toleration-act, it was unlawful to devife any legacy for the fupport of Diffenting Congregations, or
for the benefit of Diffenting Minifters ; for the Law knew no
fuch affemblies, and no fuch perfons ; and fuch a devife was abfolutely

---

* Mr. Baron Perrot.

folutely void, being left to what the law called fuperftitious purpofes.   But will it be faid in any Court in England, that fuch a
devife is not a good and valid one now ? And yet there is nothing faid of this in the Toleration-act. By that Act the Diffenters are freed, not only from the pains and penalties of the laws
therein particularly fpecified, but from all ecclefiaftical cenfures,
and from all penalty and punifhment whatfoever on account of
their Nonconformity; which is allowed and protected by this
act, and is therefore in the eye of the law no longer a crime.
Now if the Defendant may fay he is a Diffenter; if the Law
doth not ftop his mouth; if he may declare, that he hath not
taken the facrament according to the rites of the Church of
England without being confidered as criminal; if, I fay, his
mouth is not ftopped by the Law, he may then plead his not-
having taken the facrament according to the rites of the Church
of England, in bar of this action. It is fuch a difability as doth
not leave him liable to any action, or to any penalty or punifhment whatfoever.

I t is indeed faid * to be " a maxim in law, That a man fhall
" not be allowed to difable himfelf." But when this maxim is
applied to the prefent cafe, it is laid down in too large a fenfe;
I fay, when it is extended to comprehend a legal difability, it
is taken in too great a latitude.   What! fhall not a man be allowed to plead, that he is not fit and able? Thefe words are inferted in the By-law, as the ground of making it ; and in the
Plaintiff's declaration as the ground of his action againft the Defendant: it is alledged, that the Defendant was fit and able,
and that he refufed to ferve not having a reafonable excufe. It
is certain, and it is hereby in effect admitted, that if he is not
fit and able, and that if he hath a reafonable excufe, he may
plead it in bar of this action. Surely he may plead, that he is
not worth fifteen thoufand pounds, provided that was really
the cafe, as a circumftance that would render him not fit and
able.   And if the law allows him to fay, that he hath not taken
the facrament according to the rites of the Church of England,
being

* Mr. Baron Perrot.

being within the defcription of the Toleration-act; he may plead that likewife, to fhew that he is not fit and able : It is a reafonable, it is a lawful excufe.

My Lords, the meaning of this maxim, " That a man fhall " not difable himfelf," is folely this, That a man fhall not difable himfelf by his own wilful crime : And fuch a difability the law will not allow him to plead. If a man contracts to fell an eftate to any perfon upon certain terms at fuch a time, and in the mean time he fells it to another ; he fhall not be allowed to fay, Sir, I cannot fulfil my contract; it is out of my power ; I have fold my eftate to another. Such a plea would be no bar to an action, becaufe the act of his felling it to another is the very breach of contract. So likewife a man, who hath promifed marriage to one lady, and afterwards marries another, cannot plead in bar of a profecution from the firft lady, that he is already married; becaufe his marrying the fecond lady is the very breach of promife to the firft. A man fhall not be allowed to plead, that he was drunk, in bar of a criminal profecution, though perhaps he was at the time as incapable of the exercife of reafon as if he had been infane ; becaufe his drunkennefs was itfelf a crime; he fhall not be allowed to excufe one crime by another. The Roman foldier, who cut off his thumbs, was not fuffered to plead his difability for the fervice, to procure his difmiffion with impunity ; becaufe his incapacity was defignedly brought on him by his own wilful fault. And I am glad to obferve fo good an agreement among the Judges upon this point, who have ftated it with great precifion and clearnefs.

When it was faid * therefore, That " a man cannot plead " his crime, in excufe for not doing what he is by law required " to do;" it only amounts to this, That he cannot plead in excufe what, when pleaded, is no excufe : but there is not in this the fhadow of an objection to his pleading what is an excufe, pleading a legal difqualification. If he is nominated to be a

Juftice

* Mr. Baron Perrott.

Juſtice of the Peace, he may ſay, I cannot be a Juſtice of Peace, for I have not an hundred pounds a year. In like manner a Diſſenter may plead, I have not qualified, and I cannot qualify, and am not obliged to qualify; and you have no right to fine me for not ſerving.

It hath been ſaid*, That " the King hath a right to the ſer-" vice of all his ſubjects." And this aſſertion is very true, provided it be properly qualified. For ſurely, againſt the operation of this general right in particular caſes, a man may plead a Natural or Civil diſability. May not a man plead, that he was upon the high ſeas? May not idiocy or lunacy be pleaded? which are Natural diſabilities: Or a judgment of a court of law? and much more, a judgment of Parliament? which are Civil diſabilities.

It hath been ſaid † to be " a maxim, that no man can plead " his being a lunatic, to avoid a deed executed, or excuſe an " act done, at that time; becauſe," it is ſaid, " if he was a lu-" natic, he could not remember any action he did during the " period of his inſanity." And this was doctrine formerly laid down by ſome Judges; but I am glad to find, that of late it hath been generally exploded; for the reaſon aſſigned for it is, in my opinion, wholly inſufficient to ſupport it; becauſe, though he could not remember what paſſed during his inſanity, yet he might juſtly ſay, If he ever executed ſuch a deed, or did ſuch an action, it muſt have been during his confinement or lunacy; for he did not do it either before or ſince that time.

As to the caſe, in which a man's plea of inſanity was actually ſet aſide; it was nothing more than this: It was when they pleaded *ore tenus ;* the man pleaded that he was at the time out of his ſenſes. It was replied, How do you know that you was out of your ſenſes? No man that is ſo, knows himſelf to be ſo. And according his plea was upon this quibble ſet aſide ; not be-

M m caufe

---

* Mr. Baron Perrot.　　　† Mr. Baron Perrot.

caufe it was not a valid one, if he was out of his fenfes; but becaufe they concluded, he was not out of his fenfes. If he had alledged, that he was at that time confined, being apprehended to be out of his fenfes; no advantage could have been taken of his manner of expreffing himfelf; and his plea muft have been allowed to be good.

As to Larwood's cafe; he was not allowed the benefit of the Toleration-act, becaufe he did not plead it. If he had infifted on his right to the benefit of it in his plea, the judgment muft have been different. His inferting it in his replication was not allowed, not becaufe it was not an allegation that would have excufed him, if it had been originally taken notice of in his plea; but becaufe its being only mentioned afterwards was a departure from his plea.

In the cafe of the Mayor of Guildford, the Toleration-act was pleaded, the plea was allowed good, the difability being efteemed a lawful one; and the judgment was right.

And here the Defendant hath likewife infifted on his right to the benefit of the Toleration-act in his plea; he faith he is bona fide a Diffenter, within the defcription of the Toleration-act; that he hath taken the oaths and fubfcribed the declaration required by that Act to fhew that he is not a Popifh Recufant; that he hath never received the facrament according to the rites of the Church of England, and that he cannot in confcience do it; and that for more than fifty years paft he hath not been prefent at Church at the celebration of the eftablifhed worfhip; but hath conftantly received the facrament, and attended divine fervice, among the Proteftant Diffenters. And thefe facts are not denied by the Plaintiff: though they might eafily have been traverfed, and it was incumbent upon them to have done it, if they had not known they fhould certainly fail in it. There can be no doubt therefore, that the Defendant is a Diffenter, an honeft confcientious Diffenter; and no confcientious Diffenter can take the facrament at church; the Defendant faith he cannot

not do it, and he is not obliged to do it. And as this is the cafe, as the Law allows him to fay this, as it hath not ftopped his mouth; the plea which he makes is a lawful plea, his difability being through no crime or fault of his own; I fay, he is difabled by Act of Parliament, without the concurrence or intervention of any fault or crime of his own; and therefore he may plead this difability in bar of the prefent action.

The cafe of " Athiefts and Infidels"* is out of the prefent queftion; they come not within the defcription of the Toleration-act. And as this is the fole point to be enquired into, in all cafes of the like nature with that of the Defendant, who here pleads the Toleration-act; Is the man bona fide a Diffenter within the defcription of that Act; If not, he cannot plead his difability in confequence of his not having taken the facrament in the church of England: if he is, he may lawfully and with effect plead it, in bar of fuch an action. And the queftion, on which this diftinction is grounded, muft be tried by a jury.

It hath been faid †, that " this being a matter between God " and a man's own confcience, it cannot come under the cog- " nizance of a jury." But certainly it may: and though God alone is the abfolute judge of a man's religious profeffion, and of his confcience; yet there are fome marks even of fincerity; among which there is none more certain than confiftency. Surely a man's fincerity may be judged of by overt-acts: It is a juft and excellent maxim, which will hold good in this as in all other cafes, " By their fruits ye fhall know them." Do they—I do not fay go to Meeting now and then—but do they frequent the Meeting-houfe? Do they join generally and ftatedly, in divine worfhip with diffenting congregations? Whether they do or not, may be afcertained by their neighbours, and by thofe who frequent the fame places of worfhip. In cafe a man hath occafionally conformed for the fake of places of truft and profit; in that cafe I imagine, a jury would not hefitate in their verdict. If a man then alledges he is a Diffenter, and claims

M m 2 the

---

* Objected by Mr. Baron Perrot. † Mr. Baron Perrot.

the protection and advantages of the Toleration-act; a jury may juftly find, that he is not a Diffenter within the defcription of the Toleration-act, fo far as to render his difability a lawful one: If he takes the facrament for his intereft, the jury may conclude, that his fcruple of confcience is a falfe pretence when fet up to avoid a burthen.

THE Defendant in the prefent caufe pleads, that he is a Diffenter within the defcription of the Toleration-act; that he hath not taken the facrament in the Church of England within one year preceding the time of his fuppofed election, nor ever in his whole life; and that he cannot in confcience do it.

CONSCIENCE is not controulable by human laws, nor amenable to human tribunals. Perfecution, or attempts to force confcience, will never produce conviction; and are only calculated to make hypocrites, or—martyrs.

MY Lords, there never was a fingle inftance from the Saxon times down to our own, in which a man was ever punifhed for erroneous opinions concerning rites or modes of worfhip, but upon fome pofitive law. The common law of England, which is only common reafon or ufage, knows of no profecution for mere opinions: For Atheifm, Blafphemy, and reviling the Chriftian Religion, there have been inftances of perfons profecuted and punifhed upon the common law; but bare Nonconformity is no fin by the common law: and all pofitive laws inflicting any pains or penalties for Nonconformity to the eftablifhed rites and modes, are repealed by the act of Toleration; and Diffenters are thereby exempted from all ecclefiaftical cenfures.

WHAT bloodfhed and confufion have been occafioned from the reign of Henry the Fourth, when the firft penal ftatutes were enacted, down to the Revolution in this kingdom, by laws made to force confcience! There is nothing certainly more unreafonable, more inconfiftent with the rights of human nature, more contrary to the fpirit and precepts of the Chriftian Religion,

on, more iniquitous and unjuft, more impolitic, than Perfecution. It is againft Natural Religion, Revealed Religion, and
found Policy.

S A D experience, and a large mind, taught that great man
the Prefident De Thou, this doctrine: let any man read the many admirable things which, though a Papift, he hath dared to
advance upon the fubject, in the dedication of his hiftory to
Harry the Fourth of France (which I never read without rap-
ture); and he will be fully convinced, not only how cruel, but
how impolitic, it is to perfecute for religious opinions. I am
forry, that of late his countrymen have begun to open their eyes,
fee their error, and adopt his fentiments: I fhould not have
broke my heart, (I hope I may fay fo without breach of chriftian charity), if France had continued to cherifh the Jefuits, and
to perfecute the Huguenots. There was no occafion to revoke
the Edict of Nants; the Jefuits needed only to have advifed a
plan fimilar to what is contended for, in the prefent cafe: Make
a law to render them incapable of office; make another, to
punifh them for not ferving. If they accept, punifh them (for
it is admitted on all hands, that the Defendant in the caufe before your Lordfhips is profecutable for taking the office upon
him): If they accept, punifh them; if they refufe, punifh them;
if they fay, yes, punifh them; if they fay, no, punifh them.
My Lords, this is a moft exquifite dilemma, from which there
is no efcaping; it is a trap a man cannot get out of; it is as bad
perfecution as the bed of Procruftes: If they are too fhort,
ftretch them; if they are too long, lop them. Small would
have been their confolation to have been gravely told, The Edict
of Nants is kept inviolable; you have the full benefit of that act
of Toleration, you may take the facrament in your own way
with impunity; you are not compelled to go to Mafs. Was this
cafe but told in the City of London as of a proceeding in France,
how would they exclaim againft the jefuitical diftinction! and
yet in truth it comes from themfelves: the Jefuits never thought
of

of it : when they meant to perfecute, their act of Toleration, the Edict of Nants, was repealed.

THIS By-law, by which the Diffenters are to be reduced to this wretched dilemma, is a By-law of the City, a local corporation, contrary to an Act of Parliament, which is the law of the land ; a modern By-law, of very modern date, made long fince the Corporation-act, long fince the Toleration-act, in the face of them : for they knew thefe laws were in being. It was made in fome year of the reign of the late king : I forget which ; but it was made about the time of *building the Manfion-houfe*. Now if it could be fuppofed, the City have a power of making fuch a By-law; it would entirely fubvert the Toleration-act, the defign of which was to exempt the Diffenters from all penalties; for by fuch a By-law they have it in their power to make every Diffenter pay a fine of fix hundred pounds, or any fum they pleafe ; for it amounts to that.

THE profeffed defign of making this By-law, was to get fit and able perfons to ferve the office : and the Plaintiff fets forth in his declaration, that if the Diffenters are excluded, they fhall want fit and able perfons to ferve the office. But were I to deliver my own fufpicion, it would be, that they did not fo much wifh for their fervices, as for their fines. Diffenters have been appointed to this office, one who was blind, another who was bedridden; not, I fuppofe, on account of their being fit and able to ferve the office. No ; they were difabled both by Nature and by Law.

WE had a cafe lately in the Courts below, of a perfon chofen Mayor of a Corporation, while he was beyond the feas, with his Majefty's troops in America ; and they knew him to be fo. Did they want him to ferve the office? No, it was impoffible. But they had a mind to continue the former Mayor a year longer, and to have a pretence for fetting afide him who was now chofen, on all future occafions, as having been elected before.

IN

In the caufe before your Lordfhips, the Defendant was by law incapable at the time of his pretended election: and it is my firm perfuafion, that he was chofen becaufe he was incapable. If he had been capable, he had not been chofen; for they did not want him to ferve the office. They chofe him, becaufe without a breach of the law and an ufurpation on the Crown, he could not ferve the office. They chofe him, that he might fall under the penalty of their By-law made to ferve a particular purpofe: In oppofition to which, and to avoid, the fine thereby impofed, he hath pleaded a legal difability grounded on two Acts of Parliament: As I am of opinion, that his plea is good, I conclude with moving your Lordfhips,

THAT the Judgment be affirmed.

THE Judgment was immediately affirmed, *Nemine contradicente;* and the entry in the Journal is in the following words:

Die Mercurii 4 *Februarii* 1767.

IT is ordered and adjudged by the Lords Spiritual and Temporal in Parliament affembled, That the Judgment given by the Commiffioners Delegates appointed to hear the Errors in a Judgment given in the Sheriff's Court London, and affirmed by the Court of Huftings, reverfing the Judgment of the Sheriff's Court and Court of Huftings, be and the fame is hereby affirmed; and that the Record be remitted.

F I N I S.

TO THE SONS OF SCIENCE IN *AMERICA.*

R O B E R T   B E L L, Bookseller, of *PHILADELPHIA,*
N o t i f i e t h, that in the F a l l of this present Year 1773,

H E   W I L L

PUBLISH by *SUBSCRIPTION,*

F E R G U S O N's

ESSAY on the History of CIVIL SOCIETY.

This is a living Author of much Estimation, whose elegant Performance will greatly delight, by giving an Opportunity of being intimately acquainted with the *Sentiments of the Man,* whom Sir John Dalrymple, (Author of the celebrated Memoirs of Great-Britain and Ireland) is pleased to stile, " one of the greatest of *Modern Philosophers.*"

N. B. The Book will be handsomely printed in one Volume Octavo, with neat binding and lettering, at the Price of TEN SHILLINGS Pennsylvania Currency, to the Subscribers.

Those who subscribe for SIX Copies, will be allowed a SEVENTH, GRATIS.

** Intentional Encouragers who wish for a Participation of this sentimental Banquet, are requested to send their Names and Residence early, to ROBERT BELL, Bookseller at Philadelphia, or to any of the Booksellers in America.

–––––– ––––––

SUBSCRIPTIONS are also received by said ROBERT BELL, and the Booksellers on the Continent, for RE-PRINTING,

A SECOND *AMERICAN* Edition of Judge BLACKSTONE's *Commentaries on the Laws of ENGLAND* in Four Volumes *Quarto,* at *Three Dollars* each Volume.––––These Gentlemen who were Subscribers to the First Edition in *Octavo,* and now choose to possess the *Quarto* Edition, shall have their *Octavo* (if not abused) exchanged for the *Quarto,* on paying the Difference between the Prices.